RHODE ISLAND POLITICS AND GOVERNMENT

MAUREEN MOAKLEY AND ELMER CORNWELL

Rhode Island Politics and Government

UNIVERSITY OF NEBRASKA PRESS

LINCOLN AND LONDON

⊗
Library of Congress
Cataloging-in-Publication Data
Moakley, Maureen.
Rhode Island politics and government /
Maureen Moakley and Elmer Cornwell.
p. cm.—(Politics and governments of the American states)
Includes bibliographical references and index.
ISBN 0-8032-3218-7 (cloth: alk. paper)—
ISBN 0-8032-8270-2 (pbk.: alk. paper)
1. Rhode Island—Politics and government.
I. Cornwell, Elmer E.   II. Title.   III. Series.
JK3216.M63   2001
320.9745—dc21
00-048838

To the memory of my mother, Frances Keegan
M. F. M.

For Penny
E. E. C.

CONTENTS

ILLUSTRATIONS

Series Preface

The purpose of this series is to provide informative and interesting books on the politics and governments of the fifty American states, books that are of value not only to students of government but also to general citizens who want greater insight into the past and present civic life of their own state and of other states in the federal union. The role of the states in governing America is among the least well known of all the 87,504 governments in the United States. The national media focus attention on the federal government in Washington DC, and local media focus attention on local government. Meanwhile, except when there is a scandal or a proposed tax increase, the workings of state government remain something of a mystery to many citizens—out of sight, out of mind.

In many respects, however, the states have been and continue to be the most important governments in the American political system. They are the main building blocks and chief organizing governments of the whole system. The states are the constituent governments of the federal union, and it is through the states that citizens gain representation in the federal government. The federal government is one of limited, delegated powers; all other powers are possessed by the states and their citizens. At the same time, the states are the empowering governments for the nation's 87,453 local governments— counties, municipalities, townships, school districts, and special districts. As such, states provide one of the most essential and ancient elements of freedom and democracy: the right of local self-government.

Although for many citizens the most visible aspects of state government are state universities (some of which are the most prestigious in the world), and state highway patrol officers with their radar guns and handy ticket books, state governments provide nearly all domestic public services. Whether elements of those services are enacted or partly funded by the federal government and actually carried out by local governments, it is state government that has the ultimate responsibility for ensuring that Americans are well served by all their governments. In so doing, all of the American states are more democratic, more prosperous, and better governed than most of the world's nation-states.

This is a particularly timely period in which to publish a series of books on the governments and politics of each of the fifty states. Once viewed as the "fallen arches" of the federal system, states today are increasingly seen as energetic, innovative, and fiscally responsible. Some states, of course, perform better than others, but that is to be expected in a federal system. Each state is unique in its own right. It is our hope that this series will shed light on the public life of each state and that, taken together, the books will contribute to a better, more informed understanding of the states themselves and of their often pivotal roles in the world's first and oldest continent-sized federal democracy.

Authors' Preface

Rhode Island politics offers one fascinating variant of politics among the fifty American states and we thoroughly enjoyed the challenge of trying to provide a coherent overview of the political life of the state. It is our good fortune that thinking and writing about Rhode Island has provided us, as political scientists, with a wonderful opportunity to connect the outstanding theoretical and research efforts of scholars to one of our fondest interests— the history, development, and day-to-day activity of politics in the Ocean State.

Any endeavor of this sort involves considerable intellectual debts and we are delighted to acknowledge those who contributed to our efforts. First we want to recognize the late Daniel J. Elazar, not only for his research on political culture (which helped transform the study of state politics and certainly informs our study), but also for his initiation of this series. We also are indebted to many outstanding political scientists, most of whom are cited in this book, for providing the intellectual framework for the study of state politics. Their research efforts have contributed to the growing recognition of the importance of the role of states in the American political system. We also drew on the work of some outstanding historians, also cited, whose work helped us to link the present with the past.

Special recognition should go to Thomas Anton of the Taubman Center a Brown University, who took the time to read an entire draft of this book and provided insightful comments and suggestions as to the revisions. Also, John Kincaid, the series editor, read, critiqued, and edited the manuscript and provided invaluable help for the final revision. Because of the efforts of these two outstanding scholars and colleagues this is a much better book. Colleagues at the University of Rhode Island, including Al Killilea, Joel Cohen, and Norman Zucker read and commented on various parts of the manuscript, and some talented students—Scott Harris, Richard Santore, Michael Cerbo, and Matthew Ulricksen—lent a hand in doing research and tracking down data. Sharon Woodmansee provided heroic assistance in guiding the entire process to completion and Penny Walker offered a constant source of help, effort, and encouragement.

Our other critical resource was the many men and women who are engaged in the real world of politics and public service in Rhode Island and who shared their insights and experiences with us. Much of the information and our conclusions came from collective years of listening, observing, reading, and marginal involvement in and about the political life of the state. While we conducted a few formal interviews, many of our findings are the result of countless chats with innumerable others about politics. Formal interviews were conducted with former governors Phil Noel and Bruce Sundlun, and U.S. Senator John Chafee. We also engaged various other political folk along the way. Our thanks to Paul Crowley, Thomas Deluglio, Guy Dufault, Christine Ferguson, William Fisher, Joseph Walsh, Darrell West and others for either commenting on various subjects or reading sections of the chapters for comment. Scott Mackay provided useful insights into the politics at the statehouse and he, along with other statehouse reporters, produced some first-rate news articles that informed this study. Bill Humphreys offered special encouragement. Justice Robert Flanders kindly read and commented on the chapter on the courts, and Michael O'Keefe offered invaluable comments and suggestions on the budget chapter. Gary Sasse opened his office and research materials to us anytime we needed them and Peter Merino patiently guided us through some of the details of budget and education material.

In the end a book belongs to its readers, and we hope that people from other states will enjoy reading about Rhode Island as an interesting example of politics in one American state. For students our goal is to provide an engaging and useful "case study" in the field of federalism and state politics. But we especially hope this book will resonate with the people of Rhode Island. To the extensive number of people who actively contribute to the public life of the state, we hope we have done justice to the fascinating enterprise in which they are engaged. We also want to acknowledge the many Rhode Islanders who follow politics as a spectator sport, continually discussing, praising, critiquing, and kvetching about political events of the day and to the many others who, while they may not follow politics closely, seem to intuitively understand that we are all part of a continuing "lively experiment." This book belongs to them.

RHODE ISLAND POLITICS AND GOVERNMENT

CHAPTER ONE

Rhode Island in Transition

Nowhere have the results of a betrayal of trust, and the unethical conduct it manifests, been more devastating than here in Rhode Island. In recent months, the very civility that in the past insured reasonable public discourse has been lost as the intensity of the anger and despair some . . . feel grows over their government's failure to perform its duties and keep faith with the people.

Ethics Task Force, 1991

Rhode Islanders are increasingly pleased with the way things are going in the state. Eighty-three percent of voters believe the state is headed in the right direction, while 10 percent think it is on the wrong track. That is the highest 'right track' rating Rhode Island voters have given in any Brown [University] poll in at least a decade.

Darrell West, 1999

The first day of January 1991 marked a watershed in Rhode Island politics. On that brilliantly sunny day, Democrat Bruce Sundlun was sworn in as governor, succeeding a three-term Republican, Edward DiPrete. In a state that generally votes Democratic, such an event might appear to be politics as usual. But two other events of that day signaled a critical shift in the character of Rhode Island politics and marked the beginning of a transition, the effects of which are still unfolding.

The first involved a banking crisis of massive fiscal and political proportions. The pageantry of the inaugural was cut short so that the newly elected governor could hold a news conference. He declared the first "bank holiday" since 1933, closing thirty-five credit unions and ten banks. The Rhode Island Share and Deposit Indemnity Corporation (RISDIC), a private insurance corporation under the supervision of the Department of Business

Regulation, was declared insolvent and the deposits of about 300,000 Rhode Islanders (within a state of just under one million people) were frozen.

The other event, obscured somewhat by the drama of the banking crisis, was the signing of an ethics-in-government executive order. After Sundlun was inaugurated his first official act was to sign a new code of ethics for government officials. The code set stricter and clearer standards of behavior in public office and established a task force that resulted in, among other things, the most powerful state ethics commission in the country. Although the timing of this order was clearly political and symbolic, the tone of the order signaled a fundamental understanding among political elites at all levels of government that "politics as usual" was no longer possible in the Ocean State.

PRELUDE TO CHANGE

As with most major turning points, the events surrounding Sundlun's in-auguration were the culmination of long-term demographic, economic, and political trends that came together at the end of the 1980s and irrevocably changed the course of Rhode Island politics. Until that time the state was a bastion of "old style" patronage politics which in many ways resembled a classic political machine in the context of a small city-state.

"Little Rhody," the smallest state in the Union, has a total land area of 1,045 square miles. The state extends approximately fifty miles north-south and has an east-west width of thirty miles; motorists en route to Boston from New York can drive through the entire state on the Interstate 95 corridor in less than an hour. The drive provides a glimpse at the variations in the state's topography. First, one encounters vast stretches of undeveloped scrub pine that suggest a proximity to the Atlantic Ocean, a considerable amount of undeveloped land (over 50 percent of the state's land mass is considered forest), farming areas, and rural towns.[1]

Then, as a prelude to the impressive Providence skyline, gritty stretches of older commercial development appear on the outskirts of the city. Further along, at the end of Narragansett Bay and at the confluence of two rivers, one encounters the city of Providence. A short distance beyond the city is the Massachusetts state line.

Narragansett Bay, the largest body of water in the state, covers about 25 percent of the state's land area and, with over four hundred miles of shoreline, provides the rationale for Rhode Island's title as the Ocean State. The bay provides spectacular vistas that impressed even the state's earliest visitors. Looking up the bay from the ocean one sees a large land mass, Acquidnick Island, from which the name Rhode Island was derived. Historians believe the name came from the Italian explorer Giovanni da Verrazano, who sailed around the area in 1524 and named the place Rhode Island because it reminded him of the Isle of Rhodes.[2] The official name of the state, "Rhode Island and the Providence Plantations," harkens back to colonial times because although Newport on Aquidnick Island was the thriving center of the state, the colony also included plantations in and around the city of Providence, at the end of the bay, that were settled by Roger Williams.

With a population of just over a million, Rhode Island is the second most densely populated state in the country, with an 86 percent urban population. The state has the largest Roman Catholic population percentage in the nation (over 60 percent), many of whom came from large ethnic communities of working-class origins.[3] While the state moved into the top fifteen of the fifty states in per capita income after the 1980 census, the population remains older and less educated than the national average. In many ways Rhode Island retains the atmosphere of a working-class city-state.

Until the suburbanization of the 1960s and 1970s, about two-thirds of that population was concentrated either in the city of Providence (the state capital) or in the adjacent urban towns of Providence County. The Democratic party, creating a system akin to the wards of a large urban city, controlled most of these towns. Although segments of the population have since moved out to what were once rural areas, particularly in the southern part of the state, Providence and its environs retain about half the population and the metropolitan area remains the dominant political, economic, and cultural center of the state.

The political and social character of Rhode Island has often been described as incestuous because in this small concentrated environment everyone seems to know everyone else. Particularly among the business and political elite, overlapping associations and interests put them in continuous contact with each other and politicians seem to be everywhere. It is not uncommon to find the governor, state general officers, members of the state's congressional delegation, and key state legislative leaders mingling at any number of political and social events around the state. They interact regularly with business and media folk, and any interested voter has ample opportunity to meet politicians personally at various venues throughout the state.

This face-to-face style breeds a parochial politics that retains traces of group and class divisions. The "we" were originally multigenerational ethnic groups, mostly of Catholic working-class background, who by sheer force of number came to dominate the political system under the Democrats in the mid-1930s. The "they" were old-guard Republican "Yankee" elites who still control key sectors of the business and media establishment, and

Figure 1: Population Distribution in Rhode Island, 1990

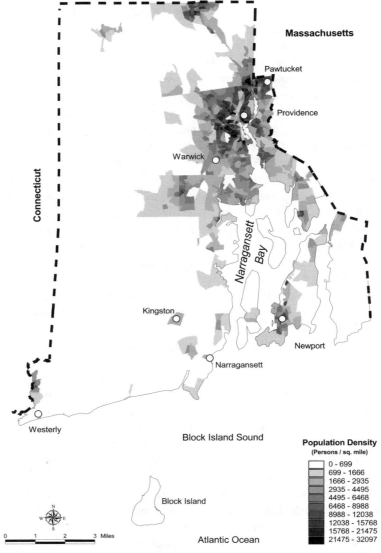

Source: U.S. Census 1990, RIGIS. Map prepared at URI Environmental Data Center.

Table 1: Population of Rhode Island by County, 1950 and 1997*

County	1950	1997
Bristol County	29,079	48,970
Kent County	77,763	161,742
Newport County	60,807	82,598
Providence County	574,973	574,429
Washington County	49,274	119,690
State Total	791,896	987,429

Source: U.S. Bureau of the Census, Rhode Island Statewide Planning Department
* Estimate

scattered pockets of rural white Protestants, sometimes referred to as "swamp Yankees." For the most part these divisions, until quite recently, fell along partisan lines.

The roots of these divisions go back to the post–Civil War period when the Republican party spawned a series of masterful political bosses who managed various political machines throughout the state that were designed to protect the interests of a Yankee establishment. The core strategy was the disenfranchisement and underrepresentation of a large and ever-expanding working-class population that sustained the industrial base of the economy. Long after they had become a minority the Yankee Republicans dominated politics through an egregious system of political, social, and economic discrimination. Their time ran out, however, with the coming of the New Deal.

The Democrats, supported by large numbers of ethnically disparate working-class groups, finally took political control in 1935 and slowly began to promote the interests of their constituencies. They too established and managed an extensive machine system based in the urban environs of Providence, a system that only began to unravel during the late 1970s. These social and partisan divisions bred a strong patronage-based system of interpersonal politics with a built-in measure of corruption. Jobs, favors, and appointments were routinely doled out on the basis of political connections and compliance. Appointments and public contracts often involved financial and political kickbacks. While the Democrats managed to accommodate the central concerns of the business elite up through the late 1980s, political agendas favored the interests of Democrats' supporters, particularly the unions.

This type of politics continued to support an "amateur" type of system that resisted the trend toward the professionalization and modernization of state government apparent in many other states since the 1960s.[4] Why streamline and professionalize the bureaucracy when friends and supporters need public jobs? Why expand merit systems in an interpersonal world where loyalty matters most? Why reorganize and reform the lines of authority between the legislature, the executive, and the courts when the present system grants extraordinary constitutional and statutory authority to the legislature and its leadership, and allows a Democratic political elite to, for all intents and purposes, manage the system?

As the excesses of the system became apparent, the voters, caught in a curious bind, also resisted change. Having grown increasingly cynical about the system, they were suspicious of any "reform" that might lengthen terms in office, professionalize government—particularly in terms of salary—or that might shift authority to or among public officials. Rhode Islanders, with a long history of radical populism, were comforted by the "short leash" theory of representation whereby terms of office for governor, general officers, and the General Assembly were kept at two years, and compensation for service, especially in the legislature, was nominal. This disposition provided cover to a political establishment that, especially in the legislature, rarely faced electoral competition and managed quite nicely to develop a system of substantial perks of office to supplement their meager salaries.

Whatever its excesses, this system produced some remarkably progressive policies. If the "we" were the poor and the working class, the Democrats took care of them. On all surveys Rhode Island ranks in the top ten states on measures of welfare efforts, welfare as a percentage of state general expenditures, and the adequacy of public assistance under the old Aid to Families with Dependent Children (AFDC) system.[5] The state also ranks high among states in health services, with innovative medical service and insurance programs for indigent people; the number of medically uninsured is the seventh lowest in the country. These data are fairly impressive, considering that Rhode Island ranks ahead of progressive states like Wisconsin, Massachusetts, and California on many of these measures. The political glitch to many of these policies, however, is that by the early 1990s this type of progressive, liberal largesse was neither politically popular nor fiscally affordable.

The state also ranks high on various measures of civic capacity and government performance. Aspects of civic performance include a general index that ranks the "livability" of the state and includes Rhode Island among the states with low crime and notably low homicide rates.[6] Performance standards include progressive tax policies that generally take care of the needy and the capacity of the state to make relatively effective decisions. One result of these policies is that among all states, Rhode Island scores second highest in the country on an equality score—meaning that the gap between the rich and the poor, based on after-tax income, is narrower here than in all other states except Vermont.[7]

The Democrats also took up the cause of the unions in this "Labor State," although their record was not nearly as strong as one might expect. After they took over in the late 1930s, many of the early Democratic leaders were conservative and pro-business; only later did the party gradually take up the cause of labor. When it did the party offered protective legislation that improved the working and living conditions of industrial workers, providing them with a decent standard of living, job opportunities, and extensive workers' and unemployment compensation. However, their support left industrial workers relatively weak, especially compared to public sector unions.[8] This in turn permitted employers of unionized and non-union workers to pursue a "low-wage, low-skill" strategy of low wages, negligible job security, and little on-the-job training for coping with changing technologies. These traditions left private sector workers vulnerable to low wages and layoffs whenever the economy turned sour.

These early patterns set the framework for a kind of "politics of accommodation" between majority Democrats and business elites, an accommodation that unraveled only when a recession hit in the late 1980s.[9] Each side got something. The old guard got a cheap, stable, and compliant work force, it retained control of key business and media establishments, and it retreated to its side a of fairly bifurcated educational and social world. As the majority party the Democrats, composed mainly of Catholic ethnic groups of working-class backgrounds, took control of state government and enjoyed—with considerable acumen—the perks and power of office. They also began to hustle up their own educational and social ladder, and the lore of Rhode Island is rich with wonderful tales of when and how these two social worlds bumped into each other.

If the Democrats supported the interests of private sector unions, they also offered extraordinary (and many would say excessive) support and protection to public service employees. Rhode Island ranks about average in the number of state employees but this ranking belies their political strength.[10] State and municipal unions formed an active core of support for the party. In return, the Democrats, who consistently held huge majorities in the General Assembly of this "weak governor" state, took care of them. Beginning with the passage of the Public Sector Act (1941), which compelled bargaining with public employees through their unions, successive legislation up through the 1980s secured for state and municipal workers well-paid employment with generous benefits. The unions, in turn, improved their own positions because many of these public employees also ran for party positions or public office. A part-time, amateur legislature provides an ideal service setting for many union employees.

Most observers agree, however, that the party leadership in the legislature went "over the top" during the 1980s. After having achieved just about every on-the-job benefit one could expect, the public employee unions, with support from the legislature, turned their attention to pensions, disability benefits, and salary credits for continuing education. Comforted by the policy that mandated secrecy of state records for reasons of privacy (in place since 1936), the legislature continued to pass what became lavish provisions for state workers and municipal employees to enhance their published salaries and retirement credits. Various provisions allow state workers to receive hefty annual bonuses for continuing education, even classes and training programs taken on state time. Other legislation permitted state workers to "buy," for a nominal rate, time in a pension system—a system that is not linked to actuarial rates—getting credit for a range of other kinds of employment in order to boost their lengths of service. Retirement credits could be claimed for part-time summer jobs, private school or out-of-state teaching, out-of-state work for which the employee was already receiving a pension, and, in one case, for time spent in prison!

Many of these special provisions applied to the legislators themselves. A constitutional convention held in 1986 underscored a pervasive public resistance to any movement toward a full-time, decently paid professional legislature. As a result there appears to have been a tacit agreement among Rhode Island's leaders that legislators would get their due through other jobs and appointments within the state system, as well as through expanded pension benefits. In one stunning example a state senator was able to combine various stints at public employment for a total of seventy-nine years of service for an annual fixed pension of $106,000 and retire at the age of fifty-two. Perhaps the height of arrogance came with a bill that entitled union leaders, who do not work for the state, to buy into the state system and receive generous *state* pensions, some in excess of $75,000 per year.[11]

CHANGES IN THE LANDSCAPE

By the late 1980s a number of factors rendered this system obsolete. Foremost was a changing demographic picture. A suburban middle-class constituency had emerged in this urban blue-collar state. Census data indicate that Rhode Island was twenty-sixth in per capita income in 1970 but jumped to fourteenth in both the 1980 and 1990 censuses. Moreover, suburbanization shifted people from the core cities to surrounding country areas. Executive home developments flourished in towns like East Greenwich and Barrington, and wealthier "good government" folks, many of whom came into managerial jobs from other states, demanded a more-effective education system and a more efficient and professional politics. These groups were highly critical of and vocal about the kind of political machinations to which many Rhode Islanders, perhaps, had become inured.

Rumors about the character of the pension provisions, as well as media revelations about selective abuses in the municipal and state workers' disability systems, fueled the efforts of various community and reform groups. These, along with some first-rate investigative reporting by the *Providence Journal* on selected excesses in the system, began to feed an undercurrent of public resentment. Here a unique feature of Rhode Island becomes critical in understanding contemporary politics. The close-knit character of the state combined with the enormous influence of the *Providence Journal*—the only statewide paper which appears to control the better part of the political agenda—creates a situation where a few well-placed, articulate, or wealthy individuals can have considerable impact on the system.

And taxes continued to go up. The state initiated a fairly hefty income tax in 1971, and taxes continued to escalate during the 1980s. Local communities found their budgets strained by the demands of the education system and by the costs of the municipal unions, which in turn forced up property taxes as well. Pressed on all sides, the Democratic legislature then increased corporate taxes. Business leaders chafed under these policies, especially after federal cutbacks and the relocation of select defense-related industries to other states, and a general economic downturn related to a lingering regional recession further dampened the economic climate.

By that time the defects of the low-wage, low-skill strategy and a lack of business investment came home to roost for the business community.[12] While small sectors of the economy related to executive and administrative jobs improved (compared to the national economy), the labor market remained concentrated in the secondary sector. For years low expectations and opportunities among factory workers, who were still able to make a decent living, sustained negative attitudes about education and training. Younger workers, who had traditionally found many opportunities in low-wage factory jobs, could no longer achieve a viable standard of living in this labor market. In this changing economic environment the economy stagnated to the point that by 1990 some observers argued that Rhode Island resembled a "mature third-world economy."[13]

One attempt to counter this trend was the development in 1984 of the

Greenhouse Compact, an ambitious public-private economic development plan intended to link technology with training to "grow" more developed segments of the economy. Intended to produce better jobs and economic development, the compact received strong support from business and labor leaders, the media, the governor, and the legislature, and was put to voters. However, the plan was overwhelmingly defeated in a referendum by an increasingly cynical public that doubted the compact would help anyone but the elites who supported it.[14]

The aftermath of the Greenhouse failure, coupled with a declining economy, caused the politics of accommodation—the *modus operandi* for the business community and the political establishment—to fall apart. In 1988, for example, a group of representatives of the business community marched on the statehouse demanding statutory reform of a workers' compensation program whose escalating rates had caused many insurance companies to stop doing business in the state. Business leaders joined nascent reform groups in demanding the reform and restructuring of the political system. The *Providence Journal*, generally supportive of business interests, turned the heat up with a more-aggressive posture toward the political elite, initiating a series of stinging investigative reports that were particularly critical of the Democratic leadership in the legislature.

Many politicians, however, failed to sense the shifts on the political landscape. Some legislative leaders, inured to the idea that they might ever be held accountable, continued to permit or promote inappropriate legislative and political concessions and favors to political kin, public unions, and key constituents. Such obtuseness, however, was bipartisan and not confined to the legislature. Edward DiPrete, a Republican governor elected in 1984 after a bruising Democratic primary, missed the drift of events and continued to indulge in questionable practices regarding campaign contributions, appointments, and a tradition of "honest graft" reminiscent of the nineteenth century. In a now notorious land transaction, a holding company which the governor and his family owned obtained a building variance on a piece of property and then sold the property the next day for a huge profit. What was most telling about the incident was that the governor initially took umbrage at the notion he did anything questionable. He only formally apologized to the voters in a 1988 television campaign ad when it was clear his reelection hung in the balance. After DiPrete left office he and his son were indicted on multiple felony counts of bribery and extortion. In 1998 they both pleaded guilty in return for a fine for his son and a short prison term for the governor.

THE 1990S: A DECADE OF CHANGE

When Bruce Sundlun took office in 1991 it was apparent that the rules of the game had changed.[15] The massive public outrage over the banking failure certainly moved things along. Subsequent investigations into the collapse of the banking system and some criminal indictments during the year revealed lax regulations, conflicts of interest, and a series of unsound business loans, many of which went to politically connected people. Publicly it was revealed that a few legislators were involved at several points in the failure process; privately it is known that proposals by various legislators and other public officials to have the General Assembly seek federal insurance for the credit unions were squelched by members of the political establishment who were either connected to the existing system or felt that exposure would cause a bank run. Given the title of the insurance network—the Rhode Island Share and Deposit Indemnity Corporation (RISDIC)—most citizens did not realize that these savings institutions were privately insured. Nonetheless, depositors in vocal, visible, and nasty public encounters made it strikingly clear that they expected the state to assume responsibility for their losses and return their funds.

In order to meet the costs of the banking crisis as well as a huge and previously undisclosed inherited budget deficit from the DiPrete administration, Sundlun and the General Assembly were forced to dedicate a portion of the sales tax to the Depositors Economic Protection Corporation (DEPCO) *and* to cut aid to local governments for education—during a lingering recession. Seizing the moment, reform groups like the Rhode Island Public Expenditure Council, Common Cause, and Operation Clean Sweep, with the support of investigative reporting by the *Providence Journal*, escalated the campaign for statutory and constitutional reform. In response the legislature did pass "revolving-door" legislation that prohibited immediate appointments to other state positions by former officeholders. In addition, the Sundlun administration developed and the legislature passed workers' compensation reform legislation that essentially saved a collapsing system and produced one of the best systems in the country today.

Then the second shoe dropped. While investigations into the banking scandal continued, and plans to return depositors' money were being developed, public anger was palpable. During this extremely volatile period Governor Sundlun, in response to a court challenge by the *Providence Journal* to open the state's pension records, ordered the records opened. The Rhode Island Federation of Teachers sought an injunction, but the state supreme court found for the governor and allowed state pension records to be opened to the public.[16] Citizens were exposed to almost daily coverage of case after case of extreme manipulation of the system for the benefit of insiders, most of which emanated from the past leadership of the General Assembly.

During this particularly tumultuous period, the *Journal* initiated, in 1993, a high-profile and somewhat sensationalized investigative series on the state court system and its sitting chief justice, Thomas Fay, as well as on the chief court administrator, Matthew Smith, which created a classic media feeding frenzy of alarming proportions.[17] The series, for which the *Journal* received a Pulitzer Prize, revealed an expensive and patronage-riddled system and disclosed transgressions on the part of Smith and Fay that appeared, in the scheme of things, relatively minor.[18] While Justice Fay and Matthew Smith were definitely a part of the "old boy network," the irony was that Fay's court had supported the opening of the pension records, had upheld the revolving door ban, and had issued the advisory opinion that essentially legitimated the role of a powerful ethics commission. Nonetheless, by this time public outrage was so pervasive and so free-floating that voters seized on the incident and Justice Fay was driven from office with little regard for due process. Reform groups, which by now had become a formidable force in public debate, kept up the pressure. Fay essentially became a pawn in the reform effort to force the legislature to place a constitutional amendment on the 1994 ballot that would change the judicial selection process for state supreme court justices. Formerly the legislative leadership basically controlled the old, highly political system, whereby all members of the legislature sat as a grand committee and elected a candidate. This was changed, via the constitutional amendment, to a form of merit selection. The amendment also mandated merit selection, instead of gubernatorial appointment, for all other judges in the state court system.

REFORM AND CHANGE

In this climate reformers were successful in initiating other statutory and constitutional reforms that significantly altered the system. Voters approved a four-year term for the governor and general officers but left in place a two-year term for members of both houses of the General Assembly. In addition, an omnibus constitutional amendment was approved that eliminated legislative pensions and raised legislative pay from five dollars a day to $10,000 per year. The amendment also provided that, after the 2000 U.S. Census, the General Assembly would be downsized: the house would go from one hundred members to seventy-five and the senate from fifty to thirty-eight. The legislature had also redressed some of the excesses of campaign money in 1992 by creating public campaign financing for statewide offices and other campaign finance legislation that eliminated some questionable practices of the past.

These changes reverberated throughout the system and the operation of the bureaucracy improved greatly. After Governor Sundlun issued the ethics order, most state agencies responded with improved standards of ethics and professionalization; members of the state bureaucracy acknowledged that "things really changed" during that administration. Increasingly, administrative appointments and evaluations were based on qualifications and merit rather than on whom you or your legislator knows, and agency heads monitored their operations with greater scrutiny toward conflicts of interest and inappropriate personnel behavior.

Continued cynicism and distrust of government and politics lingered among voters, however. Although Democrat Bruce Sundlun proved to be an able and decisive leader during the particularly difficult period of 1991 through 1994, a lingering recession in New England combined with voter cynicism and a perception of arrogance on the governor's part caused him to lose the following Democratic primary. Voters elected instead Republican Lincoln Almond, a former U.S. Attorney known principally as an anticrime and anticorruption prosecutor. In the legislature many of the old-style pols sensed the changes in the system and opted out. In fact, from 1990 to 1996 about a third of the membership was replaced.[19] Under new leadership that came to power in 1992 the General Assembly developed, supported, and enacted some strikingly innovative and responsible social and fiscal policy initiatives, especially those related to "New Federalism" whereby the federal government has devolved responsibility for various social programs to the states.[20] Although power and politics are never far from the surface in Rhode Island, most political struggles now appear to be more related to sharp institutional and partisan rivalries and less to the patronage and profiteering of the past.

By 1997 the economy had rebounded and voters sensed the changes. Polls indicated increased confidence in government, although the public remains wary of initiatives that involve public spending and are susceptible to conspiracy and collusion theories that might emanate from reform groups or the media.[21] One should also note that increased voter confidence and assessments of the state being on the "right track" appear in tandem with a growing economy; by 1999 the biggest budget issue for consideration was how to spend the surplus.[22] Another boost to voter confidence was the stunning success of the redevelopment of Providence, the heart of the city-state.

THE PROVIDENCE RENAISSANCE

Since the American Revolution, Providence has been the urban center of the state. As a major port it was at the center of the industrial revolution that began in Rhode Island in the 1790s. By the post–Civil War period Providence had achieved preeminence as the economic hub of the state. Population growth followed economic growth and peaked in 1925 when about 40 percent of the state, from a total population of fewer than 700,000, lived within the city's boundaries. After the Great Depression, population and economic growth began a downward slide that continued until 1980. Like the core cities in much of the Northeast, Providence suffered from the combined effects of substantial immigration of poor and unskilled groups, even greater "white flight" to the suburbs, a statewide decline in manufacturing activities, and a deteriorating downtown shopping area.

Gradually during the 1980s and 1990s the city began to experience a remarkable renaissance. First, a new civic center, which opened in 1973, began to draw huge crowds into a deserted downtown for rock concerts and sports events. Then, just as the department stores and other merchants were fleeing to the malls, several new office buildings sprang up, three of them built by existing banks.

Following these beginnings, the city and the state, working together, launched four massive redevelopment plans. The first involved moving the railway tracks that had formed a barrier—often called the "Chinese wall"—between the state capitol and its environs and downtown. In late 1978, with prodding from a few key business and political leaders, an imaginative plan was developed; it proposed using federal money, which had been earmarked for upgrading existing tracks and railroad stations, to reroute the tracks, build a stunning new railway station, and eliminate the freight yard adjacent to them.[23]

The successful implementation of this plan released a large area, strategically located near the heart of the city, for economic development. By 1983 this area, under the auspices of the Capitol Center Commission, allowed private developers, with help from state and federal funds, to invest in new office, retail, housing, and convention facilities in this prime area. Shortly after this project was underway a massive river relocation, planned in 1984, was set in motion with substantial federal funding. Two small rivers join and then flow into the Providence River and harbor area. Between their confluence and the bay they flow between the eastern edge of the downtown business and financial district and the "East Side," an upscale residential area of the city where Brown University is located. This area, particularly near the riverbanks, is the location of many exquisite examples of late eighteenth and early nineteenth century residential architecture, some of which dates back to colonial times. As the city declined these older areas were bypassed during earlier periods of development. When developers began to eye them in the 1970s, they were protected from demolition largely through the efforts of Antoinette Downing and the Providence Preservation Society, and private philanthropic efforts spearheaded by Elizabeth "Happy" Chace. As the city rebounded, many buildings were beautifully restored either by individual owners or by Brown University, which for the most part has artfully expanded without diminishing the overall character of the area.

The river plan was to clean out the two streams, relocate the confluence to a more convenient spot, then develop the banks of the resulting water courses for green space, recreation, boating, and the like. By the late 1990s the aesthetic impact of these changes in the heart of the city was enormous. On summer evenings literally thousands of people stroll the riverbanks, participate in city-sponsored artistic and cultural events, and dine in restaurants and cafes on or near the river.

The third project was a convention center, which was created with substantial state financial assistance. It was initiated during the recession of the early 1990s and amid great skepticism on the part of the general public. The final project involved another controversial decision to locate a multistoried shopping mall on part of the land near the state capitol that was made available by the railroad relocation.[24] The mall, located within walking distance of the downtown area, was to be the final piece of a plan that would boost the viability of the convention center because a bridge will link the two and provide shopping and entertainment opportunities for convention attendees as well as residents. Progress and development have bred more progress and more development. In 1998 a downtown outdoor skating rink in the center of the city square was completed, bringing hundreds of people to downtown during the winter months. New plans for more hotels and apartment complexes are on the drawing boards and loft renovations in the former jewelry district are revitalizing another section of the city.

Much of this development has been presided over by an ebullient and savvy mayor, Vincent "Buddy" Cianci, a legendary character in Rhode Island politics. Elected mayor as a Republican in 1974 after a divisive Democratic primary had weakened the ticket, he was reelected for two terms as a Republican and then as an independent in 1982. He was then forced to, as he says, "take a sabbatical" upon a felony conviction for assaulting his wife's lover. He came back to office in 1990 as an independent and has faced only token opposition since that time. However, a looming scandal in city hall initiated in late 1999, dubbed Operation Plunder Dome by federal investigators, has cast a long shadow on his continued political viability. Nevertheless, during this period Cianci proved to be an able leader. Beyond overseeing these structural achievements, Cianci was especially effective in implementing tax policies and rent-subsidized loft redevelopments to encourage the expansion of the arts in the city. Anchored by a nationally renowned repertory company, Trinity Rep, a theater network in the city continues to expand. The Rhode Island School of Design, located on the banks of the river, has given the city a rich legacy of museums, galleries, and a thriving community of working artists, many of whom make Providence their home upon graduation. In addition to its architecture, Brown University contributes significantly to the intellectual, aesthetic, and artistic diversity of the city. Johnson and Wales University college has added a Providence campus downtown, providing new life to a formerly declining area. Its culinary institute, along with a rich tradition of ethnic cooking, has encouraged an array of outstanding restaurants to open throughout the city. All of these developments add to the vibrant and diverse environment of this splendid city.

The Providence of the opening years of the new millennium may be very different than it was three of four decades ago, but not all its problems are being solved. As in similar northeastern cities, educating the poor children, especially the large number of immigrants who continue to settle there, is a costly and to date an unmet challenge. Tax breaks for companies that helped create much of the new development, and the sheer number of nonprofit institutions located in the city, create a narrow tax base and high property tax rates in a city where 50 percent of the potential tax base is exempt. Moreover, an expensive and extensive municipal pension system appears to be underfunded. These issues, and the role the state will play in improving education and developing the blighted areas beyond the city center, still loom on the horizon.

FUTURE POLITICAL ISSUES

Although there is no doubt that the reforms of the 1990s have gone a long way toward creating a more professional, accountable, and efficient system of state government, some of these changes raise new and challenging questions.

Rhode Island now has the dubious distinction of having the strongest ethics commission of any state in the nation. It is the only government agency, state or federal, that can create laws without legislative approval and then investigate and adjudicate complaints, impose fines, and remove from office any violators of the code. Many of the new and ever-expanding regulations created inadvertent difficulties for well-meaning public officials. In the year 2000, however, newer appointees to the commission scaled back some of the more stringent restrictions, causing reform groups to cry foul. Vacancies in races for the state legislature remain high, but reformers hope that the downsizing of the General Assembly, scheduled to be implemented after the 2000 election, will create more competitive districts. Moreover, it appears that the culture of reform has not yet filtered down to some municipal levels. In 1999 federal authorities began an extensive investigation, "Operation Plunder Dome," into the workings of Providence city hall, yielding indictments and convictions for bribery and corruption from the tax assessor's office. As the investigation broadened it became apparent that millions of dollars were being siphoned off from tax collections in a city in desperate need of funds, especially funds for public education. During that same period some questionable machinations in the Providence police department, some related to personnel problems and others related to missing or "lost" confiscated property—jewelry, cars, and cocaine, some of which suddenly got "found" prior to the investigations—are reminiscent of a B-movie script and suggest serious problems in that department. In 1999 the department also became the subject of intense criticism resulting from the inadvertent shooting of an off-duty black police officer by fellow officers. One result was the formation of a gubernatorial commission that was directed to explore the question of institutionalized racism in that department.

By 1998 it was also obvious that the judicial merit-selection system, which was supposed to remove "politics" from the process, was not the panacea expected by reformers. Recent appointments to the court have become mired in political wrangling between the legislature and the governor or subjected to public and press pressure on behalf of minority candidates. Politics remains a part of the system, but—given the diffuseness of the selection system—accountability is now less obvious. Moreover, by removing gubernatorial appointment power for all other state court judges other than those on the state supreme court, the reforms have further weakened the hand of an executive in an already weak-governor system. As an editorial in the *Providence Journal*, long an vocal advocate of reform of the judicial selection process, ruefully noted, "[T]he law of unintended consequences, so often the bane of would-be reformers, has a way of working with a vengeance when the reforms are aimed at eliminating politics from what are inherently political processes."[25]

However one construes these changes, they represent the end of an era; as it moves into the twenty-first century Rhode Island is evolving, albeit belatedly, toward a more modern system of government. At one level the changes were inevitable. States no longer are the weak links in the American federal system and the New Federalism, whereby state governments assume more responsibility for managing their own variants of federal programs like welfare, health care, Medicaid, and Medicare, demands professional and accountable state government. Moreover, Rhode Island is facing increased responsibility on issues like economic development, education quality, and environmental regulation. Even though the state has scored some stunning successes in initially reshaping some of these programs, a complex policy agenda continues to expand. In this context an amateur, patronage-based system simply becomes an inappropriate vehicle for politics.

These observations, however, raise a more interesting question. Although it is fairly obvious that the political style of politics has changed, it is not at all clear that these shifts represent an enduring change in the political *culture* of the state. There can be no doubt that the impulses of many Rhode Islanders emanate from a good-government vision of the commonwealth that sees a moral imperative in the quality of public life. But one could also argue that these shifts in the political system represent a restructuring of the marketplace of politics where, for a number of reasons, the cost of doing public business the old way got too high and, much like corporate restructuring, new systems had to be established to correct the situation.

The latter evaluation appears persuasive in light of the fact that since its founding the political culture of the Ocean State has been essentially individualistic. As in all other American states, the political culture—the orientations and expectations about government and politics—is rooted in the early beginnings of the state and then evolves with changing populations and environments. Although there have certainly been changes in the system, it is rare that one can look to the past, to the inception of a state, and trace a clear line of continuity in values and ideas about the public realm as one can find in Rhode Island. Thus, in order to understand the contemporary culture and politics of the Ocean State, one needs to begin at the beginning.

CHAPTER TWO

Political Culture in the Ocean State

A landed interest, a manufacturing interest, a mercantile interest, a moneyed interest, with many lesser interests, grow up of necessity in civilized nations, and divide them into different classes actuated by different sentiments and views. The regulation of these various and interfering interests forms the principal task of legislation, and involves the spirit of party and faction in the necessary and ordinary operations of the government.

James Madison, 1778

We want to play the game the way everybody else plays it. We think we are coming of age and are ready.

Pablo Rodgriguez, President, Latino
Political Action Committee, August 1998

Atop the Rhode Island statehouse, one of the largest and most elaborate edifices in the state, is a curious statue of a lone, nameless individual. The statue, entitled "The Independent Man," speaks volumes about the political culture of the state and suggests why it holds a unique place in New England insofar as, since its inception, Rhode Island has developed and sustained a highly individualistic political culture. The particular patterns of early settlement, the founding ideals of church-state relations, and the course of economic development created a colony, and then a state, that differed considerably from other states in the region in terms of its values and orientations toward public life.

Political culture is generally defined as the orientations and expectations of the general public and politicians about the purpose and conduct of government. In a pathbreaking analysis of political culture in the American states, Daniel J. Elazar notes that insofar as the United States shares a common culture, it is defined by two different strands of ideals and values about government and politics.[1] The first, a utilitarian view, sees the political order as a marketplace in which individuals or groups interact and bargain in order to promote their self-interests. The second perspective sees the political order as a commonwealth in which citizens participate in order to promote shared values of the common good rooted in moral principles. Definitions of political culture are shaped, in part, by how these common perspectives play out in regions or states with different ethnographic and demographic histories.

Out of these shared and contrasting visions of the public order, Elazar identifies three distinct political subcultures that evolved in various regions of the country: moralistic, individualistic, and traditionalistic.[2] These subcultures are based on the shared historical experiences and patterns of migration in particular regions or states. A moralistic culture was generally dominant in the rural and homogeneous settlements of New England, an individualistic culture was typical of the more heterogeneous and commercial Mid-Atlantic states, and a traditionalistic culture was commonly found in the hierarchical world of the plantation South.

The moralistic political culture grew out of the Puritan understanding of a commonwealth in which the role of the church and state were bound together to promote a good society. Participation in public life was seen as a positive moral obligation in the interest of a community of believers. The early world of New England was a homogeneous theocracy wherein leaders like John Winthrop "defined the particular covenant of New England in terms . . . [that] demanded that New England produce the best possible human state, the best possible men, the most perfect of human fraternities."[3] This does not mean that ideas about benevolent self-interest, which allows individuals to accumulate wealth and power, were not part of the ethic, but rather that the dominant strain in early New England reflected a moralistic vision of politics.

The individualistic subculture views the public sphere as a utilitarian marketplace designed to serve the secular needs of the people. As Elazar notes, "The individualistic political culture holds politics to be just another means by which individuals may improve themselves socially and economically."[4] In the public sphere politics is a business, and individuals or groups compete to advance individual or group interests. This view of politics, it should be noted, is fairly consistent with the ideals of the American Founders, especially James Madison, who rejected the notion of the religious state and argued instead for a secular form of interest-group politics that is the bedrock of our system. Moreover, this general culture does not preclude the idea that many individuals, driven by goals to promote a good society, will participate in civil society, but rather that the dominant pattern is one of interest-group politics.

The traditionalistic political subculture, which evolved in the hierarchical, plantation structure of the South, developed a paternalistic concept of politics wherein an elite assumed political and economic decision-making responsibilities on behalf of citizens of less-established backgrounds and families; the object of politics was to preserve the status quo.

Elazar traces the patterns of migration across the United States through which migrant groups brought these basic ideas about politics, and subsequent variations, to all regions in the country. While these political cultures represent ideal types that have been muted and melded over time, what is fascinating and remarkable is that despite the passage of time, enduring aspects of these cultures remain salient. Systematic research has found that even in contemporary politics the factor of political culture based on Elazar's model can be used to explain much of the variations in the politics, public opinion, and policy choices of different American states.[5]

RHODE ISLAND: DISSIDENTS AND MISFITS

From the onset it is apparent that Rhode Island did not fit the traditional mold of New England beginnings because its *raison d'être* was explicitly at odds with the Puritan ideal (which forms the basis of the moralistic political culture). In 1636 Roger Williams, a religious dissident, was banished from New Salem and established a settlement in what is now Providence. He was soon followed by other dissidents who, in turn, established other independent settlements around the area, which together came to be known as Rhode Island and the Providence Plantations.

In preparation for the Puritan settlement in America, Winthrop wrote that the new society they were founding was to be a model of Christian charity wherein positive moral obligations would compel members of the covenant to obey and live by the laws of a biblical community. He meant to create a "city on the hill" that would be a beacon of the Old World in the New World.[6] Roger Williams came to reject this link between church and state, and appealed instead to private moral insight. This perspective posed a fundamental threat to the theocratic order in New England and eventually caused Williams to be tried and banished from New Salem.

For the Puritans the weak inclinations of human nature justified compelling believers to adhere to the covenant. To allow other interpretations only promoted a conception of the individual that was fundamentally at odds with the Puritan ideal. Hence, as Carey McWilliams notes, Winthrop, who was a much less self-righteous leader than many of his Puritan counterparts, was uncharacteristically adamant about the breach Williams promoted and was anxious to "pursue the 'errors' of Williams and Anne Hutchison out of the Commonwealth" because the implications of their doctrine "led directly to individualism."[7]

It would appear that Winthrop's concerns were well founded. In short order Rhode Island became the "most liberal, the most entrepreneurial, and the most modern of the eighteenth century colonies," one that encouraged a culture in which secular interests dominated the public realm.[8] This form of politics fits squarely within the American marketplace tradition; it can be a highly efficient and effective form of representation that promotes mobility and pluralism in the system. Indeed, one of the most notable features of public life in Rhode Island early on was an impressive tolerance for all views and religions, which encouraged the striking diversity and pluralism that are among the hallmarks of a mature political system. But the underside of tolerance can be a moral indifference to the character of public life or a lack of "public regardingness" which, one could argue, has also been a dominant strain in the public life of Rhode Island since its founding. The historical record lends some validity to this second perspective.

Throughout the founding period of roughly 1636 to 1690 Williams remained a staunch supporter of the separation of church and state. Indeed, he argued for a view of government that was astoundingly secular. Historian Edmund Morgan notes: "Although Williams' principal concern in the separation of church and state was to preserve the church from worldly contamination, he also believed that government suffered when diverted from its proper functions by the church. . . . Whether pagan or Christian, *so long as government protected the people who created it, in their persons and their property, it did what government ought to do*" (emphasis added).[9]

This view of the role of government had profound implications for the social and political character of the state. The liberal heterodoxy of the colony encouraged multiple dissentions from one sect—and social system—to others. Given that Rhode Island had no formal charter until 1663, most settlers held a skeptical view of *any* political authority that attempted to make and enforce laws, levy taxes, or settle land disputes. In short, Rhode Islanders "lacked that communal sense of purpose that gave stability and order to the other colonies." Furthermore, Williams's ideas about leadership and his reluctance to impose any common vision about church and community on the settlements "gave a very egalitarian and individualist cast to Rhode Island's infant plantations. Indeed, they were at first almost anarchic."[10] Gordon Wood echoes this view when he notes that this tiny corporate entity "was the most faction-ridden colony of all."[11]

These patterns were, of course, in sharp counterdistinction to civic and religious developments in other New England colonies where religious and political authority was clearly defined, mandated, and enforced. The unique character of Rhode Island during this time, and the fact that it became a refuge for outcasts from other colonies, encouraged a regional disdain for the colony (see chapter 3) and nourished a tradition of separatism that further contributed to a radical populism and hard-nosed individualistic politics. Traditions of civic and religious individualism, separatism, and democracy might be appealing to modern sensibilities, but they were regarded with considerable alarm in the other New England colonies.[12]

Roger Williams himself came to lament the fruits of the liberal and tolerant foundations of the colony. Although he never abandoned his belief that civil government should never impose moral constraints on society, at the end of his life he bitterly denounced the contentious and fiercely individualist strain that characterized the social and political order.[13] One of his last public acts involved rowing across Narragansett Bay in 1672 and engaging in a heated public debate with Quaker leaders and followers of George Fox, the founder of the Quaker sect, who visited Newport that year. Although the Quaker belief in an individual calling based on one's conscience was consistent with Williams's vision of religion, Williams found the Quakers' determination to impose their moral vision on the colony objectionable and meddlesome.[14]

ECONOMICS AND DIVERSITY

If tolerance, pluralism, and factionalism provided the milieu for a secular and individualistic culture, economic development in the colony only reinforced these patterns. Although Williams's original settlements were small farming plantations in Providence, farming did not remain a major industry. During the colonial period Newport was the dominant city. After 1710 it became an imperial center of trade, commerce, and shipbuilding. Happily, the demands of commerce provided for a measure of internal cohesion; after 1690 the trend toward a market economy encouraged legislative initiatives that promoted commerce and the cooperative building of roads, bridges, and ferries to help move goods to market.[15] During this period primary sources of wealth were the sugar trade, fisheries (primarily whaling), and, of course, the infamous and lucrative slave trade.

In some ways this tiny colony was remarkably progressive by colonial standards. Rhode Island became a refuge for religious groups not welcome in other parts of New England. By mid-century, while most other colonies were attempting to impose conformity with one church that was supported by religious taxes, the doctrine of religious freedom in Rhode Island resulted in an extensive network of churches of several denominations. The state essentially acted as a "safety valve for dissenters from the Puritan colonies."[16] A substantial Baptist community developed around the state, as well as Anglicans and Congregationalists. In addition, an extensive Jewish community prospered in Newport until the Revolution. In fact, the oldest existing synagogue in the United States is the Touro Synagogue in Newport, a testament to the region's liberal beginnings.

A large and influential community of Quakers also prospered in Rhode Island. The first Quakers arrived in Boston in 1656. These early settlers, who were regarded as dangerous fanatics, were imprisoned, persecuted, and often banished from the Massachusetts colony. A steady stream found their way to Rhode Island, where they were not only permitted to settle peaceably but were also allowed to participate in voting and officeholding. Managing to get around religious restrictions on "war preparation," the Quaker community became an extensive and influential force in Rhode Island's social and political life. Many prominent and influential Rhode Islanders, finding the Quaker inclinations toward social and civic responsibility appealing, converted to the Friends. A series of prominent Quakers served as governor and other high officers, while other members became a vocal moral force in the state, especially in the campaign against slavery. Indeed, to the extent there was a tradition of fusion between private moral obligations and public life that created a moralistic strand in the political culture, these foundations go back to the ideals of the Quakers.

Regardless of how the ideals of Christian and civic responsibility were construed, the entrepreneurial spirit of this corporate colony dominated life. Objections to public lotteries were put aside so that these events became a popular and accepted way of raising local revenues. The mandates of the civic order never included restrictions against smuggling, which became something of an art form in and around Narragansett Bay during the British regency. Groups of Congregationalists and Baptists joined the Quakers in a campaign against slavery, but many of their efforts in the legislature were stymied by influential wealthy merchants who profited from the slave trade.

A telling example of the tensions between moral and economic concerns in the public sphere centered on the Brown family, one of the renowned first families of the state. The three Brown brothers, Moses, Nicholas, and John, were wealthy entrepreneurs during the revolutionary period. In 1773 Moses became a Quaker, sold his slaves, and joined a reform movement to outlaw slavery and abolish the slave trade. His group was successful in proposing and passing a bill for gradual manumission that was eventually adopted by the legislature in 1784. Moses's brother John, who at the time was profiting from the trade, managed to use his influence to get sanctions against the slave trade deleted from the bill. A few years later, when the trade was finally outlawed in the state, John engaged in various machinations to continue it, including registering his ships in other states to allow him to continue his business. Finally, in 1796 Moses brought suit against his brother for these transgressions, but a jury was apparently not willing to convict such a notable citizen.[17] Along with being responsible for funding early initiatives at industrialization at Slater Mill, Moses left a legacy that also included Moses Brown School and Moses Brown Meeting House, outstanding Quaker institutions that still thrive in Providence. John and his other brother Nicholas became the principal benefactors of the famous Brown University, just a few blocks away.

During the transition from colony to state, individualistic or interest-group politics developed around various factions, all of which attempted to gain control of the legislature. One, led by Samuel Ward and generally centered in the southern part of the colony, was favorable to the interests of Newport merchants; another, led by Stephen Hopkins, tended to be supported by the interests of a growing commercial class in Providence. Although certain religious and social groups tended to favor one or the other of these factions, historians generally find no clear class or ideological core to the emerging parties and suggest that they were loose associations based on commercial interests. These groups represented the beginnings of organized parties of opposition which early on indulged in vote buying and a system of patronage that supported their interests in the legislature and in local governments.

Thus Rhode Island got an early start in the development of political parties. As David Lovejoy notes, "Factional government, based on a number of local issues, was a stage in political growth which Rhode Island experienced earlier than most colonies owing to its large degree of political independence and the particular conditions that existed there."[18] By the time of the Revolution in 1776, the state had reached a "surprising level of political maturity," and resistance to the Crown was based not only on concerns about the autonomy of state and local government but also about the encroachments against a mature and profitable system of party politics.[19]

INDIVIDUALISTIC POLITICS AND THE ERA OF INDUSTRIALIZATION

After the Revolution Newport never regained its commercial importance. Maritime, economic, and social power had shifted to Providence. The city's location at the head of Narragansett Bay and the confluence of three of the state's largest rivers made it the center of manufacturing as well as trade. The opening of Slater Mill in 1790, financed in part by Moses Brown, brought manufacturing and the factory system to Rhode Island. With these developments came huge increases in the population of Providence and its environs as immigrant workers who worked the mills settled in and around the city and in mill towns in Providence County. In political terms these events encouraged a Yankee middle-class mentality of hunkering down to protect one's interests against a growing immigrant class of what was initially mostly poor and uneducated Irish Catholics.

Ironically, the liberal charter of 1663, which was essentially adopted as the state constitution after independence was won, became the vehicle for restrictions against immigrants. By 1840 a state that had been founded on principles of tolerance and participatory politics became one of only three states in the Union—Virginia and Louisiana being the others—that denied its citizens universal male suffrage.[20] It took a civic insurrection in 1842, popularly known as the Dorr Rebellion, to force a constitutional change; yet the new constitution, adopted in 1843, retained a property requirement or a hefty tax for all non-native-born citizens who wished to register to vote. As a result, the open and egalitarian aspects of the state's early traditions were thwarted as the Yankee elite grew increasingly more conservative and maneuvered to maintain their commercial dominance, growing wealth, and social status as well as to prevent the newcomers from accessing the political system.

This period marked the beginning of the particular "we-they" divisions and tough partisan politics that remained evident in the state until fairly recently. Broadly speaking, native, white Anglo-Saxon Protestants of all classes lined up against an exploding number of ethnic and Catholic working-class constituencies who manned the factories and had little economic or political clout. Rhode Island by the 1860s was the most industrialized state in the union. Less than 3 percent of the workforce was involved in maritime activities, more than 50 percent was engaged in manufacturing, and 10 percent was engaged in farming.

After the Civil War and through the turn of the twentieth century, the state reached its economic and political pinnacle as the era of the robber barons dawned throughout the greater Northeast. During that time this "most densely populated, most heavily industrialized and urbanized state in the Union, was ruled by a small minority of business oligarchies and rural voters."[21] The vehicle for control was the Republican party, which created a system of rural political machines that allowed the GOP minority to retain power up through the 1930s. The Yankees were finally outmaneuvered by the Democrats in 1935 in an organizational coup known as the "Bloodless Revolution."

The coup took hardball politics to a new level. Democrat Theodore Francis Green was elected governor in 1932. In the 1934 election the Democrats managed to also take control of the lower house in the assembly as well as reelect Green for governor and Robert Quinn as a Democratic lieutenant-governor. At the January 1935 opening legislative session, the Democrats, through a parliamentary maneuver that required Quinn to preside over the state senate's organizational meeting, were able to invalidate the elections of two Republicans to the senate, giving them a majority in both houses. Drawing on reorganization provisions in the state constitution, they then went on to dismiss and replace the entire state supreme court, eliminate the commission of finance (which was controlled by the General Assembly), and pass omnibus legislation that completely reorganized state government and gave a figurehead governor meaningful budget and other statutory authority.

After they consolidated power the Democrats indulged in a melee of patronage politics by removing many Republicans from administrative positions and replacing them with Democrats. The old-line Yankee, T. F. Green, however, exerted a measure of restraint over his Irish colleagues by insisting that they attempt to bring other ethnic groups into the coalition. They even appointed two Republicans to the new supreme court.[22]

This pattern of individualistic politics was fairly typical in other states when and where immigrant or minority populations finally broke into politics. Understandably, such groups do not get into politics to make the world a better place or promote "good government" ideals. They get into politics to get for themselves and their constituents a slice of the political, social, or economic pie that has eluded them, usually due to discrimination or lack of opportunity. The history of the American states is replete with a number of these transformations in political culture, when significant groupings of previously disadvantaged populations came to dominate the political system.

In New England, for example, the political cultures of both Massachusetts and Connecticut were essentially melded into more individualistic patterns as the immigrant classes came to power in those states. The difference in Rhode Island was that the ascendancy of the Democrats represented a shift in power but a continuity in a political culture that was already dominated by individualistic inclinations.

ETHNIC POLITICS IN AN INDIVIDUALISTIC CULTURE

The "we-they" gap between the Yankees and the immigrant groups ob-
scures significant and long-standing political and social divisions among
various ethnic groups themselves. These endured until well into the twentieth
century, although most of these groups ultimately coalesced around the
labor movement, the presidential nomination by the Democrats of an urban
Catholic (Al Smith in 1928), and the ascendancy of the Democratic party
at the national level during the Great Depression. In a fairly typical pattern,
early ethnic divisions were related to intergroup loyalty and a parochial
perspective of the "other," to the sequence of migrations ("who got here
first?"), and to different interpretations of the Catholic tradition.

The first group to settle in the state in significant numbers was the
Irish. Although a small cadre of generally well-educated Irish Protestants
were evident in Rhode Island from colonial times on, the deluge of poor
immigrants came after 1835 as a result of the potato famine. Between 1815
and 1835 a sizable wave of Irish Catholics emigrated to America as a result
of the English policies of eviction and disenfranchisement of Irish Catholic
tenant farmers; of some potato crop failures in 1818 and 1822; and of the
liberalization of passenger restrictions and fares to America. These groups
coalesced into a poor farming class with some resources and usually a
rudimentary education. Toward the end of the 1830s, however, as the famine
became more severe, huge numbers of destitute (and usually illiterate) Irish
were encouraged to flee to America by laws that would have placed them in
workhouses had they chosen to remain in Ireland.[23]

This influx prompted the first explicit nativist public reaction, as Henry
Anthony began an intense campaign in the *Providence Journal* against the
"foreign vagabond." The campaign was in no small measure a backdrop
to the anti-nativist and anti-Catholic opponents of reformer Thomas Dorr
of the Dorr Rebellion. The campaign contributed to discriminatory and
restrictive voting regulations for non-natives that were incorporated into the
new constitution of 1843. Nonetheless, by 1850 the Irish comprised almost
70 percent of the foreign-born persons in the state. They made their way
up the social and political ladder and began to gain influence through the
Democratic party.

Another significant ethnic group in Rhode Island was the French. Early
French migration included an unsuccessful Huguenot farm settlement in
1686 and small groups of prominent Huguenots who settled in the state
during the colonial era. The French were also a prominent presence during

the Revolutionary War, when a force of six thousand troops under the command of Gen. Jean Baptiste du Rochambeau were garrisoned at Newport to assist the Americans in the war effort. Several other prominent Frenchmen, including the Marquis de Lafayette, volunteered their services, and the French provided critical assistance in several key battles during the war. The exemplary presence of the French promoted intercultural communication and went a long way toward dispelling an anti-Catholic bias that generally characterized colonial New England.[24]

The most substantial number of French immigrants, however, were working-class French-Canadians; about seventy-five thousand settled in Rhode Island between 1860 and 1930. Most were drawn to the emerging textile industry and established communities throughout the state. As with other immigrant groups, they were subjected to prejudice and suspicion exacerbated by the fact that they did not speak the language and they resisted assimilation insofar as they were intent on retaining their own languages and customs.

As is often the case with successive immigrant groups, the French did not align with the Irish and some rancor developed between the two groups. One point of contention was the differing conception of Catholic parish life: the French were accustomed to local parish autonomy and resisted the more authoritarian Irish pattern of religious authority that vested power with the bishops. Given that the church hierarchy was dominated by Irish Catholics, this rift caused the French to insist on their own French-language parishes and churches. Moreover, in political terms the custom in many French communities was to follow a more ascriptive tradition and support the politics of their employers, the mill owners. They also shared the Yankee antipathy toward lower-caste Celtic peoples and, given the slightly elevated position of the Irish, class envy exacerbated these tensions. Thus, before the 1930s the French tended to be Republican. The GOP, playing on these divisions, courted the French by giving them places on electoral tickets. Between 1909 and 1928 Aram Pothier, a prominent banker, served six terms as a Republican governor during a period when that office enjoyed little influence. During the Great Depression, however, the French alliance with the Republicans became frayed and a significant switch to the Democrats occurred.

Italians are proud of the fact that the first European reported to have come to Rhode Island was the Italian explorer Giovanni da Verrazano. However, significant immigration to the state did not begin until around 1880. Although 1900 census data indicate that nine thousand Italian immigrants were in the state, the boom came later; records indicate that from 1898 to 1932 almost

Table 2: Ethnic Populations in Rhode Island

1990 Population	Rhode Island: 1,003,464		
	Urban: 863,467		
	Rural: 140,037		
Ancestry:			
Total Reported:		1,276,935	
Irish:		213,801	16.7%
Italian:		199,190	15.6%
English:		161,001	12.6%
French (except Basque):		134,177	10.5%
Other:		114,322	9.0%
Portuguese:		94,650	7.4%
German:		73,482	5.8%
French Can.:		72,843	5.7%
Polish:		47,227	3.7%

Source: Rhode Island Department of Administration, Division of Planning, *"Census 90" Selected Social Characteristics for Rhode Island Counties, Cities, and Towns*, April 1992.

sixty thousand Italians arrived at the port of Providence.[25] Census data from 1990 indicate that Italian-Americans were the second largest ethnic group in the state.

Like groups that preceded them, assimilation for the Italians was not easy. Communities of strong families with guild orientations settled throughout the state, with large concentrations in and around Providence, Bristol County, and Westerly, where settlers originally worked in the quarry mines. Because of language differences, Italians experienced suspicion and hostility that encouraged them to remain in tightly knit communities. They, too, chafed under the hierarchical version of Catholic parish life developed by the Irish clergy, and fought for community parishes and priests. Moreover, as is the case in several other northeastern states—including New York, New Jersey, Connecticut, and Massachusetts—political infighting, especially with the Irish (who dominated Democratic party organizations) created enduring pockets of Republicans among Italian-Americans.

As they moved up the socioeconomic ladder, Italians made their mark in business, the professions, and politics. Although today large numbers are elected locally and to the state legislature, and significant numbers of Italian-Americans can be found in high appointed positions, electoral success in statewide races remains more difficult. Unfortunately, the New England headquarters of the Mafia under the Patriarca family was until recently located in Providence. This, no doubt, created some electoral obstacles for Italian-Americans.

The most common problem was simply one of association. In a close-knit ethnic and social environment, influential Italian-Americans might have had longtime childhood, family, or community associations with people connected to the Mafia. In a culture where loyalty to one's own is highly valued, it is sometimes difficult to avoid some contact with these individuals. Elected representatives and other public or business leaders might socialize in or around these circles, sometimes inappropriately so. The most famous case was the long-time association of State Supreme Court Chief Justice Joseph Bevilacqua with people connected to the Mafia. His continued associations with such people while chief justice ultimately resulted in impeachment hearings and his resignation. By the late 1980s, however, the influence of organized crime under the control of the Patriarca family ended in Rhode Island.

Although the outstanding public service of notable Italians has done much to dispel a lingering stereotype, their electoral image suffered a series of setbacks again in the 1990s. The administration of Republican Governor Edward DiPrete (1985–1990) was clouded with scandal. After he left office the governor was indicted on several counts of bribery and extortion. During the same period, investigations into the 1991 credit union scandal revealed a preponderance of Italian surnames, many of whom were involved in questionable networks of influence peddling and illegal activities. Unfortunately these events can cast a shadow on the statewide political aspirations of the many talented and capable Italians-Americans who serve in government.

Other ethnic groups played a vital part in the political development of the state. Rhode Island has long been a home to a small but thriving Jewish community. As noted earlier, the state's tendency toward freedom of religion allowed Jews to settle in colonial Newport as early as 1658, and by 1770 one quarter of the entire population of Jews in America was settled in that city. After the Revolution a few families settled in the commercial heart of Providence, but significant growth came after 1880 when immigrants began to arrive from Eastern Europe.[26] Given the small size of the Jewish community (approximately twenty thousand), data on the political preferences of this group are hard to come by. Anecdotal evidence suggests, however, that Jews, perhaps because of their small numbers, never united politically as a group. Instead, their political associations tended toward their socioeconomic status and interests. Thus, wealthier families tended to support Republicans while working-class Jews aligned with the

Democrats. Despite their small numbers, in addition to attaining prominence in business and the professions they have been a strong force in politics. In 1992, for example, three of the five elected general officers (including the governor) were Jewish. The Jewish community has also provided significant leadership in the political reform movement of recent years.

The Portuguese were another sizable ethnic group that settled in Rhode Island during the early twentieth century. Among the first Portuguese were Jewish families, many fleeing the Inquisition, who settled in the state in 1658. Later, groups of Portuguese drawn to the fishing industry came from the Madeira Islands as the whaling industry developed; a steady stream continued to settle in Bristol, Fox Point, Pawtucket, and Central Falls from 1897 to the 1920s. The initiation of federal quotas blunted these migrations beginning in 1924, until they were lifted in 1965. Most Portuguese immigrants to the state now come from the Azores and Cape Verde Islands. Recently, Cape Verdans asserted their separate status as a distinct ethnic group. Because of these racial, ethnic, and regional divisions, Portuguese-Americans tend to be stratified by place of ethnic origin or social class, as reflected in various and distinct "social" clubs throughout the community.[27] They remained, until quite recently, politically diffuse.

CONTEMPORARY INDIVIDUALISTIC POLITICS

The experience of these immigrant groups suggests a core dynamic of individualistic politics in the behavior and loyalties of ethnic groups. Voters became aware that gaining representation in local and party offices was important, and thus began to support names on the ballot that reflected their groups. The dominant Republican Yankees and Irish Democrats came around, rather grudgingly, to the awareness that opening doors to the newer groups was politically advantageous and even necessary. Eventually both parties developed ethnically balanced tickets for statewide office. In recent decades, as the children and grandchildren of immigrants have moved up the socioeconomic ladder and often moved out to the suburbs, ethnic voting tendencies have weakened among many groups as their interests became defined by economic or social issues relevant to their changing status.

In fact, in an era when political parties no longer organize ethnically balanced tickets and individual candidates control nominations, ethnic politics at the beginning of the twenty-first century have taken some curious turns. In 1996 an Italian-American, Joseph Paolino, who was formerly the mayor of Providence and then ambassador to Malta, ran in a congressional Democratic primary. In a district with a sizable Italian population, his strategy appeared to focus on securing the Italian vote in the three-way primary and then going on to broaden his appeal in the general election. Unfortunately, in a letter inviting Italian-Americans to a campaign dinner, an aide (without Paolino's knowledge) issued a blunt appeal to this constituency that stated that it was about time we had "one of our own" in Congress. The press got hold of the letter and Paolino lost big in the primary. A telling fact about the incident was that this blatant appeal angered Italian-Americans as well as other voters.

U.S. Representative Patrick Kennedy has forged another variant of ethnic politics in his bids for Congress. In a brilliant strategy Kennedy first organized ethnic awareness and support among the Portuguese. Using family connections in Washington, Kennedy invited the prime minister (president) of Portugal and other high-level representatives of that country to visit Rhode Island ostensibly on trade missions. By doing so he tapped into this politically diffuse group, raised awareness of their common identity, and created strong political ties with this constituency. In a similar effort he used his family connections to invite the prime minister of Italy to Rhode Island, raising the awareness of the common bond among Italians—in a most benign and celebratory way—*across* party lines. This strategy, of course, has the potential to reap broad electoral benefits should Kennedy run for statewide office in the future.

The newer variant of individualistic politics continues among groups that are presently defined by race. African-Americans are one of the oldest groups in the state in that they preceded most other groups; indeed, there are extended families, especially in and around Newport, who can trace their lineage in Rhode Island back to colonial times. During the Revolutionary War, for example, former slaves were mobilized into the Black Regiment that fought heroically in the Battle of Rhode Island. Presently blacks represent about 5 percent of the population. They have been fairly successful in local and legislative races, and representatives of the black community and other supportive groups lobby hard for appointments to the courts and other administrative offices. Nonetheless, the insidious residue of racism remains evident. In 2000, prompted by the minority community's reaction to the accidental shooting of an off-duty black police officer, the governor appointed a commission to address questions of institutionalized racism that continue to hamper the progress of these Rhode Islanders.

Meanwhile, Hispanics are the fastest-growing ethnic population in the state. They are beginning to make inroads in local and state legislative races and have also begun to lobby for positions in the courts and government agencies. As table 3 indicates, 2000 Census estimates of the Hispanic population put them at about 8 percent of the population. (Some of the

Table 3: Population Based on Race in Rhode Island, 1990–2000

	1990	2000*
Total Population	1,003,464	988,500
White Population	869,000	851,000
Black	38,861	54,000
Asian	18,325	28,000
Native American	4,071	4,000
Hispanic Origin**	45,752	76,000

Source: U.S. Bureau of the Census: Rhode Island Division of Planning.

*Estimates based on census projections

** Hispanics may be of any race

estimation difficulty stems from counting Hispanics as part of either black or white groups, regardless of whether or not Portuguese are included, and the national disparateness of these groups.) Early on most Hispanics emigrated from Puerto Rico and sought integration into the white community. Later immigrants and their families, mainly from the Dominican Republic and Costa Rica, are both black and white and are becoming more active and visible in politics as they attempt to access the system in support of their constituencies. In an attempt to consolidate their influence they formed a Latino political action committee (PAC) in 1998.

Other recent immigrants are Asian Americans, whose numbers increased significantly after the Vietnam War ended in 1975 when Cambodian, Laotian, Hmong, and Vietnamese refugees made Rhode Island their home. These groups are less politically active and visible because, in total numbers, they are about 2 percent of the population and, given the histories of their countries of origin and a legacy of political repression, they are reluctant to "register" for anything.

Finally there is the legacy of the original or oldest Americans, the Native Indian population of Rhode Island. Represented mainly by the Narragansett Indians, their history within the state is a long and tragic one (see chapter 3) and their claims are part of some intense and fairly hardball interest-group politics over casino gambling (currently being played out in the state and federal arenas).

Thus it would seem that a culture of individualistic politics remains alive and well in the Ocean State. Although ethnic associations have for the most part been subsumed under partisan and interest-group politics, the clash of these interests and the resolution of group demands still define the parameters of Rhode Island state politics. Although the rules have changed to reflect a demand for more open, accountable, and efficient government, politics continues to reflect who gets what, when, where, and how within the framework of various government institutions, jockeying for position and power. Whatever its flaws, it is a thriving, modern, representative system that is inherently political and one which James Madison would surely understand.

CHAPTER THREE

Rhode Island and the Federal System

Hail, realm of rogues, renowned for fraud and guile,
All hail, the knaveries of yon little isle . . .
The wiser race, the snare of law to shun,
Like Lot from Sodom, from Rhode Island run.

Connecticut newspaper, 1787

Treaties were broken and that, in a modern frame . . . is what is happening here.

Lawyer for the Narragansett Indians, 1997

A significant feature of the landscape of Rhode Island is miles and miles of beautiful stone walls that line the roads and mark property lines throughout the state. Most of these walls were built by hand from stones dug from the relatively flat, rocky, and unfriendly land on which early Rhode Islanders settled, endured, and prospered. This small state, with limited natural resources, found itself in a hostile civil environment as well. The original colonies and then states in the region long regarded Rhode Island as a "rogue state." To some extent that stereotype endures.

Given this legacy, there are several aspects to consider in attempting to assess Rhode Island's place in the federal system. First, we will explore the roots of the outsider legacy up to the present day. We then look at the contemporary relations of the state to the federal government and neighboring states. Finally, we consider the state's relationship with the Narragansett Indians who, given their federal status, are from but not of Rhode Island. Although early relations with the Indians were remarkably cooperative, the inevitable and tragic clash of cultures marginalized the status of the Native population, creating hostilities between the state and the Narragansetts that are unresolved even today.

EARLY BEGINNINGS: REALM OF ROGUES

From the beginning the state's relationship with its neighbors was contentious. As a refuge for social and religious outcasts, the early settlements around the state were regarded as objects of scorn by neighboring colonies, which questioned the legitimacy of Rhode Island as a separate entity. Although Roger Williams established the colony in 1636, a few years later the four neighboring colonies of New Haven, Massachusetts, Plymouth, and Connecticut established a confederation that purposely excluded Rhode Island.

To fend off intrusions from the colonies in the confederation, Williams sought and obtained a patent from England in 1644. Unfortunately, the patent did not establish clear geographical boundaries. This ambiguity, added to the lack of internal agreement among the various Rhode Island settlements themselves on forming a unified colony, encouraged continued encroachments by the surrounding colonies. Some boundaries were clarified in the more comprehensive Royal Charter of 1663 that established Rhode Island and the Providence Plantations, but active boundary disputes continued for nearly a hundred years more. Although the major outlines of the state were established in 1747, the final demarcation of the state was not settled until 1862 when a disputed land issue with Massachusetts was resolved.[1]

These boundary disputes were symptomatic of the lack of regard the surrounding colonies had for the state and its settlers, whom they considered misfits and outcasts. In many ways this was an apt description of the independent and somewhat ornery folk who, by dint of their wits and determination, had carved out a thriving maritime and commercial economy by the time of the Revolutionary War.

Having turned to the sea and maritime trade for a source of much of its livelihood, the colony developed a strained relationship with the British authorities, particularly after 1763 when the Crown ceased to overlook the cavalier manner in which Rhode Islanders ignored tariff and trade regulations. Smuggling, especially as it related to the production of rum and molasses, had been commonplace, and merchants chafed when the British sent ships into Narragansett Bay to enforce the payment of duties. The state soon become known as the "spearhead of the Revolution."[2] In 1772 dissidents burned the British ship *Gaspee* and shot the captain. Although other issues colored the colonists' responses to English efforts to regain control of the colonies, the huge commercial stakes and the tradition of almost radical self-determination that did not exist in other colonies (and certainly not elsewhere in New England) made the state a leader in the movement toward independence. The General Assembly led an early call for a Continental Congress, colonists joined the armed resistance early on, and on 4 May 1776—two full months before the signing of the Declaration of Independence—the General Assembly voted a form of political independence from the Crown.

True to its independent inclinations, although the state was "first in war" it was "last in peace" insofar as the state declined to send delegates to the constitutional convention in Philadelphia and refused to ratify the federal constitution of 1787.[3] Much to the consternation of its neighboring states, Rhode Island had issued its own paper money to pay off war debts and remained engaged in a lucrative smuggling enterprise. Fearful that a federal authority would intrude on these systems and concerned about issues of individual freedom, the state was wary of ceding authority to a nationwide federal government. Deadlocked by intense internal partisan politics the stalemate continued, only reinforcing the rogue image of the state. National notables such as George Washington, Thomas Paine, and James Madison expressed disgust at the recalcitrance of the state and its continued refusal to join the union, thus provoking the newspaper epigram quoted at the opening of this chapter.

After threats from the Continental Congress to treat the state as a foreign nation and the realization among political elites that joining the union was the best course for postwar economic development, the state finally ratified the constitution in a tight convention vote in 1790. But one condition of approval was a list of amendments protecting individual freedoms, which, along with similar petitions from other states, eventually became part of the U.S. Bill of Rights.

After the Revolutionary War the center of economic and political power shifted from Newport to Providence and its environs where, by 1790, the beginnings of the Industrial Revolution were underway. Eventually this shift brought considerable growth and prosperity to the state. In a curious twist it also encouraged an unfortunate integration of Rhode Island into the established order in New England, insofar as the social and political elite abandoned the state's tolerant traditions.[4] Rhode Island "joined the ranks" of other states in the region during this period in displaying intolerance for "foreigners" and an intense anti-Catholicism that spawned a Know-Nothing Party movement. In 1855 that party swept the elections in the region and, like in Massachusetts, Connecticut, and New Hampshire, completely dominated in the Rhode Island legislature. The movement faltered later on with the advent of the Civil War and the ascent of the Republican party.

Historian William McLoughlin argues that the state "was not a vigorous antislavery state," although abolitionist movements developed as early as 1770 promoted by Quakers and other religious groups. In 1835 the president of the Providence antislavery society, William Chace, led a call for immediate abolition. Yet interests led by Benjamin Hazard in Newport, which were friendlier to the South, attempted to have abolitionist literature suppressed and discouraged congressional representatives from supporting abolition. A core debate centered around the economic links between cotton interests in the South and the textile industry in New England, as well as among many old-line Yankees who found slavery repugnant. When the war broke out, however, the state vigorously supported Lincoln's call to save the Union and supplied a record number of volunteers to the war effort.[5] One surviving letter (which received national attention in a television series on the Civil War) was written by a Maj. Sullivan Ballou as he awaited the battle of Bull Run; it provides a moving testament to the valor and patriotism of the many soldiers from the Ocean State who fought to preserve the Union. Moreover, returning veterans became part of a twenty-year effort to eliminate property requirements for those who had served in the war. This legislation was finally passed in 1886. Two years later the legislature passed the Bourn amendment, which eliminated the property tax qualification for naturalized citizens.

Despite the inspiring efforts one encounters by some Yankees during this period, from the postwar period up to the mid-1930s the "rogue" status of the state was maintained through the machinations of the Republican party, which sustained a rural political machine controlled by a Yankee elite that fostered patronage, favoritism, and a high level of corruption. Although this type of party politics was fairly typical of other states at the time, the extent and pervasiveness of corruption practiced by Rhode Island's political establishment prompted muckraker Lincoln Steffens to dub it a "State for Sale" in a now-famous 1905 article in *McClure's* magazine.

When the Democrats took control in 1935 they followed these established patterns by creating their own machine and pursuing individualistic politics; they continued the reputation of the state, which along with Massachusetts and Connecticut, was by this time at odds with the more moralistic political culture in the rest of New England. The parochial cast of politics—which continued well into the 1980s—as well as events like the RISDIC scandal that broke in the early 1990s, the scandals involving two sitting chief justices of the state supreme court, and the protracted discovery process and imprisonment of former Governor Edward DiPrete which finally played

out in 1999—has only reinforced a lingering stereotype about the character
of state politics.

RHODE ISLAND'S PLACE IN THE FEDERAL SYSTEM

When prosperity came after the Civil War the state sent powerful political figures to Washington who became significant players in national
politics. During this period Rhode Island developed a pattern familiar to
southern states where, because of one-party rule, members elected to the
U.S. Congress remained in office and built up seniority and political clout.
Historically, because of the influence of these key political figures promoting
Rhode Island in the federal system, the state has fared quite well despite its
small size and small number of voters.

Nelson Aldrich, who served in the U.S. Congress from 1879 to 1911
(two years in the House and just over twenty-nine in the Senate) moved up
through the ranks and became known as the "General Manager of the United
States." The state's remarkable transformation into a thriving industrial and
manufacturing state during the nineteenth century was certainly facilitated,
if not entirely made possible, by the high tariffs that protected U.S. products
from foreign competition. As head of the Senate Finance Committee Aldrich
promoted high-tariff policies; the Payne-Aldrich Tariff Act of 1909 bore his
name. He became a spokesperson for business interests and the mediator
between the often conflicting interests of vast business conglomerates across
the country. Toward the end of his tenure he helped create the Federal Reserve
System. Yet, while concerned with these national goals, Aldrich still managed
to protect local textile and manufacturing interests and funneled considerable
federal patronage to his home state.

After the Democrats took over in 1935, T. F. Green played an especially
significant role in federal politics. Elected to the Senate in 1937, Green became a partisan of the Roosevelt coalition and a force in national Democratic
politics. With the decline of the state's textile industry that began in the 1920s,
a desperate need developed for a new basis on which the economy could rest.
The shift from Republican to Democratic loyalty of the voters undoubtedly
encouraged the flow of New Deal program money into the state. Moreover,
Green's loyal support for President Franklin D. Roosevelt facilitated that flow
and helped trigger the massive expansion of naval activity in Rhode Island—
which sustained a significant portion of the state's postwar economy. Green
served for twenty-four years, retiring at age ninety-four. He was followed
by Democrat John O. Pastore, who served for twenty-six years (1950–1976)
and by Claiborne Pell, who served from 1961 to 1996.

These federal representatives were able to protect federal patronage until Richard M. Nixon began to close down naval operations in Rhode Island after his 1972 election, moving the destroyer fleet home base and most other naval operations (except the War College) to the South, with its emerging Republican inclinations. The move dealt a severe blow to the economy when the largest single employer of Rhode Islanders pulled out of the state. It also signaled a partisan and demographic shift in federal influence away from the Ocean State and New England. While the GOP has made gains in other regions of the country, the Northeast, and certainly Rhode Island remain a bastion of Democratic support.[6] Thus, the Republican takeover of Congress in 1994 and recent demographic shifts in the region create problems for the federal-state relationship in all the New England states, including Rhode Island.

In political terms, the state's congressional delegation does not enjoy the clout it once had. Over the course of the history of the Republic, population shifts have altered the size of the New England congressional delegation: the number has dropped from the more than 25 percent of the House of Representatives in 1790 to five percent in 2000. Going beyond the percentage of representatives, New England was still able to produce a raft of congressional leaders like John McCormick, Tip O'Neill, and George Mitchell, who continued to protect the interests of the region. In Rhode Island powerful figures like Claiborne Pell and John Chafee were able to help sustain the flow of federal monies into the state. In fact, in a balance-of-payments analysis of federal budget documents from 1981 to 1995, Rhode Island received more in federal aid than it paid in federal taxes. (The balance was a plus $420 per capita in 1981 and a plus $390 in 1995.) During much of that period Rhode Island personal income was below the national average and, with its large elderly population (the third highest in the country), the state received high Social Security payments as well as high Medicaid and welfare reimbursements.[7] A more recent study found that in 1998 the pattern still held: for every tax dollar the state sent to the federal government that year it received $1.15 in federal aid. The study cited the large elderly population and a relatively large percentage of legal immigrants as reasons for this trend.[8]

After Senator Pell retired in 1996 and Senator Chafee's death in office in 1999, the congressional delegation in Rhode Island consisted of relatively junior representatives. As one would expect, the political agenda of the Republican Congress was inclined to limit federal largesse in New England and redirect it to more fertile political ground. For example, a federal transportation law—the Intermodal Surface Transportation Efficiency Act—provided federal rebates to states based on gas tax receipts sent to the federal government. Traditionally, states in the Northeast, whose roads are older and endure more wear and tear, receive a rebate above what they contribute in gas funds. Southern states are currently challenging the formula and during the year 2000, Republican budget chairs in both the House and Senate had promoted legislation to change the existing formula.[9]

NEW FEDERALISM AND SOCIAL WELFARE POLICY

Another shift in federal-state relations during the 1990s concerns the mandates of New Federalism, a federal initiative that involves a devolution of power and program responsibility from the federal government to the states. The underlying logic of the initiative is that by giving the states federal money in the form of block grants and mandating only the broad outlines of social programs, states will be free to create programs that are better suited and more responsive to the needs of the populations they serve. The expectation is that programs developed by the states will be more efficient and accountable than the federal government, and that state control will encourage innovation in the public sector as policymakers seek to design programs that reflect the needs of their constituencies. Some argue, however, that this shift is less about the devolution of power from the federal government to the states and more of a rebalancing of powers back to the states that had eroded over the years.[10] In addition, there is concern that the promise of New Federalism may not be realized because no overall consensus has been reached regarding how to effect this transformation in the context of federal officials who, with the exception of welfare reform, are reluctant to cede authority to the states. Moreover, other concerns center on the fear that when federal mandates no longer shape social programs some states will drastically cut benefits and ignore the needs of their residents.

While to date there are only limited examples of such devolution of power being fully implemented, several factors offer encouraging prospects for New Federalism in Rhode Island. In terms of social programs, the state has a long tradition of support for social welfare; there was never a concern that Rhode Island would join a "race to the bottom" by imposing minimum benefits on programs based on federal guidelines once responsibility was turned back to the states. Moreover, the progressive inclinations of Rhode Island's political leaders are manifest among both Republicans and Democrats; although there might be differences at the margins in terms of how social policy should be crafted, general consensus on the goals of social programs can be found. Also, in a small state of about a million people, the possibility of bringing key people together to develop efficient and accountable programs is greater. To date, Rhode Island appears to have had some notable successes in crafting effective policies that invest in long-term results.

In 1994 in response to federal changes in eligibility for Medicaid, the state received a federal waiver and implemented RIte Care, a program of health insurance for the poor and working poor that has become a model for the rest of the country. Through HMOs health insurance coverage was eventually extended not only to those formerly eligible under Medicaid but also to pregnant women and children with incomes up to 250 percent of the poverty level. Originally the program covered children up to the age of eight; by 1997 it was extended to all children up to age eighteen. In 1998 the Republican governor, Lincoln Almond, sought a waiver of federal rules to create a plan to extend coverage to all uninsured parents up to 185 percent of the poverty line. The stated goal of the program is to be one of the "first states to say that every single person has access to health insurance."[11]

The RIte Care program was a prelude to the Rhode Island Family Independence Act that was initiated in May 1997. In anticipation of the Temporary Assistance to Needy Families (TANF) federal block grant, which replaced the AFDC welfare program, the state crafted a package wherein most of the concern and debate was related to how much more the state would provide beyond federal limitations. While the Republican administration worked to develop a fairly progressive reform proposal, on another front some groups representing the poor and other community and business interests formed a coalition and worked with the Democratic legislature to produce an alternative plan. The legislature's plan was designed to prevent a 15 percent across-the-board reduction in welfare benefits and the elimination of food stamps for legal immigrants, both of which had been recommended by the federal administration.[12] The legislature's plan prevailed and the state, with the help of able staff at the Department of Human Services, went on to craft a program that initial studies indicate is potentially one of the most effective plans in the country. In a national study of reform programs that were likely to improve the economic security and long-term prospects of poor families, Rhode Island ranked first among the New England states in terms of benefits and second overall. It was only one of six states that received high scores on measures of support for childcare. This appears significant insofar as the study also indicated that thirty-five states have implemented policies that will make the economic situation of families worse than it was under the old welfare system.[13]

The total number of AFDC beneficiaries as of 1997 was just over 51,489 (16,557 adults and 34,932 children). Of that population more than 92 percent were U.S. citizens, slightly more than 6 percent were legal immigrants, and about 1 percent refugees. In the case of RIte Care, the population served in 1999 totaled 86,000, and plans for expansion involve another 25,000. Structuring programs that can provide adaptable rules and effective case monitoring by the state administration is probably less daunting than creating programs in New York, for example, where estimates of the welfare population run over a million and programs are administered at several bureaucratic levels to exceptionally diverse populations. For example, as the state continued to expand coverage, in 2000 the high budget projections for the cost of the program and the fact that significant numbers of people had dropped their private insurance and signed on to the public system forced the state to adjust and amend formulas for coverage.

Federal statistics in 1999 also revealed that the state's welfare caseload had dropped only 12 percent (compared to a national average decline of 42 percent), putting Rhode Island in forty-ninth place among the states. But the governor, unfazed by these rankings, argued that the state had taken the longer view and opted for a system of less draconian measures and stronger incentives (which included free health care, free childcare, job training, and provisions that allow some working mothers to remain on welfare while keeping a portion of their earnings). In addition, the state *added* to the rolls about one thousand two-parent families in order to encourage family stability. While it's too early to judge the ultimate outcome of these efforts, legislators, the governor, and the administration remain committed to the idea that this type of plan has a much greater likelihood of effecting systemic, long-term change.[14]

REGIONAL RIVALRY AND COOPERATION

The New England region came out of a long economic downturn in the mid-1990s, and strategies of economic development have created competition between Rhode Island and its neighboring states. In some ways these efforts have encouraged "parochialism and petty jealousies" as Rhode Island vies to lure businesses in the region its way.[15] Although some politicians argue for a cooperative model that avoids duplication in services and education resources, the reality is that the state's economic leaders are scrambling to capture and keep new business—with tax packages and other legislation favorable to business. Rhode Island's leaders are particularly sensitive to the proximity of Boston and the high tech Route 128 as they try to draw business and capture the shopping clientele they lose to Massachusetts just across the border.

In 1997 the state passed a budget package that included the highest tax credits in the country for new money spent on research and development, and one of the highest tax credits for investment in new equipment. In 1998 the state Economic Development Corporation targeted software as one of the most promising industries, and is attempting to lure Boston companies across the state line.[16] The state still has a higher personal income tax rate for high-end wage earners as compared to Massachusetts and Connecticut. Although Rhode Island lowered this rate recently, these other nearby states have been more aggressive in income tax reduction for earners in the highest brackets, giving them some advantage in attracting high-priced executives (and their businesses) to settle in their states.

In another competitive move, after intense public debate and controversy the legislature in 1997 also approved joint funding for the construction of a huge upscale shopping mall in downtown Providence, which opened in 1999. It was designed to enhance the state's convention trade industry and also to lure Rhode Island shoppers who formerly crossed the border to shop in a similar mall in nearby Massachusetts.

Another effort with symbolic as well as economic ramifications was the campaign to build a football stadium for the New England Patriots in downtown Providence. Voters in Massachusetts soundly rejected a 1996 proposal to build a new stadium for the Patriots in Boston to replace the aging facility in Foxboro, Massachusetts, located just off the main highway that links Providence and Boston. The Massachusetts legislature also rejected proposals from Patriots owner Robert Kraft, for expensive and extensive rebuilding of the Foxboro site. Massachusetts House Speaker Thomas Finneran noted that the taxpayers of that state had better things to do with their money than subsidize "whining millionaires." In response to this rejection the mayor of Providence, Buddy Cianci, began to court Kraft in an attempt to lure the team to Rhode Island. While initially considered a somewhat fantastic idea, the governor, sensing the political capital to be gained from the intense public enthusiasm generated by the proposal, got on board and engaged Kraft in discussions on financing a $300 million stadium in downtown Providence.[17] In the end the Patriots backed away from the deal, and after an attempt to court political leaders in the state of Connecticut Kraft was left to negotiate with a reluctant Massachusetts legislature for about $50 million to renovate the existing stadium. While it is likely that Kraft used these initiatives to gain leverage in Massachusetts, the level of energy and interest among politicians and the general public alike in "getting the Patriots to Rhode Island" suggests an interstate dynamic whereby "Little Rhody" is attempting to assert its place in the region.

Not all relations are competitive. Recently, the purchase of the Bath Iron works of Maine—that state's largest employer—by General Dynamics of Connecticut, with divisions located in Rhode Island, provided a boost to the possibility for extended submarine and surface-vessel production. This joint effort should help the region compete with Newport News, Virginia, for lucrative federal contracts.[18]

THE INDIANS IN THE FEDERAL SYSTEM

Another critical "border" issue is the competition for gambling revenues with neighboring Connecticut, where Indian tribes have established casinos close to Rhode Island state lines. No discussion of federal-state relations can ignore the difficult and contentious question of the role of Indians in Rhode Island who, given their federal status, remain of but in some ways not part of the Ocean State. As in other American states, the history of state-Indian relations, particularly the Narragansetts, is a tragic one that continues to cloud the political landscape.[19]

The beginnings were hopeful. When Roger Williams was exiled from Plymouth in 1636 he settled at the end of Narragansett Bay on land given to him by the Narragansett Indians—which eventually became the city of Providence. Williams developed warm relations with the Narragansetts, one of the less warlike Indian tribes of the Northeast who found Williams's tolerant and respectful attitude toward Native tribes to be in sharp contrast to the aggressive and contemptuous posture of the other Puritan settlements in New England. He worked among the Narragansetts and the Wampanoags, learned their language, and in 1643 published the first study of their cultures and languages.

These gentle beginnings promoted a measure of tolerance and understanding between the early settlers and the Indians. Indeed, as William McLoughlin notes, "(R)hode Islanders did not join in the annihilation of their Indian neighbors" and, thanks to Williams's efforts, sought to maintain peace.[20] Nonetheless, the aggressive conduct of the Massachusetts Bay Colony—in a blatant quest for Indian lands—culminated in 1675 in King Philip's War between the region's Indians and the colonists. Although Rhode Island attempted to remain neutral, a massacre of the Narragansetts (including women and children) at their winter camp at the Great Swamp provoked retribution by the Indians that included the burning of Providence. The Indians lost this regional war, and the survivors were either sold into slavery or in Rhode Island were typically permitted to settle on tribal lands around Charlestown, Rhode Island.[21]

In 1880 the Narragansetts detribalized, accepted U.S. citizenship, and sold off all the common reservation land in Charlestown that was not occupied by individuals. Not realizing that their new status would subject them to local and state taxes, many Indians subsequently lost their homesteads due to their inability to pay taxes. By the turn of the century the Indians pressed the state to return to them the 130,000 acres that they bargained away for $5,000. The federal government refused to intervene directly, but in 1934 Congress did pass the Indian Reorganization Act, which permitted the Indians to reestablish their tribal identity. At that time the Narragansetts numbered just under a thousand.

In 1975 the Narragansett tribe sued in federal court to regain three thousand acres of the reservation land taken under the 1880 agreement. The state settled with the Indians by way of the Rhode Island Indian Claims Settlement Act of 1978, which was enacted into federal law by Congress. In this agreement the state and the federal government together returned eighteen hundred acres of tribal lands in Charlestown to the Narragansetts who in turn agreed to follow state and local law in the disposition of that land. In essence the law permits gambling on tribal lands or anywhere else in Rhode Island only if voters approve it both statewide *and* locally where the gambling sites are to be located.[22] Voter approval of gambling in any state, particularly within local communities, is difficult to pass; in Rhode Island a history of unsavory politics and lingering fears over organized crime's influence initially made gambling an all but impossible sell. Artful wording of a constitutional referendum in 1973 did allow for a state-run lottery, but generally Rhode Islanders were reluctant to go along with any expansion of gambling in the state.

Events took a more complicated turn when, in 1988, Congress passed the Indian Gaming Regulatory Act, which grants tribes across the country special prerogatives to create gambling establishments on reservation lands as an aspect of economic development (provided the state's gambling laws are followed). Indian gambling casinos are now a major industry in many states, and the largest and most successful gambling venue in the country is Foxwoods Casino in Connecticut, just a few minutes west of the Rhode Island border. Established in 1992 on the homelands of the Pequot Indians, estimates are that the casino draws about a fifth of its clientele from Rhode Island.

The flourishing success of gambling establishments, particularly in Connecticut, has raised several issues about the role of Indians and the question of gambling in Rhode Island. First is the fact that Rhode Islanders (and their money) flock to these establishments across the border and the state does not realize any revenue from these ventures. This situation has generated support among some political leaders to expand the state's gambling activities as an added source of revenue under the auspices of the Indians. Voters, however, in a cumbersome set of statewide and local referenda in 1994, defeated proposals to establish gambling facilities in the state.

The Narragansetts continued to press their claims for gambling ventures under the 1988 Indian Gaming Regulatory Act in the federal courts. Republican John Chafee, in a preemptive move, had an amendment to federal budget legislation passed in 1996 that would specifically deny the Narragansetts prerogatives under the gaming act and force them to abide by the prior 1978 agreement that subjects them to state law and voter approval. In 1997 a federal district court found in favor of the Chafee amendment; events in that year took another unfortunate turn when Connecticut's Pequot Indians purchased extensive blocks of land in southern Rhode Island for nongambling extensions of their casinos, in order to build a complex that includes golf courses, more hotels, and a possible amusement park. Local residents seemed to favor this development as a way of boosting the local tax base in this relatively underdeveloped area.[23]

This proved to be a particularly bitter pill for the impoverished Narragansetts, whose relatively meager requests for advanced bingo establishments were stalled on appeal as the Pequots got richer by the day. The cast of this debate took on a political and partisan turn when Representative Patrick Kennedy became a vocal proponent of the Narragansetts' rights and turned the debate into a political attack on John Chafee.

By 1998 public support for the Indians began to build. Primarily, voters and many political leaders faced the reality that gambling was already an institutionalized sport in Rhode Island. The 1999 budget estimate listed over $130 million dollars in revenue from lotteries, and reports began to document revenues in Connecticut that were coming from Rhode Islanders crossing the border. State law still requires that all gambling ventures be approved by a statewide referendum as well as by a local referendum in the community where the site will be located. The Narragansetts, working with Boyd Gaming Corporation, earmarked millions for an Indian casino referendum campaign. They lobbied the legislature to change the wording of the standard ballot question to permit gambling under the auspices of the Narragansetts.[24]

As momentum for the idea began to build, reformers as well as antigambling forces became concerned that, given extensive and expensive advertising, the proposal might pass. In response the legislature had in 1998 set up yet another legal hurdle by passing a statute that requires specific enabling legislation before any referendum concerning gambling can be placed on the ballot. That legislation, along with strong resistance to a casino, enabled the legislature to quash the proposed ballot question in the 2000 election. There was considerable acrimony when the vote came down and the Indians vowed to fight for ballot access in the next election.[25]

The Naragansetts continued to pursue their cause on other fronts. In 1999 a federal appeals court upheld the restrictions that had been placed on the Naragansetts' land under federal law—leaving the tribe with the unlikely recourse of a U.S. Supreme Court hearing. Events took yet another turn when in the summer of 2000 the federal Bureau of Indian Affairs, in response to a request from the Indians, issued a ruling granting trust status to a small parcel of thirty-two acres of Indian land in the southern part of the state. Trust status removes land from state and local tax rolls and releases it from state and local jurisdiction. Instead it becomes subject to federal regulations only—which would presumably leave the Indians free to build a gaming operation on the land without legislative or voter approval. The state and the local town immediately appealed the ruling, thus initiating another protracted confrontation with the tribe and a continuation of centuries of hostile relations between the state and these first Rhode Islanders.

CHAPTER FOUR

The Constitution

And whereas, in their humble address (the people of Rhode Island) have freely declared, that it is much on their hearts . . . to hold forth a lively experiment, that a most flourishing civil state may stand and best be maintained, and that among our English subjects, with a full liberty in religious concernments; and that true piety rightly grounded . . . will give the best and greatest security to sovereignty.

Royal Charter granted by King Charles II, 1663

Thus, Rhode Island's [constitutional] history is that of a quintessential system of parliamentary supremacy.

Rhode Island Supreme Court, 1999

The variety of constitutional traditions among the fifty states is considerable. This is true not only of the content and matters dealt with, but also in terms of the number of successive constitutional documents and major revisions written and ratified by the states. In some the production of successive constitutions and revisions almost has been a local cottage industry. Having four or more constitutions has not been unusual in some instances.[1] In tabulated lists Rhode Island is in a small group that displays relative stability. The state's first frame of government was the Royal Charter of 1663, which the colony retained as its constitution until the state adopted its first homegrown document in 1843.[2] The latter, with very substantial modifications (including fifty-nine amendments) has remained in place ever since.

THE ROYAL CHARTER OF 1663

The charter granted by King Charles II in 1663 is actually a quite remarkable document. It was extraordinarily liberal for its day. It is most often noted for its strong assertion of freedom of religion, unquestionably the result of the influence of Roger Williams and of the fact that the colony was settled initially by refugees from Massachusetts Bay where Puritanism was the established church and orthodoxy was enforced by the government. As a result, the charter mandates that "no person within the said colony, at any time hereafter shall be anywise molested, punished, disquieted, or called in question, for any differences in opinion in matters of religion."[3] This was acceptable to the royal authorities in part, no doubt, as a result of the bitter experiences England had gone through during its recent civil war. It is also undoubtedly true that granting this freedom (not available in the mother country) was acceptable for a very small and distant colony.

More important for present purposes was the extraordinarily democratic frame of government established by the charter. That it fell short in some respects of contemporary beliefs about democracy in no way detracts from the fact that it was remarkably liberal for its day. In this and other respects it set precedents that reappeared in the 1843 constitution and that have pervaded the political culture of Rhode Island since.

The document created "a body politic or corporate" for the group that had petitioned the crown, "and all such others as . . . shall be made free of the company." That is, the functional equivalent of "citizen" in that era was "freeman," a status automatically granted to original householders and to others whom those householders later made freemen. The charter then created the offices of governor, deputy governor, ten so-called assistants, and representatives of the several towns, all to be elected by the freemen. The first twelve elected were to "take care for the best disposing and ordering of the general business and affairs" of the plantation and government of the colony. In a rough way they were the executive branch. Twice a year these dozen, plus the elected town representatives, would meet together as the General Assembly, which in turn would admit freemen and "elect and constitute such offices and officers" as they felt necessary to manage the colony's affairs. Moreover, the General Assembly was empowered "from time to time, to make, ordain, constitute or repeal, such laws, statutes, orders and ordinances . . . as to them shall seem meet, for the good and welfare of the said Company, . . . so as such laws, ordinances and constitutions, so made, be not contrary and repugnant unto, but as near as may be, agreeable to the laws of this our realm of England." The Assembly was directed to create courts and appoint judges, regulate elections, establish towns beyond those already existing, and institute penalties for offenses.

Beyond these grants of authority, the assembly could remove officials "for any misdemeanor or default," fill vacancies, and provide for military officers and the calling forth of the inhabitants for military service. In short, the charter established government institutions, provided for elections to fill offices, and conferred upon the resulting government broad and sweeping powers to act for the good and welfare of the inhabitants of the colony. The only limitation was that laws enacted by the General Assembly should not be repugnant to those of England, though even that was qualified by the clause "considering the nature and constitution of the place and people there."

The words of the Rhode Island Supreme Court, quoted at the beginning of the chapter, have a solid basis in the charter as well as in the 1843 constitution, which was modeled to a large extent on the broad themes found in the charter. The legislative power, in Rhode Island practice, has always been seen as broad and unconfined. Historically that power has embraced directly or indirectly much that later generations have considered the executive role, and indeed the role of the courts. The General Assembly, under both the charter and the 1843 constitution, had almost unlimited freedom to create and empower executive organs and courts on just about any basis it chose. The only limits on the legislative authority formally recognized in the Rhode Island constitution were those also found in the U.S. Constitution.

In light of the provisions of the royal charter, it is not surprising that rather than do what most of the other colonies-turned-states did following 1776 (that is, write a constitution for state government), Rhode Island instead retained the charter, doing no more than abolishing the oath of allegiance to the Crown. For more than sixty years the charter remained the state's organic document. Presumably Rhode Islanders felt that they had a system in place (having avoided royal colony status and the imposition of a royal governor) that already involved direct popular control. Coincidentally, it was also one that had long possessed a prime characteristic of the sort the other states were building into their new systems: a weak executive subservient to a popular assembly.

The charter was broad and general enough, and sufficiently open to interpretation, that changes could be made when needed. Moreover, with England out of the picture, changes that might previously have required sanction from London could be made at will. Curiously, the state emerged from the Revolution with something akin to the British concept of a constitution as a partially written but largely unwritten document and set of traditional practices. The resulting flexibility is well illustrated by the action, taken in 1696, of creating a bicameral assembly by mandating that the governor, deputy governor, and assistants would meet as one chamber while the town representatives would meet separately as the other chamber under an elected speaker.

Another critically important adaptation of the charter, which represented a more conservative direction in the character of the document, was the importing of a property qualification to vote. The charter mentions freemen but without also mentioning the criteria for their designation. In 1723 the assembly passed an act that for the first time linked property ownership to the status of freeman.[4] The requirement was for land ownership worth L100, which in time translated into $134. This restriction became one of the key issues that eventually brought about the replacement of the charter with a constitution.

CONSTITUTIONAL REFORM, THE CONSTITUTION OF 1843

The reform process began with a shift in the state's economy from commerce and agriculture to manufacturing. This shift had profound political implications. It produced a massive population movement when people left the small agricultural towns to work in the mills in the towns where the industrial transition was centered.[5] Naturally, in the mill towns the proportion of land owners and thus voters declined sharply. In fact, there was a general decline as the population grew and free land became less available. This in turn made representation in the assembly increasingly inequitable. The charter set six seats as Newport's share; four each for Providence, Portsmouth, and Warwick; and two for each of the other towns. By 1840 the average population that each assembly member represented in the expanding towns was 2,590; among towns with static populations it was 1,074; and for those with declining numbers, 665.[6]

Thus the franchise and apportionment in the assembly were two sources of agitation for constitutional change. Two others, important but less salient, were the lack of a bill of rights and a separate judiciary. The latter was one of the results of the charter's granting of all power, including, effectively, judicial authority, to the legislative branch. The structure of the court system was completely under the control of the assembly; that body elected all judges for very short terms and could remove them at will. Moreover, the assembly itself acted as a court of appeal to which resort against unfavorable court decisions could be had.

The story of the fight for reform and the eventual adoption of a constitution in 1843 is too long and involved for more than a brief summary here.[7] Thomas Wilson Dorr became the reform movement's key leader and sparked the calling of the Peoples' Constitutional Convention, over the opposition of the charter-based government, in the fall of 1841. The convention produced a constitutional document that would have achieved most of the reformers' objectives. Dorr and his group organized a referendum on the basis of manhood suffrage, which was approved by a wide margin.

The supporters of the existing government, the "Charterites," insisted that all such reform was illegal. (The Charterites were the conservative, well-to-do and often nativist elements in the population who benefited politically and economically from keeping the status quo. The term "Charterites" implies that strong support for the governmental system and distribution of power that was based on the royal charter still existed.) The Charterites called a constitutional convention that produced a rival document to the People's Constitution. Their constitution was a conservative one that would have preserved the status quo. It, too, was put to referendum and narrowly defeated. Nevertheless, encouraged by this near miss as evidence that support for the reformers was declining, a third convention was called which, with a few concessions, adopted the present constitution in November 1842. Referendum approval came later that same month. Earlier that year the "Dorr War," a rather halfhearted coup attempt by the reformers to install a government under the People's Constitution, had failed and further strengthened the Charterites' "law and order" cause. The government under the new constitution was organized in May 1843.

In broad outline the new frame of government tracked the principles on which the charter government had been based.[8] It did include, as the first article, a Declaration of Rights and Principles. Of critical importance was Article II, "Of Qualifications of Electors." The article stated that native-born citizens with property could vote in all elections, while those without property could vote (upon payment of a $1.00 tax) for all offices except Providence city council, and on all questions except those related to imposing a tax or expending money in any town. Naturalized citizens, however, all remained subject to the property qualification to vote.

The General Assembly retained its powerful central position in the system despite a genuflect in the direction of separation of powers in Article III: "The powers of the government shall be distributed into three departments: the legislative, executive and judicial." The legislature's position was buttressed in a number of ways. Of special interest is section 10 of Article IV, "Of the Legislative Power," which reads: "The General Assembly shall continue to exercise the powers they have heretofore exercised, unless prohibited in this constitution." That, of course, locked in the sweeping mandate granted to the assembly under the charter. Moreover, unlike many state constitutions, Rhode Island's in fact placed very few restrictions on assembly power. Those few restrictions included the requirement of a special majority for appropriations for private purposes, a limit on borrowing without referendum, a ban on lotteries, limits on taking private land for public purposes, and limits on creating corporations. There were no limits on taxation, spending, or the like, and no provisions relating to executive departments or functions that would inhibit the legislature.

The weakness of the position of the governor in itself, of course, strengthened that of the assembly.[9] As to the powers of the governor, one finds little mention that is specific. The governor was to be commander in chief of the military forces, could grant reprieves (but not pardons, until the addition of Amendment 2, and then only with senate approval), and could fill vacancies pending assembly action. The chief executive could also adjourn the assembly when its two houses could not agree, could call special sessions, and could sign commissions, but that was about it.

Article X ("Of the Judicial Power") provides for a supreme court and "such inferior courts as the General Assembly may, from time to time, ordain and establish." Only the selection of supreme court justices was provided for in the constitution: election by the two houses of the General Assembly sitting jointly in what was called the Grand Committee of the Assembly. Appointment of all other judges and, indeed, of virtually all other officers (judicial and otherwise) was vested in the grand committee by language in Article VIII ("Of Elections"), section 3. That section mandated that town clerks would bundle up and certify all votes cast at general elections and deliver them to the grand committee, whose duty was that of "counting and declaring said votes, and of electing other officers."

The last clause of the foregoing passage was the lineal descendent of the grant of authority in the charter for the General Assembly "to elect and constitute such offices and officers, . . . as they shall think fit and requisite." In practice it meant grand committee election of the members of all boards and commissions (the bodies charged with such administrative chores as existed at the time or were created thereafter), and of all judges and other officials. The governor thus played no role through power to appoint or authority to direct the work of any of these appointees. As to the roles of the other elected statewide officers—secretary of state, general treasurer, and attorney general—the constitution merely said (in Article VII, section 12) that these individuals shall have the same duties and powers "as are now established, or as from time to time may be prescribed by law." In other words, even these constitutional offices were subject to the will of the assembly.

A useful way to highlight the brevity of the Rhode Island Constitution (about nineteen thousand words) and the omission of many subjects (which, if expressed, would have represented limits on legislative power), is to look at a typical state constitution table of contents.[10] The Rhode Island

Constitution does have, as noted, a bill of rights and legislative, executive, and judicial articles. It also has articles on education, suffrage, and the amending procedure. It does *not* have headings on finance and taxation; banking and corporations (save a limit on the power to incorporate); land and the environment (though eminent domain is referred to); public services; health, housing, and social services; labor; local government units; apportionment (briefly dealt with); initiative, referendum, and recall; or intergovernmental relations that are commonly found in other state constitutions.

REVISIONS BY AMENDMENT AND CONVENTION

This then was the general shape and content of the 1843 constitution. Forty-two amendments were added in the years up through 1973, some of which made quite substantial changes that need to be noted briefly. Until 1935 there was no other way to amend the constitution save through the rather cumbersome process (delineated in Article XIII) that required assembly approval of any proposed amendment by majorities of all the members of each house twice with a general election in between, and then approval by three-fifths of the citizens voting in a referendum. The supreme court had held that because the constitution made no provision for change in the document by a constitutional convention, no convention could be called.[11]

In the aftermath of the "Revolution of 1935," the newly installed supreme court justices who replaced those voted out of office reversed that decision and held that conventions could be called.[12] From then on most amendments added up to 1973 emanated from brief (usually one-day) constitutional conventions, because a convention proposal went directly to the voters for referendum and required, it was held, only a simple majority to be adopted. Thus the Article XIII process (of constitutional amendment) was avoided.

The first open constitutional convention since 1842 with no limit on the subjects it could consider convened in 1964 and sat, with some breaks, until 1968! It produced a substantially revised and rewritten new constitutional document, which the voters turned down. This defeat had little relation to the overall theory or theories it offered, but rather was blamed on two or three very specific and relatively minor items, such as the repeal of the ban on lotteries. Not until 1986 was another such open convention approved and called by the voters. In 1973, however, a thirty-day limited convention was held that proposed and secured approval of some major changes.

A quick review of constitutional amendments added between the first in

1854 and those from the 1973 convention shows that of the thirty-seven approved, eighteen, or almost half were related to the franchise and voting, voter registration, absentee voting, and other closely related matters. The constitution of 1843 may have grown out of the struggle to broaden the franchise, but it merely represented an early stage in a struggle that continued up to the approval of one of the key proposals of the 1973 convention.

The other important changes among these thirty-seven amendments involved, to a large extent, modernizing certain structural arrangements in the document. The twice-a-year assembly sessions were reduced to one (passed in 1900); pay was increased from one dollar to five dollars a day for sixty days (1900); the state borrowing limitation and incorporation restrictions were modified; revisions were made in the apportionment provisions for both assembly chambers; the veto was given to the governor, who had had none before (1909); provision was made for two-year rather than one-year terms for state executive and legislative officeholders (1911); some amendments were added on land acquisition and redevelopment; and home rule was provided to cities and towns, thus introducing the first constitutional language relating to local government (1951).

The 1973 limited constitutional convention was mandated to deal with a number of important and long-simmering issues. Perhaps most important, a new brief article was prepared that dealt with suffrage, voter registration, and absentee voting, to replace the tangled mass of amendments and amendments to amendments that had accumulated as the state worked its way during more than a century toward a simple universal suffrage system. The convention also revised the provision requiring indictment by grand jury to allow suspects to be charged by information only in most cases. The lottery prohibition was modified with some rather opaque language that at least allowed a state lottery. Less noticed but of great continuing importance was a complete rewrite of the amending process article so that majorities of all members of each house can now propose amendments which then go to referendum at the next general election and can be adopted by a simple majority of those voting. This same revision requires that the calling of a new convention be placed on the ballot every ten years.

Needless to say, the result of all this revising and tinkering produced a constitution whose main body had much material that was superseded by amendments (or a series of amendments), many that were themselves obsolete. The clutter of suffrage and election language was particularly confusing. Consequently, the only way the constitution could be read for current meaning was backward—starting with the newest amendments first.

CONSTITUTIONAL REFORM, THE 1980S AND 1990S

The first referendum on the holding of a convention pursuant to the new 1973 revision language was held in 1984, and the voters approved the call. When the convention met one of the major tasks it set for itself was the preparation of what was referred to as a "neutral rewrite" of the document. By this was meant a thorough editing that would delete obsolete and superseded language from the body of the constitution, and insert at appropriate points amendment language that was currently effective. One new article, Article XIII, "Home Rule for Cities and Towns," had to be added to reflect the fact that the old constitution made no provision, explicitly, for local government. A couple of other articles were relocated to place rules regarding suffrage, qualification for office, and elections adjacent to each other at the beginning of the document.

When the work of the convention was completed, the voters confronted fourteen questions on the November 1986 ballot. The first was the acceptance of the "neutral rewrite," which passed with no difficulty. Of the remaining thirteen changes, seven passed and six failed. In brief terms, the seven were:

New declaration of rights language on due process, equal protection, non-discrimination, free speech, and crime victims' rights;

Establishment of an ethics commission with broad powers; limits on campaign spending and contributions; and expanded impeachment language;

Governor's authority to submit a budget, and speaker to succeed lieutenant governor;

Guarantee of rights to the shore, and environmental protection;

Restrictions on felons holding office and voting;

State mandate to promote libraries; and

Limitations on rights to bail.

The six that failed would have reformed judicial selection, provided a higher level of legislative pay, instituted four-year terms for governor and general officers, provided for voter initiative, strengthened home rule for local governments, and guaranteed the right to life.

Reviewing these lists it is quite clear, in the first place, that the voters were much concerned with ethical reform and citizens' rights. The provision on ethics called for an ethics commission with power to write an ethics code, and to receive complaints of violation, adjudicate them, and pass sentence. In an advisory opinion the supreme court confirmed this interpretation of the new language despite expressed concerns that it violated the separation of powers.[13] Other new language instructed the assembly to legislate limits on campaign contributions, establish voluntary public campaign financing, and set spending limits for candidates.[14] Convicted felons were barred from running for or holding public office until three years after their sentences had been served, and from voting while still serving a sentence. New language was inserted to tighten up the impeachment process.[15] The new bail language had "tough on crime" motives.

The other thread that seemed to run through the voters' minds as they marked their ballots was the protection of individual rights. They approved language that inserted guarantees into the state bill of rights parallel to those found in the federal constitution, plus nondiscrimination language. The inclusion of a victims' bill of rights was also in accord with popular concern about crime. Shore rights and environmental protections were also strengthened.[16]

Granting the budget power to the governor sounds important in light of the weak office set up in the original constitution, but in practice governors have been preparing budgets for submission to the assembly since the 1930s. This involvement was statutory and replaced the prior situation under which the assembly dominated the process and the governor played virtually no role. Thus a minor step has been taken in providing a broader constitutional basis for a stronger governorship.

One need only look at the things that the voters declined to approve to place the approved amendments in proper perspective. Each of the rejected reforms could have had a substantial impact on the operation of the state's governmental system. Clearly, it was this kind of operational proposal that an apparently suspicious electorate declined to support. One could speculate on the reasons in each case—the desire to be able to get at elected officials every two years and not have to wait for four years, deep-seated suspicion of legislators and the assumption that they steal so there is no need to pay them, too, and a general feeling that change itself is risky. "The devil you know is likely to be better than the devil you don't know" may sum up these feelings.

Surprisingly, several of these rejected proposals secured approval within less than a decade of their original introduction. Why the change of mind? Again, one can only speculate. Undoubtedly the rash of highly disturbing and disillusioning events played a major role in persuading the electorate that reforms were in order. The crisis that closed all state-insured credit unions and banks in 1991 brought turmoil and anger that in turn triggered a powerful reform thrust. There was also a drumbeat for reform as a result of scandals in 1992 related to the arrest of the mayor of Pawtucket and a superior court judge (each for taking bribes), and the forced resignation of two chief justices in 1986 and 1993. These and the seemingly constant news of corruption gave the forces pushing for reform ammunition and growing support.

The General Assembly proposed and the voters approved an amendment to the constitution that appeared on the November 1992 ballot, again proposing four-year terms. The proposal came as a carefully crafted package. It applied only to the statewide elected officials and not to members of the assembly, and was coupled with the first recall provision adopted for state officials. Any general officer under felony indictment or against whom the ethics commission was proceeding could be recalled by petition followed by referendum. Unquestionably, the electorate was persuaded to accept the doubling of term length knowing that they could resort to the recall process when necessary.

Another big reform year was 1994. Court scandals provided fertile soil for reform of judicial selection. A proposal was worked out for "merit selection" to replace the grand committee election of supreme court justices, and applied to the selection of judges for all other state courts. The language called for the creation by statute of a judicial nominating commission to screen candidates for all judicial vacancies and recommend a short list from which the governor must select nominees. Nominations for supreme court were to be confirmed by both the house and the senate and, for other courts, by the senate only. Besides its obvious purpose, this new language had the effect of conferring an important constitutional appointive power on the governor for the first time, which voters approved by a better than two-to-one margin at the November election.

Also on the ballot was a complex and again carefully crafted set of changes in the constitution relating to the legislative branch. This was largely the work of a blue ribbon commission appointed to study the assembly and the legislative process. Perhaps the key objective of the framers was to once and for all break the logjam on legislative pay. They wrote in a provision for a salary of $10,000 per year with cost-of-living increases. This was sweetened in two major ways. First, the scandal-plagued legislative pension system was to be phased out; it would only benefit those already serving. New members were allowed only salary. Second, the size of each chamber was to be reduced following the 2000 census: the house from one hundred to seventy-five, and the senate from fifty to thirty-eight. This proposal was approved by a narrow margin of about ten thousand votes, underscoring the deep suspicion voters feel for the assembly and the wisdom of other changes conjoined with the salary increase.

At the same 1994 election the voters added language to the 1973 lottery amendment, which did nothing to clear up the confusion in that provision but was intended to ensure that any newly approved type of gambling could only be instituted following referendum approval both statewide and in the community or communities in which the facility would be located. Gambling, and particularly the drive to establish an Indian casino, has kept the pot boiling on that issue for some time.

THE CONSTITUTION AT THE TURN OF THE CENTURY

Over the years since 1843, what major changes had the voters wrought on their constitution? The answer is relatively modest ones, ones that changed the basic characteristics of the system very little. Franchise reform merely allowed Rhode Island to plod slowly toward goals that had been achieved much earlier elsewhere. Most of the rest of the changes were also designed to allow the state—often belatedly—to catch up with the rest of the country. Especially significant changes were the governor's veto gained in 1909, home rule in 1951, and a simplified amendment process in 1973. Each of these was important but not earthshaking.

The decade beginning in 1985 brought a real thaw to the ice of constitutional tradition: ethics, judicial selection, legislative pay and membership, and four-year terms were all addressed. But even these had little impact on the most fundamental of the constitutional principles with which the state had lived since the seventeenth century: a virtually all-powerful legislature, a vague and weak separation of powers provision, and a relatively weak governorship with virtually no administrative authority. A careful reader of the constitution might still conclude that the state governed itself through a flawed system, by modern standards. The Jacob and Vines' Index of the Formal Powers of Governors put Rhode Island very near the bottom of the list as having among the weakest governorships in the country. Their study, however, was based on a tabulation of gubernatorial powers spelled out in respective state constitutions. If statutory power grants were added to this index, the picture for the state would be very different.[17]

This point recalls a suggestion made earlier, that historically Rhode Island has had a constitutional tradition that in some ways resembles the British unwritten constitution, a tradition sharply different from that of many American states. The norm, particularly outside of the Northeast, tends to be that of writing much longer and more detailed constitutions that cover many subjects and structural provisions which Rhode Island's document omits and thus leaves to the powerful legislature (recall the standard table of contents cited earlier). Actually, this more common tradition is almost the polar opposite of Rhode Island's in that not only does it deal with the governmental system in a very detailed and didactic manner, but in so doing it constitutionalizes much that is essentially "legislative" material. In many states, hard-won policy achievements and compromises are routinely embalmed in multiple constitutional amendments to place them beyond legislative reach. Only in the franchise area did this happen in Rhode Island.

The fact of the matter is that if one does take into account statutory enactments, one finds that the state has, for some decades, been developing a potentially stronger governorship with considerable independent status and power, and a judicial system quite effectively separated from the involvement of the legislature. Admittedly, in these areas what the assembly has given it can also take away, but in practical terms this has become as unlikely as it would be for the British Parliament to tamper with statutes that have become part of their "constitution."

In summary, as of the mid-1990s the combination of a few key amendments, particularly those from the 1986 convention and others adopted since, plus a pattern of statutory adaptation has given Rhode Island a governmental system that compares favorably in many respects with currently approved models. And this was accomplished while leaving in place the fundamental principle of legislative dominance and a permeable system of separation of powers.

In the latter 1990s a new and determined reform movement arose led by Common Cause and similar groups. For the first time the focus was directly on legislative supremacy and the perceived deficiencies in the state's adherence to the separation of powers principle. Specifically, reformers attacked the practice followed by the General Assembly of creating regulatory and other bodies, then conferring appointive power to those bodies on itself and often providing that some positions be filled with sitting legislators. This practice, it was argued, thrust the legislative branch into the executive realm where it did not belong and gave it an improper role in executing some of the laws that it had passed.

Following the abolition of the pre-1935 boards and commissions and the establishment of the new department system, the demarkation between legislative and executive realms seemed clearer than it had ever been. Then, with mounting pressure for Rhode Island to undertake new regulatory roles—often for environmental protection purposes—new boards and commissions were devised not unlike the federal independent regulatory commissions, to which the assembly made appointments, often of its own members.

The reformers' challenge was founded on the basis of the separation of powers "violation" involved, the resulting alleged conflicts of interest and malfeasance, and the weakening of the proper role of the governor. A major prong of the attack emerged when the newly formed ethics commission was persuaded to promulgate a regulation that would have prohibited any legislator from sitting on such a body or from participating in making board and commission appointments.

Clearly the ensuing struggle was about power and its distribution in the system. The reformers and the governor were pitted against the General Assembly and its allies. Constitutionally, this was the most fundamental attack on the structure of the traditional Rhode Island pattern of governance since the 1840s. If the reformers won, the ensuing changes in that system would be profound indeed.

Seeking a judicial resolution of the issues, the governor requested an advisory opinion from the supreme court, posing three questions: 1) Was the ethics commission regulation constitutional? 2) Should not separation of powers in Rhode Island match the federal model with respect to legislative appointments on boards and commissions? and 3) Does the separation of powers principle impose any limits on legislative appointments and/or membership on boards and commissions?

The questions were extensively briefed on both sides and argued before the court in November of 1998. The court rendered its opinion in June 1999. By a four-to-one margin it found that the ethics commission had exceeded its powers. It declined to address the other two questions until litigated cases came before it. However, in its answer to the first question it set the stage for answering the other two.

Stripped to its essentials, the advisory opinion of the majority cited the three hundred years of effective legislative dominance stemming from the royal charter. They noted that the framers of the 1842 constitution, whose language was readopted in 1986, conferred on the assembly the powers it had enjoyed under the charter minus only explicit exceptions, and did not follow the federal constitution by including a dual officeholding prohibition for legislators or giving to the governor the appointive power enjoyed by the president. Thus, the operational bases of separation of powers on the national model are different in Rhode Island's constitution. Indeed, it was in this decision that the court explicitly characterized the model as that of a "quintessential system of parliamentary supremacy."

In the summer of 2000 the state supreme court essentially reiterated this position in *Lincoln C. Almond v. Rhode Island Lottery Commission*, when it overturned a superior court ruling that argued that legislators, sitting as a majority on the lottery commission, were circumventing the legislative process. The supreme court ruled that under the constitution legislators not only have the power to create and staff the commission but can also, sitting as a majority, set and implement regulations regarding the conduct of state lotteries.[18] The court went on to say that whereas the people of the state had accepted and ratified at the ballot box the existing distribution of governmental powers, if sentiment to change that distribution arises the proper means would be via constitutional amendment. Until appropriate amendments are approved, the existing constitutional arrangements are likely to remain in place.

CHAPTER FIVE

The General Assembly

Historically, the power of the General Assembly in this state, as in other states, has been plenary and unlimited, save as this authority may have been limited by the Constitution of the United States and the Constitution of the State of Rhode Island.

Rhode Island Supreme Court, 1999

In the end, the people of Rhode Island ultimately will decide how best to divide the power pot that lies at the center of our state government. Shall the powers of our state government be checked and balanced? Or shall they be unchecked and imbalanced, with one player holding almost all of the aces and wild cards?

Justice Robert Flanders, dissenting opinion, 1999

Legislative practice and tradition in Rhode Island are a veritable museum of modes of operation and leadership, from the most democratic to the most centrally controlled. But a constant factor involved in any changes in operations and leadership is the significant power that first the charter and then the constitution gave to the General Assembly. This reality was affirmed, with one strident dissent, in a 1999 opinion by the state supreme court. In a fundamental sense, whoever controls the assembly controls Rhode Island. Therefore, throughout the state's history the stakes have been high in the struggle for control, and the rewards of success have been considerable.

The Royal Charter of 1663 allocated six representatives to Newport, four each to the other original settlements (Providence, Warwick, and Portsmouth), and two to each subsequently organized town. The representatives were to be elected by their fellow citizens in town meetings held every six months. The record suggests that townsmen gave their representatives, at times, strict orders on what positions to take and how to vote. There were two annual assembly sessions; thus, one fell within each of the six-month terms.

This pattern of representation provided as close an approximation to a statewide "town meeting" of all citizens as any delegate assembly could achieve—in theory, and apparently to a large extent in practice. We have little information about legislative operations during the first century under the charter. However, David Lovejoy, in a fascinating book about the factional politics that prevailed in the decade or so before the American Revolution, paints a picture that Rhode Islanders two centuries later would recognize as familiar.[1]

Factions (parties in all but name) had coalesced to compete for control of the colony's government, which meant control of the assembly. This, in turn, also meant access to all of the appointive positions ("patronage," in modern terms) because the legislature made all appointments. It also gave the winners the power to restructure the apportionment of property taxes, which supported both the colony and town governments. Assembly members could lighten the burden on the towns they had carried and shift it to their opponents' communities.

By the 1760s (if not earlier) party-like management of the assembly had thus replaced more freewheeling legislative management. In the early nineteenth century the representative quality of the assembly began to decline sharply. By late century this helped to make possible the advent of the Brayton Machine, under which total external control was exercised over the assembly by boss Charles Brayton and his clique of Republican leaders. Eventually Brayton's influence waned as the twentieth century opened. Following the Green Revolution in 1935 there was a period of quite tight party and gubernatorial control of the legislature, replaced in mid-century with a pattern of internal majority leadership domination of the legislative process during the speakerships of Harry Curvin and Joseph Bevilacqua.

Popular control was thus determined by external dictation from bosses, and then by internal autocratic power. It would not be much of an exaggeration to say that the proper source of control and leadership, which democratic theory postulates for legislatures—and as exercised by the members of a legislature—did not emerge in Rhode Island's tradition until the successive waves of reform that began in the late 1970s. Presently the legislative system is more open and participatory than at any other time in the past two centuries, but the legislative leadership still retains a measure of control that allows them to manage the process.

INSTITUTIONAL STRUCTURE

The changing shape and structure of the Rhode Island legislative institution has had a profound impact on the distribution of power both within the General Assembly and throughout the governmental system as a whole. From 1663 to the 1690s the colony essentially had a unicameral legislative system. Town representatives met with the ten assistants who had been elected at large, with the governor in the chair. Later the assistants sat separately as an embryonic senate, and the representatives remained as the other chamber. Terms, mode of election, and apportionment remained essentially (and formally) the same, until the constitution was adopted in 1843. As indicated in the discussion of the constitutional history of the state, the legislative branch continued to enjoy broad powers.

Both the apportionment of the assembly and the franchise restrictions on voting for the state's elected officials were chronic areas of dispute and the targets of reform efforts until recent decades. The constitution of 1843 liberalized legislative apportionment to a limited degree. The house membership, keyed to the towns as before, was set at seventy-two.[2] Two important provisos were included, however: each city and town was to have a minimum of one representative, regardless of population, and no city or town could have more than one-sixth of the total number. Both rules had the effect of perpetuating much of the malapportionment that had resulted from the charter formula.

By 1905 and just before a constitutional amendment again revised the apportionment, population growth and shifts had increased to twenty-five (out of thirty-eight) the number of towns that were overrepresented, even though Providence, still limited to twelve, would have been entitled to thirty of the seventy-two seats! Rapid urbanization continued to distort the allocation of seats in favor of the small towns and against the growing cities.

A constitutional amendment adopted in 1909 made modest changes in house apportionment by increasing the total number of seats to one hundred but setting a new ceiling for any city at one-quarter of the total (rather than one-sixth). This latter change helped Providence somewhat, but as of 1910 the city had about 41 percent of the state's population and thus would have been entitled to that same percentage of house seats rather than its twenty-five.

The situation in the senate was far more inequitable. The 1842 constitution allocated one senator to each city and town regardless of population size. As of the effective date of the constitution there were thirty-one cities and towns. The sixteen smallest, which together elected a majority of the senate, contained about one-fifth of the state's population. Just prior to a 1928 minor reform of senate apportionment, the twenty smallest towns (among the then-total of thirty-nine) could elect a senate majority though they contained only about 7 percent of the state's population!

A 1928 amendment provided a slight and obviously grudging concession to the grossly underrepresented cities and large towns. It provided that "any town or city having more than twenty-five thousand qualified electors shall be entitled to an additional senator for each additional twenty-five thousand qualified electors . . . and for any fraction exceeding one-half the factor."[3] No city or town was to be entitled to more than six senators, however. Where a city was entitled to more than one, senators were to be chosen by district. As of the total reapportionment following the U.S. Supreme Court's 1962 *Baker v. Carr* decision—and *Sweeney v. Notte*, the local counterpart case—the senate had forty-six members, with five from Providence and two each from Cranston, Pawtucket, and Warwick.[4]

We have dwelt in some detail on the reapportionment history of the General Assembly because, as a discussion of Rhode Island legislative politics will make clear, the impact of those arrangements—and of franchise limits and changes—has been very great over the years. Throughout most of the state's history, power has been predominantly in the hands of, first, the landed and mercantile interests, later in the proprietors of the textile and manufacturing enterprises, and then, in the late nineteenth century, the railroad, other traction interests, and their allies.

In general, each of these groups governed through reliance on the Yankee stock in small towns and by withholding as much power as possible from the blue-collar "ethnic" masses in the cities and industrial towns. Each adjustment in the apportionment scheme made prior to the 1960s, though granting small concessions to the severely underrepresented urban and industrialized communities, nonetheless retained much of the preexisting distribution of power and representation.

One curious and ironic fact about all this, viewed in light of the effect that *Baker v. Carr* had in most states, was that in Rhode Island rural overrepresentation did not mean disproportionate power and influence for the agricultural segment of the state. By the mid-nineteenth century the agricultural sector of the economy was minimal. Rural dwellers had become the willing bulwark of the urban industrial and financial interests against the inundation threatened by the urban masses. By the time "one man one vote" came to Rhode Island in the 1960s, universal suffrage had been achieved, the Democratic party had become the vehicle of a now dominant working-class majority, and even the senate was going narrowly Democratic. Thus, what court-mandated equality of representation had achieved in many other states was already in place in Rhode Island by the mid-1950s. Reapportionment had the effect of reducing the GOP, already the minority party, to little more than a rump in both chambers from then on.

A few current structural changes also need to be mentioned. In 1992 the voters approved four-year terms for the governor and the other state executive officers. One obvious effect of this change is that because legislative terms run for two years, all senators and representatives stand for election at general elections that fall in the middle of the governor's term as well as in gubernatorial election years. It was thought that these off-year elections could have the effect of focusing more attention on the record of the General Assembly and its members, whose campaigns had been overshadowed by those for governor, though thus far this does not seem to be the case.

In 1994 a lengthy and complicated reform of the General Assembly was approved by the voters through amendments to several articles of the constitution. One long-sought change was the provision of a $10,000 annual salary for representatives and senators instead of the $5 per day for sixty days they had been receiving. It is possible that, in time, this could alter the composition of the assembly by making it possible for some categories of people who have not been able to accept the financial sacrifice of serving to do so (for example, women, blue-collar workers, and minorities).

The other major change wrought by the 1994 reform was the reduction of the number of house members from one hundred to seventy-five, and the number of senators from fifty to thirty-eight. These reductions will take effect in the 2002 general election, which will be conducted on the basis of new districts drawn using the 2000 U.S. Census data. The reductions in size were put forward by a study commission that framed these proposals anticipating that the voters would see them as a cost-saving measure and make the salary hike more palatable.[5] Obviously the money saved will be insignificant, but the symbolism was probably important. Ironically, at least in the short run, the real impact will probably be to decrease the number of Republicans, minorities, and perhaps women in the assembly as the larger districts with more constituents may dilute the strength of these existing minority groups. Another change will be to increase somewhat the number of constituents per district, and thus the legislator's task of keeping in touch. It will almost certainly increase the cost of campaigning. Each house member will represent roughly thirteen thousand people, and each senator, twenty-six thousand (both of which are still small numbers by the standards of most states).

The reduction in the number of legislators from 150 to 113 will increase the workload of each and may lead to a greater tendency to professionalize the assembly. Commission recommendations for more legislative staff, which did not appear on the ballot, may be underscored as the workload rises. A drive toward professionalization may be stimulated, along with a greater degree of "careerism" likely to be injected by the new salaries. The salary figure, however, is still far too low to tempt anyone to make legislative service his or her sole occupation.

LEGISLATIVE POLITICS

During most of the nineteenth century Rhode Island legislative politics were shaped by the vast economic and demographic changes that engulfed the state. In 1800 the total population was 69,122; by 1900 it had multiplied more than six times to 428,566. These changes—caused by shifts within the state and immigration from abroad—were indispensable to the industrialization of the state's economy, but were also a potential threat to the political power of the proprietors of the textile and other manufacturing establishments during the early and middle decades of the century, as well as to the parallel interests of the newer capitalist ventures of later on: railroads, streetcar lines, telephone companies, and generators of electric power.

In a word, the business elite that replaced the landholding and commercial elite of the late eighteenth century needed the newcomers as employees as well as the political power to maintain what, today, we would call a "favorable business climate." That is, they needed the kinds of legislation that would allow them to do what they needed to do—lay tracks, string wires, dam streams, and the like—and also protect them against child-labor reform that would prohibit a ten-hour workday and similar legislation that threatened their management prerogatives and their profits.

They had to control the state government, and that meant the General Assembly. Lincoln Steffens, writing in 1905, described how they did it. Legislative malapportionment was the key. (Restricted voting rights were important, too, but by disenfranchising urban dwellers, where relatively few assembly seats were to be filled anyway, they had but a modest impact.) The crucial votes were found in the small towns where the rich harvest of house seats, and especially senate seats, were to be found. Political power was to be had by whomever could reap that harvest.[6]

The year 1876 is cited as the date representing the start of General Charles Brayton's career as state Republican boss. Five years later, Nelson W. Aldrich was first elected to the U.S. Senate, where he served until 1911. Brayton was Aldrich's "man in Rhode Island," the one who built and operated the political machinery that supported Aldrich's career as a national figure and protected the economic and financial interests of the other proprietors and business beneficiaries of the machine.

How did the machine work? It rested on the voters in the small towns, who were, apparently, almost invariably "purchaseable." The "Boss" rejected the term "bribery" in an interview, which Steffens quoted: "the voters are paid for their time, because they have to leave their work and come down to the polls." The persistence of political traditions, good or bad, is illustrated by a passage David Lovejoy quotes from a 1763 document pledging campaign contributions to be used "to procure the free votes of the poorer sort of Freemen . . . who's surcomstances [*sic*] does not admit their time to the injury of their familys."[7] The base of the machine's power rested not on immigrant urban masses but, writes Steffens, on the "good old American stock out in the country."

The next step was identifying candidates for assembly office. Brayton had to approve names before they went on the ballot, whereupon campaign money was then made available. If a member disobeyed the Boss, Brayton would say, "That man sha'n't come back," and he very rarely did. The Boss had carrots as well as sticks. Because the grand committee filled all civil and judicial positions (from the highest to the lowest) in the service of the state, there were many appointments to which the loyal could look forward. Some, like district judges, could serve both on the bench and in the assembly. Brayton also had benefits available in the private sector that his connections allowed him to use as rewards. If a young lawyer was offered a fee by a corporation for securing passage of a bill he might count on the Boss's help and then repay with lasting loyalty.

In short, Brayton, thanks to the fact that "Legislator[s] returned by the electors came bought," controlled all of the state patronage and just about everything else. Steffens summed up Brayton's position: "Brayton has great personal power; he 'organized the Republican Party'; he systemized the corruption of voters; he chose legislators; he organized the General Assembly and ran it; he has gradually altered the government of the State." At the peak of the Boss's power the state government was virtually the private fiefdom of the business interests—those in the state, on Wall Street, and other investors who sought to extend their empires into Rhode Island.

During the 1890s legislative politics in Rhode Island resembled those of the tightest and most centralized of the urban machines of the period. The demographic base was different and some of the techniques were different as well, although loyalty (as in all machines) was cemented by a carefully developed and maintained system of rewards and punishments. The self-interest of the participants was the motivating power harnessed by the machine. And the constitutional system made it all possible: the restricted franchise, the centralization of power in the assembly, and gross legislative malapportionment. These factors made possible a Rhode Island legislative management style in an extreme form: rigid external party machine control.

General Brayton died early in the new century. His power structure gradually lost its total grip on the state governmental system. Democratic governors were occasionally elected, though the office still had little power save the addition of a veto power in 1909. The list of constitutional amendments approved during the first third of the century shows that reform forces were making some headway. In addition to those already cited, the franchise was further broadened in 1928 by the elimination of the property qualification required to vote for city council members. One still had to own property to vote in town meetings. Women's suffrage was approved by the General Assembly's ratification of the federal constitutional amendment in 1920.

All of these developments contributed to the loosening of the Republican machine's grip. The Great Depression was the final catalytic event, leading, as it did, to the Green Revolution of 1935. The impact of the revolution on the General Assembly was profound. For one thing, the role played by the governor in bringing it about unquestionably enhanced the symbolic stature of the office, whereas the decades of assembly intransigence had left it under a cloud. Furthermore, the restructuring of the administrative apparatus into departments answering to the governor obviously gave that office authority and a management role that, in a real sense, shifted the balance of power toward the executive. This same reform, by placing enormous amounts of state patronage at the disposal of the governor (and therefore at the disposal of the Democratic party), laid the foundation for a totally new pattern of legislative leadership.

Democratic governors could now call the shots and manage the assembly, not perhaps with the incredible power of a Brayton but to a degree that exceeded any previous governor. The executive became a very active and potent player in making state policy. This seems to have been particularly the case during the tenure of Governor Dennis Roberts, which began in 1951. He had been mayor of Providence for the preceding ten years, and went to the statehouse carrying with him control of the Providence Democratic organization, which gave him very substantial leverage in the assembly.

One suspects that during the years following the revolution, some restiveness developed among the assembly at its enforced subservience to the governor. Roberts lost to Republican Christopher Del Sesto in 1958 in the aftermath of the 1956 "long count," through which Roberts had won his fourth term via a court decision.[8] In 1960 Del Sesto lost to John Notte who, after a rather unsuccessful administration, in turn lost to Republican John Chafee. Chafee served three terms.

It is quite apparent that the long count and its aftermath not only paved the way for Chafee's success but also gave the General Assembly an opportunity to reassert itself against gubernatorial domination. This reassertion and the power structure that coalesced within the assembly and which again made the legislature a powerful force in the state government was symbolized by the career of Speaker Harry F. Curvin. Curvin was first elected to the House in 1930, during the waning of the long era of Republican assembly dominance. He was elected speaker in 1941 following the only interlude of Republican control of the house and governorship between 1932 and Del Sesto's election in 1958. Until Curvin, the almost invariable pattern had been for speakers to serve a maximum of four years in that office. He held office for twenty-three years.

It would be nearly impossible to tease out of the scanty record the process by which Harry Curvin became the all-powerful leader of the house and the key figure in the legislative branch. His political skills and powerful personality were certainly major factors. The system of legislative politics that prevailed during his tenure, and until the internal reform revolution in the house in 1977, represents another in the succession of power models in the assembly.

The Curvin control system was, in some ways, not unlike that under Boss Brayton. Its base, however, was the dominant position now enjoyed by the Democratic party and the leadership in the assembly. This dominance stemmed from the final release, in the 1920s, of the long pent-up voting power of the majority blue-collar, low-income, ethnic portion of the population. Franchise restrictions were now gone, and the inhibiting apportionment inequities had been largely overcome as the weight of the new majority increased and spread outward from the urban centers. The Democrats did not have to buy votes (though they probably would have if they had needed to) because the votes were there for the asking. Not only were these newly activated groups loyal to the Democratic party because it was perceived as standing up for their interests, but also because of anger and bitterness against the Republican party and its "mill owner" stalwarts. Resentment of the treatment meted out to workers and ethnics, both in blocking their political involvement and by preventing the passage of legislation to ameliorate the brutalities of the industrial system, would not fade for a couple of generations.

Within the chambers of the assembly these same loyalties and attitudes helped ensure the solidarity of the Democratic party—and, defensively, of the

GOP as well. Active followership was elicited by the new majority leadership in much the way Brayton had gained and held it. Election assistance was probably rarely needed, but rewards for loyal support and party service in the form of preferment in the committee and leadership structures, in government jobs that could be held while still serving, and in positions in the public sector for those who retired after periods of faithful service were the inducements used by the leaders. Punishments were available in the form of deprivation of benefits and denial of assistance in passing a member's bills. A powerful leader's weapon was, of course, tight control over the committee system and the legislative process generally.

This latter rested on the well-known political maxim that knowledge and information equal power. Long before the days of "open government," much of the assembly's work was conducted out of the sight of the voters and, indeed, even from legislators who were not "in favor" with the leaders. Most rank-and-file members were part of a game they could barely understand, let alone play.[9] Specifically, committee sessions were closed. A bill sponsor who was not a committee member might appear to press his proposal if invited, but, if not invited often could not find out when or if his bill would be considered and, if so, the bill's outcome. No records of committee actions were available to assembly members or to the public. Committee chairmen could dominate their committees and had, subject to leadership instructions, complete control over the agendas. Quorums were not required for action and votes, if actually taken, mirrored the position of the chairman. Given that all committee members and chairmen were speaker appointees in the house, subservience to leadership was the norm.

In most state legislatures it is generally true that if a bill is favorably reported from committee it will pass in almost all cases. Floor action was normally accomplished by voice vote; hence, save in very rare instances, no information as to who had voted how was available. Moreover, much of the floor action during a given annual session was taken in the final "all night" session—which often lasted for a full twenty-four-hour day or even longer. Bills would be gaveled through by number in rapid succession, with only the leadership and interested individuals aware of what was going on. On occasion a bill would be enacted without a body, just a title, the details to be filled in later. Exhaustion became an ally of the leadership in maintaining control over this windup melee.

The average member was clearly little more than an automaton, unless a legislator found favor with the leadership. Absent that favor one could only seek an audience with a committee chairman or a leader, and then plead for one's bill. If the supplicant was on the fringes of the loyal party group for any reason, or had failed to show complete loyalty sometime in the past, the cause would be pretty hopeless. If a bill had merit, it might well be reintroduced by some other, more-favored member who would then reap the credit. There would be little or no incentive to throw a bone to the disfavored member. The options were to either try to change one's ways and win favor, to not bother to seek reelection, or to become a professional maverick and critic (which during most of this period would have meant crying in the wilderness).

When Harry Curvin left office in 1964 he was succeeded, after a brief interim, by John Wrenn. Wrenn was a man of much less assertive personality. Following the 1968 election, the Democratic caucus passed over Wrenn and nominated Joseph Bevilacqua as speaker. "Joe B.," as he was almost always called, held office until January 1976 when he was elected chief justice of the supreme court. His successor, John Skiffington, only served out the term and then retired from the house.

After the 1976 election there was a prolonged and bitter struggle for the speakership. Bevilacqua had been speaker very much in the Curvin mold, and the tightness of control exhibited during the Curvin era was also the pattern of his tenure. Gradually more and more new members had been entering the house and chafing under its autocratic leadership system. The speakership vacancy gave them their chance to change things. The various clusters of dissidents banded together and supported Edward Manning, while the old guard supported Edward Maggiacomo, the majority leader. Manning won by a very narrow margin, triggering a virtual revolution in the house leadership model and procedures.

A rules committee, set up by the leaders of the reform coalition, brought in a substantially revised and reformed set of legislative rules. Knowing the oppressive and secretive system under which they had suffered during the Bevilacqua years, they systematically worked to produce a legislative system that would ensure a genuine deliberative process and a better use of assembly time to avoid the "all night" sessions.

Opening up the process meant major changes in committee operations. New rules mandated that only a quorum could act; agendas (bills to be considered) had to be posted a week in advance; no bill could be considered unless members had copies; committee meetings would be open; a record of all formal actions would appear weekly in the house and senate journals; and committee votes would be recorded by individual members. The power of the chairmen was reduced by allowing individual committee members or a bill's principal sponsor to request consideration of a bill. The electronic voting system was to be used on all votes on public bills and procedural questions. Skeleton bills and nongermane matters were banned.

Traditional scheduling practices were sharply revised: an early deadline was established for submission of all new introductions; house committees had to deal with all bills by a deadline, thereby providing enough time in the latter part of the session to consider bills from the senate; and bills reported from committee had to be on the calendar for two full days (or one full day if nearing the end of a session) before full floor consideration so that members could familiarize themselves with the bills. It was hoped that these new rules and strictly enforced daily adjournment requirements would spread out the workload, encourage thoughtful consideration, and eliminate the end-of-session pileup.

Although these changes were not always strictly adhered to, it is important to note what, in overall terms, was accomplished by this very substantial overhaul of the rules and reform effort. As noted at the beginning of the chapter, Rhode Island has gone through nearly every legislative leadership or operational style on the continuum, from something approaching a fully democratic member-managed arrangement to a pattern involving total domination by the leader of an external party machine, with the Curvin-Bevilacqua era as a variation on that latter model based on internal "machine" domination. What did the reformers of the 1970s accomplish, and where do they fit on the continuum?

Actually, the post-1976 Rhode Island legislative system landed somewhere in the middle of that continuum. Genuine and successful efforts were made to open the system up, especially to rank-and-file members. They now had full information on what was going on in committees and elsewhere, and would have means of trying to influence what happened. These changes did not mean, however, the dismantling of all leadership authority over the system. The reformers in some cases might have wanted to, but they did not end up "congressionalizing" the Rhode Island Assembly. That is, after the legislative reforms in Rhode Island the ability of the leadership to manage the process remained much stronger than the ability of the leadership in the U.S. Congress to lead effectively after the congressional reforms of 1974.

The house speaker and senate majority leader still appointed all committees and chairs, thus preserving an obvious means of enforcing management authority. And a system—probably similar to what had obtained previously—was operated whereby the leaders met with each committee chair and went over all the bills in the committee's files. The chairman was expected to return to the committee and guide it to the action desired by the leaders on bills on which the leadership had taken firm positions. This sounds like things had not changed much, and in this respect they had *not* changed profoundly.

What had changed was "the leadership" itself. From 1977 on "the leadership" included an expanded number of deputy majority leaders and all the committee chairs. This group met from time to time to discuss major issues and positions to be taken. The speaker and the majority leader still called most of the shots on a day-to-day basis, but on major controversial questions the leadership group would meet and not infrequently a caucus of all majority-party members would air the pros and cons and try to arrive at a consensus.

The key difference in leadership position and style was a subtle but important one. The new leadership could not assume that, come hell or high water, their position was secure and they could do virtually anything they pleased (the assumption during the Curvin-Bevilacqua years). The new team felt it should, and politically must, work actively to keep the troops happy through consultation and conciliation. Speaker Matthew Smith, who succeeded Manning, spent far more time talking to and listening to individual members than anyone had in the past. Joe B. came to his office for a fixed period of time before each daily session. If you could get in to see him, well and good, but if you couldn't you'd have to try again another day. The new leaders felt they must try to see all who wished to be seen and, more often than not, promise support for pet bills whether they liked them or not (since every Democratic representative would have a vote at the next post-election caucus to elect the leaders for the next two years).

Such accommodations, however, did not undermine the control held by the leadership, particularly in the house. As one of the current leaders noted of his experience in the assembly as a "back-bencher" under Matthew Smith, "Only a decade ago, if a vote was 97 to 3 for a key vote that the leadership wanted, Smith would get riled up and ask to see the three guys that didn't line up with him. Me? I need 61 votes and if I get them, I don't ask any questions." In terms of output, however, the more open system still allowed for ample amounts of old-style politics. It was during the 1980s that many of the excessive pension provisions and other legislation that granted questionable perks and accommodations for favored groups were approved. Moreover, the flaws in existing systems, like the weak regulatory provisions for RISDIC, were routinely ignored.

LEGISLATIVE POLITICS IN THE 1990S

In the aftermath of the RISDIC scandal, many legislators opted not to run for reelection. There were especially high turnover rates in 1990 and 1992 so that just under 70 percent of the legislature was elected after 1990. Many of these new members had decidedly different expectations about legislative life, which resulted in another changeover in leadership and additional reforms that gave rank-and-file members more influence and assured a more visible and open process.

There was another epic leadership struggle in the house after the 1992 election. Again, the outgoing speaker had not sought reelection and his followers had put up a candidate for speaker. The opposing candidate was supported by a coalition of members who were out of favor or out of sync with the previous leadership plus new members and others who had long been critics of the system and were pushing for further reform. The latter group, led by John Harwood and George Caroulo, won—this time with the support of less than a majority of the Democrats but aided by a number of Republicans.

A similar struggle took place in the senate in 1989. The Democratic caucus had elected Senator David Carlin as majority leader in place of the former leader who had not sought reelection. Carlin defeated John Bevilacqua (son of the former speaker). Instead of accepting his defeat, however, Bevilacqua rallied his Democratic supporters, made a deal with most of the Republicans, and gained majority control of the Senate. Using this coalition he secured adoption of senate rules that gave special privileges to the minority in gaining consideration of their bills, fulfilling a quid pro quo for their support. Throughout the sessions of 1989 and 1990 the real majority leader of the senate was Bevilacqua junior, who ultimately was elected leader in 1991.

In both of these instances Democrats won leadership positions in both houses by relying on Republican support. Many scholars see in these coalition patterns a serious further development in the "fragmentation of legislatures" and, by inference, a weakening of their ability to govern.[10] These concerns are probably well-founded. In Rhode Island these examples of bipartisan coalitions have not been disruptive in the house but have had an impact in the senate. In the house, sheer numbers are probably the explanation. There are so few Republicans and they are so weak that their support can be won without major concessions. Speaker John Harwood was supported in 1993 by the GOP members largely, it seems, in anticipation of liberalizing reforms that would benefit all rank-and-file members. Moreover, with such a large Democratic contingent it was not difficult for the new leadership to win over enough members to turn their narrow minority among Democrats into a comfortable majority. Many who voted against Harwood undoubtedly concluded later that further opposition was pointless. There is the old political saw, "if you can't beat 'em, join 'em." Thus things returned to normal not long after the new leaders were installed.

These patterns of fragmentation do appear to have had an impact in the senate, which because of the size and structure of the body gives individual members somewhat more autonomy. After Bevilacqua's term Paul Kelly was elected majority leader in 1993. Although he supported a number of internal reforms, pushed for the senate to play a greater role in budget negotiations, and was especially active in promoting women as committee chairs and to other leadership positions, his hold on the fragmented senate membership was more tenuous. Although the Democrats held a forty-two-to-eight majority in 2000, the leadership controlled a much slimmer majority. This fragmentation not only affects the influence of leaders but also the substance of legislation. Dissident members routinely vote against legislation supported by the leaders, whatever the content. When asked about his position on an important vote being held on the fate of for-profit hospitals in the state, one dissident Democratic senator noted, "I don't care one way or the other about the issue; if the leadership wants it, I vote against it." Kelly faced a serious challenge to his leadership in the summer of 2000 when one of his original supporters, William Irons, rallied a growing number of Democratic dissidents in a successful bid to take over the leadership.

Speaker John Harwood, once installed in 1993, appointed a rules committee dominated by the reformers in his group of followers. The general thrust of the committee's proposals was to shift the balance yet further in the direction of the individual member and his or her ability to influence legislation. Among the changes was a requirement to ensure that virtually all bills were heard and acted on in committee, and a device whereby a bill that received a "no passage" committee recommendation would still have to be reported to the floor. At that point the sponsor could move to change the recommendation to one of "passage." A rule was also adopted to require a delay of seven business days between the house finance committee's approval of the annual state budget bill and consideration of that bill on the floor. Previously the time lapse was minimal.

These last two rule changes would have the effect, in theory, of giving rank-and-file members more say on legislation and on the budget by allowing time to study it and to prepare amendments. The right to try to overturn a committee recommendation, if used at all, frequently would substantially undercut the role of the committees as the screeners of legislation. The budget waiting period could have the result of unleashing the parochial and special interests of individual members on a painfully compromised and fragile spending plan whose interdependent elements had been laboriously fitted together. In both cases the legislative process might well be made more time-consuming and difficult. As matters turned out, the leadership was able to reduce to a minimum the impact of both changes.

Table 4: Education and Occupation of General Assembly, 1950–1975–2000

General Assembly Members—Education Elected in:	1950	1975	2000
"Educated in Home Town Schools"*	47	2	0
High School/Trade School	30	30	6
High School/Some College	21	28	14
Bachelors Degree	24	38	48
Graduate School/Law School	18	51	79
No Answer	4	1	3
Totals:	144	150	150

General Assembly Members—Occupations Elected in:	1950	1975	2000
Small Business Operators	36	29	14
Lawyers	16	39	37
Teaching Professions	1	14	17
Managers and Executives	4	18	16
Other Professionals	7	11	9
Sales/Insurance/Real Estate	26	17	10
Retired/Housewives	8	8	14
Farmers	9	0	3
Skilled Workers	18	4	5
White Collar Workers	11	6	17
Mill Workers, Employees	4	0	0
Miscellaneous/No answer	4	4	8
Totals:	144	150	150

* No indication of grade, no mention of high school

Behind much of the reform that has been advocated for legislatures since the early 1970s lies commendable zeal for greater openness and democratization, the inevitable tension between the interests of the leaders in retaining their ability to lead and monitor the legislative process, and the keen desire of the individual members to have the greatest possible freedom to serve their constituents and their own careers. The public and the legislative institution as a whole have an interest in openness and a permeable legislative process, but also in a legislative process that can produce timely policy decisions. Clearly there needs to be a balance between individual member access to the process and the ability of the leadership to shape outcomes that are in the broad public interest. To date, changes in Rhode Island's legislative process have met this balance test reasonably well.

MEMBER CHARACTERISTICS, FACILITIES, AND RESOURCES

Table 4 presents some illustrative data on the characteristics of assembly members of selected years. The most striking changes emerge in relation to education attainment. The 1950 figures should be read with the reminder that the GI Bill's impact on the post–World War II generation had yet to be felt in most cases. Thus, in 1950 less than one-third of the legislators had reached the bachelor's degree level, while twenty-five years later nearly three-fifths had done so. The 2000 figures show 87 percent of those reporting with at least a bachelor's degree. (However, there is not necessarily a direct correlation between education and political skill or the ability to understand legislative issues. Harry Curvin, legislator and parliamentarian par excellence, lacked a college degree.)

What perhaps can be said is that during the intervening five decades—between 1950 and 2000—members have become on average less wedded to the old-style politics of patronage and strong partisan loyalties and more open to reform and modernization of the legislative process. Quite likely they have come to view their legislative careers as less important contributors to their self-esteem and less as an avenue to upward career mobility and financial security (for example, through state jobs that might be secured upon retirement). This latter point in particular gains support from an examination of occupational changes.

Occupationally, for each of the years noted there has been a decline in the number of legislators who were engaged in small business enterprises, while the percentage of members in the lawyer, teacher, or manager categories have increased. At the other end of the scale, the few mill workers who were legislators in 1950 disappeared, as did most of the skilled workers and farmers. Higher levels of education attainment led to more people in professional and related fields. This, one could argue, has increased the intellectual "horsepower" of the General Assembly, but a perhaps more important conclusion is that the legislature has become substantially less representative of the range of status rankings in the society—skewed more heavily toward the upper levels.

In broader terms the personnel of the assembly has not changed markedly over the years. A few members, by virtue of their unusually long tenures, approached the status of "professional legislators," but the vast bulk accept their roles as part-time, essentially amateur legislators. Given that compensation is meager, this has meant recruitment from a very narrow segment of the population. Most are people who are their own bosses and can spare the time, at least during part of the year, from their occupations. Since the 1960s lawyers and teachers (usually high school and some college professors) have been elected to the legislature. Wage and salary employees, business executives, and others whose time is not their own are largely absent. Lack of pay, as well as an earlier gender bias, undoubtedly have made service by women difficult, though more recently their numbers have grown markedly. There was one woman serving in 1951, eight in 1975, and thirty-seven in 2000; in 1975 only one black legislator was serving, but by 2000 there were seven.

Studies have been conducted from time to time of Rhode Island's legislative facilities, staffing, and related matters. The most comprehensive of these was completed by the Eagleton Institute at Rutgers University and published in 1968.[11] It was very thorough, detailed, and sensitive to the political realities. The old guard, still in control in the General Assembly, doubtless greeted many of the study's recommendations with skepticism. One recommendation, for upgraded staff (both in numbers and in qualifications), would have threatened leadership control, as would have the suggestion of roll calls on all major bills and other Eagleton proposals.

The major set of recommendations that was accepted from the Eagleton study's report dealt with a totally revamped committee system. The researchers found that three committees in each chamber (finance, corporations, and judiciary) dealt with nearly 90 percent of all bills, while the remaining bills were scattered among a dozen or more additional committees in each chamber. Eagleton urged that each house should have its committees consolidated into six: finance, corporations, judiciary, human resources, natural resources, and special legislation. This arrangement was accepted, though a labor committee was substituted for natural resources. At the time and given the politics of an essentially blue-collar state, the Democratic leadership, probably correctly, assumed that labor needed representation. It is also true that in that period the environment had yet to become a major issue.

Some additions to staff positions were created in the following years, but little if any true policy staff was added until the early 1990s. The finance staff has become quite substantial, but the other committees still have only a clerk and part-time counsel. The leadership staff did grow also in both chambers. The fact that the staff thus remained largely under the central control of the leadership was not accidental. No move was made to provide either staff or office space for individual members. The necessary money would simply not have been available. During the late 1980s, however, a new office building was built near the statehouse to house the Department of Administration's various branches, most of which had been in the statehouse. Much of the released space was taken over by the assembly and the expanding staff of the governor. Thus, some improvement in physical facilities was made though the impact on the individual members was indirect at best. Presently the leaders in both houses are attempting to reallocate office space and provide desks, offices, and more staff for cooperative members.

At the opening of the new century, although the governorship has made steady gains, the General Assembly remains the state's premier governing institution. It has not been professionalized to a very great degree, though there has been some movement to provide better pay, staffs, and working conditions. Within the legislative process the roles played by the rank-and-file members and those played by the committee chairs and the party leadership have been substantially modified from the highly centralized and autocratic styles of the past. A reasonable balance seems to have been struck between these competing sets of forces. Members have more rights and means of access to the system, but it is also true that the majority leadership can still manage the overall legislative process and output.

This balance appears, for the most part, to have allowed the General Assembly to respond to the challenge of an increasingly complex policy agenda in a constructive way. Having supported or acquiesced to many structural reforms that opened up the process and crafted fairly responsible campaign-finance reforms, they have been reasonably successful in promoting responsible policy choices. In terms of the budget (see chapter 10), since the RISDIC scandal they have adopted a fiscal policy that attempts to manage competing interests in taxes and spending and deal with long-term systemic problems. They have also drafted and enacted some highly innovative legislation dealing with utility deregulation, welfare reform, patients' rights, and universal health insurance for children—all of which have earned national recognition. There remains, of course, ample amounts of deals, tradeoffs, favoritism, and downright pettiness in the day-to-day operation of the institution. Moreover, regardless of policy concerns, a high-stakes institutional power game is never far from the surface, and leaders keep their sights on the stakes and the players at all times. Nonetheless, one would have to acknowledge that—at least over the past century—the legislature has done a better job of managing the messy and maddening business of representative democracy.

CHAPTER SIX

The Executive and the Administration

The framers of the constitution in 1842 and 1986 have treated executive power quite differently than did the framers of the federal Constitution. First, they included no specific appointment clause similar to that contained in the federal Constitution. Secondly, they deliberately fragmented and distributed the executive power among four elected general officers.

Rhode Island Supreme Court, 1999

Rhode Island did not really have a governorship worthy of the name until the 1930s. The office was so weak that it played, at most, a marginal role in the General Assembly–dominated government of the colony and the state. To this day, along with all other New England states except Connecticut, the Rhode Island governor ranks among the weakest of the fifty state governors as measured in terms of constitutional provisions and powers.

However, as suggested earlier, Rhode Island's constitutional tradition accounts for a good bit of the low ranking. Unlike many other states, the brief constitutional provisions have of necessity been fleshed out by statute. As a result, much of the role and many of the powers of the governor of today are statutory, and in totality compare more favorably with those of governors elsewhere.[1]

THE GOVERNORSHIP IN THE CONSTITUTION

The framers of the 1843 constitution had the clear intention of crafting a gubernatorial office that was weak in the tradition set by the royal charter. Article VII of the constitution (now Article IX in the edited and reformatted 1986 version) is entitled "Of the Executive Power." It provides that the governor shall take care that the laws be faithfully executed, be commander in chief of the state military forces, have limited power to grant reprieves and pardons, adjourn the assembly when the houses disagree, call extraordinary sessions, fill vacancies until the assembly acts, and issue commissions with the secretary of state.

This meager list, with its very significant omissions, left Rhode Island governors on the fringes of the political process at best, absent statutory additions to their powers. The very first section in the article reads: "The chief executive power of this state shall be vested in a governor." The insertion of the word "chief" as a modifier in this clause was no doubt intended to suggest that the other elected state officers each exercised a portion of the executive power.

Although the other executive offices were much more important in the years before the arrival of the administrative state in Rhode Island (that is, before the Green Revolution), even today these offices enjoy a range of executive functions. The lieutenant governor presides over the senate and the grand committee (when the house and senate sit together) and, in the event of a tie, casts the deciding vote. That individual also assumes the duties of the governor should there be a vacancy, and serves as the chair of a number of advisory councils. Recent occupants of the office have carved out a policy advocacy role, particularly on issues that deal with health care. The Department of State is presided over by the secretary of state. The office is in charge of archival records and the state library, shares responsibility with the board of elections for administrating elections, registers and maintains records of lobbyists, and deals with matters related to incorporations. The Department of the Treasury, presided over by the general treasurer, handles all revenue receipts and makes all disbursements, keeps records on bonds and bond indebtedness, and is a member of various boards (such as those dealing with state investments and pension systems). The attorney general is the state's chief legal officer for both criminal and civil matters, conducts the state's legal affairs, and represents the state in all legal proceedings. The office advises state offices and agencies on legal issues, gives written legal opinions, and sits as a member of a number of boards and commissions. Rhode Island is the only state other than Delaware that does not have district attorneys, making the attorney general an especially influential office.

All of these officers are elected for four-year terms and, depending on the person and the party of the individual, they carve out their own political agenda which may or may not support the position of the governor. Many state officers see their positions as a prelude to running for governor or other higher office.

One strongly suspects that the "chief" executive clause in the constitution was also intended to suggest that the General Assembly would exercise executive powers as well. Elsewhere in the constitution the assembly is vested with most of the appointive powers, and clearly retained within its plenary power is the authority to create and, if it chooses, to manage administrative agencies and the budget. Other than proposing the state's initial budget, there is no hint that the governor should participate in setting the legislative agenda through a state of the state message or otherwise.

Until 1909 Rhode Island's governor had no veto power.[2] The conferring of the veto power by constitutional amendment that year was the first significant step toward giving the governor any substantive power to affect state policy and governance. Even then, a three-fifths vote by each house can override a veto. To this day the governor does not have a line-item veto.

James Q. Deeley of Brown University, writing in 1928 after winding up a review of the major deficiencies of the gubernatorial office by noting that the governor did not even have any oversight or control over the state administration, concluded: "Our Governor has no such power. He controls his own office, and being ex officio a member of many boards and commissions he may offer suggestions here and there. . . . [B]ut constitutionally he has no right to give orders or to investigate any department of administration, or to demand reports from any officer unless so authorized by the Assembly."[3]

THE GREEN REVOLUTION

The Green (or "bloodless") Revolution in 1935 was the turning point for the governorship, as it was for the political parties and the balance of partisan control in the General Assembly. On New Year's Day 1935, once they had gained control of the senate, the Democratic leaders secured the enactment of some key pieces of legislation that sped through both chambers and were then signed by Governor Theodore Green.[4] The last of these was a massive bill that merged some eighty state commissions into eleven new departments. Of key importance was the fact that the governor would appoint all department directors (with senate approval) and they would then serve at his pleasure. From 1935 on, if the senate had not acted on a gubernatorial appointment within three days, instead of having the right to elect someone to fill the position the appointee would be presumed to have been confirmed.

To say that this legislation, and further fine-tuning enactments along the same line, transformed the governorship of Rhode Island would be no exaggeration. Armed with appointive power and the power to remove, the chief executive at long last became a true chief administrator. Moreover, he could control a rationalized set of departments in place of the crazy quilt of boards and commissions responsible to the assembly (if to anyone, in practice) which had passed for an administrative structure for a century or more. Beyond that, as Erwin Levine wrote, "More than altruism and devotion to the cause under lay the speedy passage of the skeleton reorganization bill on New Year's Day. Consolidating the departments and commissions of the state also meant the creation of many new jobs for good Democrats."[5]

Rhode Island had yet to enact any kind of civil service system; all jobs were potentially spoils for the victors. Their initial distribution did not go all that smoothly in 1935. Governor Green had to thread his careful way among conflicting factional demands. This massive changing of the guard was necessary, however. Democrats were gaining access to state offices for the first time ever, and the rush to benefit was understandably something of a stampede. The new leadership had a right to put its people in key positions if it was to govern successfully, and Green insisted on competence for his appointments. It was regrettable, though inevitable, that the victors and the masses they represented approached the quest for public office with the firm conviction that now "their turn" had finally come.

The lesson they had learned, one which the Republicans had taught them well, was that places on the public payroll were entitlements won by political combat. Indeed, government itself existed to benefit the people whose leaders won the political struggle. It would be a long time before the ethical assumption was accepted that public office is a public trust and that government's obligation is to provide fair and disinterested service to all citizens. Rhode Island's problem in this regard stemmed from the fact that the leaders from the time of colonial pre-Revolutionary factions and all of the power groups that succeeded them saw government as the source of particularistic benefits to the winners in the political wars.

The impact of the revolution of 1935 would be felt for decades to come. It transformed the office of governor and launched the process of tooling up the office. The legislation, passed in 1935, also set up a new department called the Executive Department, to be headed by the governor and to include his executive staff, the budget director, the comptroller, the purchasing agent, all of their respective staffs, the adjutant general, the state police, and the division of parole.[6]

The Democrats were, it turned out, well advised to move quickly and decisively in 1935 while they had the chance. In 1936 the GOP regained control of the senate and retained that control almost uninterrupted into the 1950s. Thus, if a strong beachhead of countervailing power had not been established in the office of governor, the Democratic party could well have slipped back into the frustrating impotence it had suffered for decades before the 1930s.

A key piece of legislation from the governor's point of view was the administrative reorganization.[7] The abolition of boards and commissions and their replacement with eleven departments to be headed by gubernatorial appointees who served at his pleasure meant that he really could be chief executive. The magnitude of this shift in the locus of power would be hard to exaggerate. Under the earlier system the legislatively appointed board members were quite beyond the reach of gubernatorial influence, to say nothing of its control. The resulting system doubtless partook of substantial assembly influence, as well as decentralization and fragmentation (that is, there was no "administration" or "administrative branch" as we know it today). At worst, the governor was a spectator. At best he could exert limited influence as an ex-officio board member or otherwise. In 1935 he became a genuine chief executive and chief administrator.

The General Assembly gave up an enormous amount of power, in at least two senses and perhaps three. First, it lost whatever direct influence it had exerted through the various boards and commissions now superseded by administrative departments. Second, it lost much of the control it may well have had over staffs and other appointments, that is, over state patronage. Third, it participated in the creation of a gubernatorial office that was certain to become a powerful rival and alternative source of authority in the governing system—an influence that had had no counterpart in the old assembly-centered system.

The point again is that the only way in which the General Assembly could have been persuaded to make this huge sacrifice of long-enjoyed power was through the particular set of circumstances that obtained at the time. The Democratic party, once in control of both chambers in January 1935, had no choice but to attempt to consolidate its position for the future. The apportionment arrangements were such that members had to have known that the situation was but a limited window of opportunity. The powerfully strengthened governorship thus became their hedge against future revivals of Republican control of the senate which, indeed, came as early as 1936. Theoretically the GOP could have tried to undo what their rivals had done, but this would have been well-nigh impossible without control of both chambers. Even then, legislation to turn the clock back would have faced a veto. Not until 1938 and the election of Governor William Vanderbilt did the GOP gain control of both chambers and both branches. By then the Democratic changes were deeply imbedded, and a changing generation of Republican leaders adopted a strategy of "out-reforming the reformers" by instituting a civil service system.

A change less spectacular than the administrative restructuring, albeit a part of it, was legislation that created the office of budget director and comptroller, to be appointed by the governor and to hold office at his pleasure. Whereas legislative leaders, undoubtedly at the behest of the governor, had placed the power to appoint department directors firmly in the chief executive's hands and mandated that they serve at his pleasure, in the case of the budget director they did not even require senatorial confirmation. New language, in sharp contrast to that of 1926, described the new budget-making process: "The budget director and comptroller shall, under the supervision of the Governor, prepare the annual state budget, . . . [T]he governor shall submit to the general assembly a budget containing a complete plan of estimated revenues and proposed expenditures for the next fiscal year."[8] The state as of 1935 thus acquired a modern executive budget system, and the fiscal authority the governor needed to have as chief administrator became available.

The Green Revolution was indeed a total restructuring of the power positions of the two parties in the state; it was also almost a coup d'etat in terms of the removal by the General Assembly of the whole supreme court to make way, as they saw it, for a fairer partisan and ideological composition of that body. But it was also a revolution that had a profound impact on the relative positions of the executive and legislative branches of the government.

THE GOVERNORSHIP AND THE GENERAL ASSEMBLY

Without losing any of its traditional constitutional power as the central organ of the system, the General Assembly was to be yoked for the future with governors equipped to be major players in politics and policymaking. This is not to say that the legislative institution settled comfortably and contentedly into a new and permanent partnership role with the executive. The assembly still had all of the constitutional authority it had long exercised. It would have been surprising if, in time, a restlessness had not developed to reclaim at least some of the legislature's former central position in the system. Actually it did, and the rest of the story of the governorship during the twentieth century is an account of competitive rivalries between governors and legislative leaders and the as-yet-unfulfilled quest for an agreed-upon and stable balance between the roles of the two institutions. Almost certainly a permanent balance of this kind will be impossible to find, given the deeply rooted commitment to divided government and checks and balances.

The 1935 refurbishing and empowering of the governorship did result in a strong and assertive executive that lasted until the beginning of the 1960s. Obviously, transitions from one mode or pattern to another (as will be noted) were gradual and cannot be dated with precision. Moreover, the position and influence of various governors after 1935 also depended on the leadership abilities of the governor to work with the legislature and sustain public support.

Green left office to go to the U.S. Senate at the end of his second term. In 1936 Lieutenant Governor Robert Quinn was elected to the top position. His were not a harmonious or happy two years in office, due in large part to a bitter factional fight and public brawl relating to the major racetrack in the state. Quinn was defeated for reelection by William Vanderbilt, a wealthy member of the famous family and a quite liberal and reform-minded Republican. Vanderbilt's major legislative accomplishment was the institution of the first civil service system for Rhode Island's state employees. In a way Vanderbilt's initiative could be called the GOP's revenge on the Democrats for their defeat in 1935.

Vanderbilt also served only one term, in part, it is suggested, because rural Republicans resented his legislative blow to the patronage pool they had lived on for years. Democrats then consistently won the governorship from 1940 until 1958. The incumbency of John O. Pastore from 1947 to 1951 is of interest both because he was the first Italian-American to attain that office and because later on he was the first of his nationality to serve in the U.S. Senate, which he did from 1950 to 1976. His governorship was also noteworthy for the adoption of the direct primary for the state—one of the last states to make that transition—and for the institution of a statewide sales tax (until then Rhode Island had neither sales nor income taxes).

Pastore's accomplishments underscore the assertion that the strong governorship launched by Green was still the mode. The individual who, it can be argued, brought the office to its peak of power and influence and also helped to precipitate its decline was Dennis J. Roberts. Roberts had served for ten years as mayor of Providence. During that tenure he brought his strong modernizing and reforming interests to bear on the capital city. It was during his tenure that a new, strong-mayor charter was adopted in place of the archaic one that had served the city for many years.

When Roberts was elected governor in 1950 he brought these concerns to the state government, but also brought to his new position the political clout of the Providence Democratic organizations that he had controlled and used to advantage while mayor. His handpicked successor in city hall was his administrative assistant, Walter Reynolds, whose loyalty to his former boss was unshakable. Thus Roberts could count on the Providence machine as a major political asset in the statehouse. This was no small advantage. In those days one-quarter of all the seats in the House of Representatives were held by Providence districts and typically were overwhelmingly Democratic. (The senate was still a problem because the city held only five of the total of forty-four seats.)

That the same individual should be both party boss and reformer may seem unusual, but such was the case with Roberts. So far as the governorship was concerned, he was responsible for another major innovation which, together with the 1935 reforms, was another long step toward forging a truly modern governorship.

During his first year in office he secured passage of legislation that established the state's Department of Administration.[9] The objective of this legislation was to build on the precedent of the executive department set up in 1935, bringing together all of those kinds of activities into one department headed by a director who would be a close advisor to the governor and manage staff functions on his behalf.

The idea, strongly advocated by students of public administration, was to bring together all of the staff services into one agency and thus leave the chief executive freer to devote his attention to the "line" functions of government. This latter idea, of course, meant the supervision of the programs that government provides for the citizenry and the development of policy proposals to deal with emerging problems. Accordingly, the new Department of Administration had responsibility for: preparing and administering the budget, instituting proper uniform accounting practices throughout the government, purchasing (and all that it involves), caring for the physical plant of state government and state motor vehicles, establishing and maintaining central tabulating and related services, overseeing tax assessment and collection, and operating the personnel merit system.

Roberts's partially inadvertent contribution to the weakening of the governorship came when he ran for reelection to a fourth term in 1956 and only won by a whisker after some categories of absentee ballots were thrown out by the state supreme court. With the assiduous help of the *Providence Journal*, an unfortunate sequence of events was portrayed as a stealing of votes by an unscrupulous person determined to stay in office at any cost. The fallout was extensive and had long-lasting effects. For Roberts it meant an unhappy lame-duck final term and defeat in the 1960 U.S. senatorial primary by newcomer Claiborne Pell. (Both were vying to fill the seat from which Senator Green was retiring.)

Pell was the first major candidate to wrest a nomination from a party-endorsed candidate. By so doing he encouraged a number of subsequent assaults on formerly unassailable primary candidates endorsed by the Democratic party. It is probably also true that many of the Democratic voters Roberts had angered never returned to the party loyalty they had once felt. In a broader sense Pell's victory foreshadowed the long-term decline of party strength among the voters, and hence the role of the parties in the political system.

One can only speculate as to when, during the events that followed, and for what reasons the General Assembly began to become restless in its position of relative subservience to the newly strong gubernatorial office. In retrospect it seems clear, however, that somewhere along the line during the 1960s the assembly began to reclaim its former power and role in the system. Republican Christopher Del Sesto, whom Roberts had bested in the 1956 vote recount, defeated the governor in 1958. Del Sesto in turn was defeated in 1960 by Democrat John Notte, an amiable individual but one who lacked the force or drive to check a distinct decline in the governorship and a corresponding legislative renaissance.

Then in 1962 Republican John Chafee defeated Notte and began a three-term tenure in the office, something the Republicans had not enjoyed since well before 1932. Chafee, a liberal Republican, was a very able candidate, a superb campaigner, and a strong leader. It has often been said since that it was John Chafee who taught Rhode Islanders how to split their tickets at election time. The state had always had a "master lever" on its voting machines by which the citizen could cast with one stroke a straight party vote. When Chafee was running, groups like the League of Women Voters made it their business to show people how they could split their vote for various offices. As a result, Chafee won two more terms with lopsided majorities. Quite likely this altered pattern of voter behavior (also a reflection of weakening party ties) encouraged the Republican strategy of devoting most of its resources to the top of the ticket and doing little to try to increase its very limited representation in the assembly.

Governor Chafee is credited with having extremely good relations with the heavily Democratic General Assembly. As a result, he enjoyed considerable success in getting his proposals passed. One may suspect, however, that it was during Chafee's six years that the legislature concluded it could and probably should reassert its role in the governing process. That is, under strong governors like Roberts it had yielded much of the leadership initiative to the governor. During the Del Sesto and Notte terms, gubernatorial management of policy making relaxed considerably. Then, when it became clear that the Chafee administration was to be more than another two-year interlude, it may have been clear to the Democratic leadership that a partial vacuum was being created that they could fill.

The limitations on gubernatorial leadership and the risks it can entail for a governor were brought home during the long debate on the institution of an income tax. The need for a broader-based state revenue-raising system had become increasingly apparent. Governor Notte proposed a limited tax on unearned income. His loss to John Chafee was due in part to the unpopularity of that idea and to Chafee's campaign promise that there would be no income tax. Then, during his third term, Chafee became convinced that such a tax was inevitable and he said so publicly. Frank Licht, the Democrat Chafee lost to in 1968, claimed during the campaign that an income tax was not necessary and promised to ensure that there was none. History then repeated itself. Licht was forced to the same conclusion Chafee had reached, and pushed an income tax through the assembly during his second term. The resulting outcry was such that he decided not to seek reelection.

Subsequent governors enjoyed leverage and influence vis-à-vis the legislature depending on the economic and political climate prevailing during their terms as well as on the individual leadership style of the chief executive. But the backdrop for their activities was usually an increasingly assertive legislative leadership. During the 1980s when Edward DiPrete, a Republican, was governor, the economy of the state was generally prosperous. DiPrete did not take a particularly active role in policymaking and legislative leaders of the time dominated the budget process. As a result, agreements between the executive and the legislative branches were achieved without much difficulty. At the onset of the Bruce Sundlun administration, however, the banking crisis and a large unexpected budget deficit created a political situation in which some legislative members and leaders, on whose watch these problems had developed, ran for cover. Sundlun, whose style was bold and assertive, was able to fill the political vacuum created by retreating legislative leaders. Given his success in handling the fiscal and budget crisis, as well as the open and innovative character of his administration following on the heels of DiPrete's, Sundlun enjoyed considerable leverage even after new leadership took over in the legislature after 1992.

In 1994 Republican Lincoln Almond was elected to serve the first four-year term in the history of the state. Budgetary problems were even worse and a confrontation became inevitable. First, as a Republican he faced veto-proof majorities in both houses. Second, new and particularly savvy leadership that had a firm grasp on policy and budget issues had consolidated its control in the legislature. By 1996 a confrontation over the budget resulted in the legislature creating and passing its own budget. As one legislative leader

noted, "We just realized we didn't need him; it [the budget] was our show."
Third, during Almond's tenure two state supreme court decisions reaffirmed
in bold terms the dominant position of the General Assembly. In *Sundlun v.
Pawtucket*, a 1995 unanimous decision, the court reaffirmed the sole authority
of the legislature (and *not* the courts or the governor) to deal with issues of
funding for education. The second court decision was an advisory opinion
issued in 1999 that flatly rejected the governor's attempt to eliminate or limit
the role of legislators on boards and commissions. The case was argued on
a separation of powers principle but in response the court likened the Rhode
Island legislature to a parliamentary system.

During this same period the role of the executive was further weakened by
the implementation of merit selection for all judges. While this constitutional
change eliminated the direct role of the legislature in selecting supreme court
judges and gave the governor a role in the selection process, it also eliminated
a source of influence that governors had enjoyed insofar as they formerly
had directly made all the appointments to the state court bench, except for
those to the supreme court. Finally, Almond, who was reelected in 1998,
was an amiable enough individual, but his passive leadership style created
a vacuum that the General Assembly was ready and able to fill. The new
constitutionally mandated four-year term was designed to give the governor
some political leverage over a legislature that faced reelection every two
years. Perhaps future chief executives can realize this potential.

Nonetheless, future governors will certainly play a central role, by using
both their constitutional and statutory powers, in a changing political process.
The realities of New Federalism assure that the chief executive will play a
more central and visible role in policy development and administration. The
assembly will continue to be a partner in that process, but is not likely
to assert its full prerogatives at the permanent expense of the role of the
governor. The chief executive, along with state administrators, has been and
will continue to be required to develop and manage complex policy programs
as the federal government devolves power and responsibility to the state on
a range of issues and initiatives. While the legislature may intervene on the
margins, a part-time nonprofessional legislature does not have the capacity to
develop and manage these policies and programs. Thus state administration
and administrators under the governor will play an increasingly important
role in this vital and highly visible process.

GOVERNORS IN THE POLICY PROCESS

The role of the governor as policy leader began to emerge during the tenure of

John Chafee. Chafee was not only a charismatic presence at the statehouse, he also articulated a policy vision that eventually created a potentially broader role for the executive. Chafee promoted the first environmental policy agenda, which included a successful Green Acres program initiative. He also began the push for civil rights legislation and promoted initiatives like the fair housing program. This policy focus was eventually institutionalized under Governor Philip Noel following the 1972 election and the withdrawal of the U.S. Navy from Rhode Island.

During the years between the Great Depression and the United States' entry into World War II, the navy presence in Rhode Island grew into a major element of the state's economy. The state also benefited greatly during the war as a center for shipbuilding and other forms of war production. After the war the threat of major base closings, in addition to the tapering off of military contracts, hung over a state that had become dangerously dependent on defense spending.

A push during the Nixon administration to slim down the nation's military establishment came through a drastic program of base closings. As the presidential election of 1972 approached, Rhode Islanders became increasingly worried about the impact of such a policy. True, John Chafee had gone to Washington as Nixon's Secretary of the Navy, but he had returned to Rhode Island to run for Claiborne Pell's U.S. Senate seat in 1972. The state's Democrats were unhappy with George McGovern's presidential candidacy. That, plus a promise from the Nixon administration that Rhode Island bases would be spared the axe, helped put the state into the Republican column for the first time since they had voted for Dwight Eisenhower in 1952.

President Nixon's second term had barely begun, and Governor Noel's term was still in its opening weeks, when the axe indeed fell on the Rhode Island naval establishment with devastating impact. Thousands of civilian jobs were lost both in the Newport area and at Quonset Point across the bay. The movement of the Atlantic destroyer force from Narragansett Bay to the south also meant the loss of thousands more naval personnel and dependents. The Noel administration faced a major economic crisis. The details of how it was dealt with are less important for our immediate purposes than the impact it had on the governorship.

The new governor moved to set up a policy group in the office of the governor, something that had not existed before. Unlike the traditional method of staffing the office with former campaign aides and other political appointees, Noel brought in people with appropriate professional backgrounds and training. Noel saw his "policy staff" as a way of dealing with the economic crisis and also as a necessary adjunct to the governor's office.[10]

So far as remedial economic development was concerned, the governor secured legislation to set up a Department of Economic Development and a Port Authority and Economic Development Corporation.[11] The policy staff in the governor's office was available as a major component of the overall immediate economic development effort, but it also represented a valuable long-term source of assistance to governors in their administrative and policy leadership roles.

Previously there was always a risk that the governor would become the captive of his department directors. Any new administration's directors took office as loyal associates and supporters of the chief executive. In time, however, they often became protagonists and spokespersons for their own departments. They would come to the governor with policy proposals seeking approval and he would have little basis for evaluating their suggested initiatives. Gubernatorial staffs had traditionally been limited, and they were politically rather than policy oriented in terms of both background and function.

The establishment of policy appointees represented a major reorientation of the staff and the inclusion of crucial policy development and analysis capabilities. The governor could now use these new staffers to evaluate, on the basis of professional expertise, any suggested departmental policy initiatives and to work on policy innovations for the governor to include in his programs. No longer would the chief executive be solely dependent on the policy advice of department directors, whose perspective and political needs might not coincide with his own. The governor could now base decisions on analyses prepared by people from his own political and program perspective.

A comparison of the staff roster for the office of the governor in the personnel supplement to the state budget of 1972 (with corresponding data from the 1994 Personnel Supplement) is revealing. There were twenty-four positions on the 1972 roster, not one of which had the word "program," "policy," or a similar designation in its title. By 1994 the total on this same roster had doubled to forty-eight, and eighteen of these did have one or another of those words in the position title. Recent administrations have obviously adopted and elaborated on the practice of building a strong policy capacity among the governor's immediate staff.

The size of the staff and the complexity of modern state governance have confronted each new governor with questions of staff organization and operation. With nearly fifty persons in the immediate entourage, the chief executive must decide how to deal with this array of aides as well as how to fill the role of chief administrator. The actual operation of the office of the governor under Democrat Bruce Sundlun (1991–1995) and Republican

Lincoln Almond (1995–2002) settled into a pattern. Both governors began with a kind of "open door" policy for principal aides and department directors.[12] Both began holding regular cabinet meetings with the group of directors. Sundlun continued these meetings on a generally weekly schedule throughout his period in office; Almond held them rather less frequently and settled into a once-a-month pattern.

During an interview with a person who had served in both of these administrations as a top policy staffer, the question was asked about the role played by the staff. Did the staff in fact make policy, that is, did it originate the proposals that made up the governor's legislative program? Did it serve as the filter through which policy proposals from the departments would pass before the governor made a decision about them? The answer: in general the staff is outgunned by the departments. The policy staff just does not have the resources and data to really evaluate departmental initiatives. In some cases it does develop policy for the governor. In others, especially regarding technically complex issues, the departments take the lead. Under Almond, in particular, the staff did try to exercise a quality control role, that is, it ensured that departmental proposals made sense and that the figures on which they were based were accurate.

In short, an elaborate system of gubernatorial staffing has evolved which seems to have changed little in general size and arrangement from one administration to the next. Governors of course have used this apparatus in somewhat different ways, based to a considerable extent on personality and work habits. Almond, for example, came to the office from many years as U.S. Attorney for Rhode Island, an office in which he undoubtedly relied heavily on his assistant attorneys and gave them considerable freedom to do their jobs. Bruce Sundlun came to the statehouse as an archetypal corporate executive accustomed to running the show himself. In both cases, however, an initial open door approach gave way to a much more centralized and hierarchical one. This shift probably stemmed as much from a need to have close trusted associates with whom to interact in decision making as it did from a conscious choice of one standard operating style over another.

STATE ADMINISTRATION

Table 5 gives a broad overview of the administrative structure in Rhode Island government. The left-hand column lists the new departments set up in the course of the Green Revolution in 1935. With some obvious exceptions, this structure proved remarkably durable. In most cases the original departments survive today, possibly with some changes in title or adjustments in function.

Table 5: Administrative Departments, 1935–2000

Departments Set Up in 1935 Reorganization	Transitional Departments	Current Departments (2000)
Executive		Executive Administration
State		State
Justice		Attorney General
Treasury		Treasury
Public Welfare	Social Welfare	Human Services
	Social & Rehabilitative Services	Mental Health, Retardation, & Hospitals
		Corrections
	Children & Families	Children, Youth, & Families
Public Works		Transportation
Taxation & Regulation		Business Regulation
Education		Education
Labor	Employment & Training	Labor & Training
Agriculture & Conservation	Natural Resources	Environmental Management
Health		Health
	Economic Development	Economic Development Corporation
		Elderly Affairs

Only two wholly new departments have been added, both of which appear in the current roster. Actually two minor agencies—the Department of Community Affairs and the Department of Library Services—existed for some time but were recently absorbed into other departments.

The Department of Administration represented a major addition to the list, drawing its roster of responsibilities from the Executive Department, the Department of Taxation and Regulation, and elsewhere. The renaming of the Justice Department as the Department of the Attorney General was merely a shift in title. Skipping Public Welfare for the moment, the new departments of Transportation and Business Regulation represent a reallocation of some functions from the 1935 scheme. The creation of Labor and Training represents both a recognition of the importance of vocational and technical training and the unification of two related areas of concern.

Economic Development and Elderly Affairs emerged in response to the more recent recognition of the urgent need to create and retain jobs in the state and the needs of an aging population, respectively. The proliferation of progeny from the original Public Welfare Department in 1935 indicates the one area in the list that has shown extensive growth and organizational innovation. The Green Revolution and the enactment of Social Security by the U.S. Congress occurred in the same year, 1935. Although changes in federal, state, and local responsibilities in this area were emerging, there would have been no way to predict what the term "public welfare" would come to embrace as the years went on. It was both a process of expanding activity in areas of human need that were already a concern of government (such as welfare and similar payments to the indigent) as well as movement into new areas of concern.

A dramatic example of the latter involves programs for and about children. The original 1935 legislation set up divisions of mothers' aid and children's care in the Department of Public Welfare. Eventually, when it was decided that a separate department was needed, the Department of Children and Families was established in 1974. Then in 1991, following the issuance of a major study commission report on child neglect and troubled youth, further legislative action was taken. The result was a reorganization of the department and the insertion of the word "youth" into its title.

In short, table 5 depicts both the continuing importance of traditional state governmental functions and the agencies set up to carry them out, and the areas in which new responses have been needed. The principal one among these areas of new need has been that of social services for various groups at risk, from the youngest children to the elderly. The structure of state government has changed over the years to reflect its efforts to meet these needs.

STATE EMPLOYEES

Although the merit system or civil service movement began at the federal level with the Pendleton Act in 1883, it caught on more slowly among the states. New York set up a Civil Service Commission for the state in 1894, and mandated the use of such systems for all its cities. As of the mid-1930s a dozen states had civil service commissions. Actually, the movement went forward more rapidly among counties and cities. As of 1934, 450 cities had some kind of civil service system.

Rhode Island climbed, somewhat reluctantly, on the bandwagon during the governorship of William Vanderbilt (1939–1941). Vanderbilt had campaigned as a reformer and for civil service in particular. The "old guard" rural Republicans (as noted) were adamantly opposed to civil service per se, though the governor was able to push through his merit-system legislation. His success at passing the legislation doubtless contributed to his failure to secure reelection.

Local communities were slow to follow the state's lead, although the state act did offer help to cities and towns in setting up merit systems of their own. With the coming of municipal home rule in 1951, the reformers who wrote the first charters for the older industrial cities were much more sympathetic to this and to other reform ideas (see "Local Government," chapter 12). Actually, the Providence legislative charter adopted in 1940 contained a civil service provision under which, via a Civil Service Commission, "The city of Providence is hereby authorized, empowered and directed to institute, establish and maintain a civil service system of employment for its employees." The passage of an appropriate ordinance was called for, though only a brief summary of the provisions it should contain was included in the city charter. There is, in fact, no record that this mandate was carried out.

The Pawtucket "home rule" charter also mandated civil service, but provided much more detail—virtually a full-blown plan. The Woonsocket home rule charter adopted around the same time also mandated a civil service system. In short, at both the state and city levels there was a strong impulse stemming from reform elements to institute merit systems. Even so, the traditions and the political culture of Rhode Island supported the long-standing patronage method of filling offices, with the result that the forms of civil service were adopted but the traditional practices were yielded only grudgingly.

In the years following the establishment of the state merit system in 1939, a number of amendments were made to the system. These amendments can be interpreted either as desirable injections of flexibility or as making it more permeable to political or other "nonmerit" kinds of appointments. Given the dominant position that the Democratic party had achieved after 1935, there was less concern for ensuring appointments to state service on the basis of partisan political grounds than other kinds of preferment. That is to say, governors and others who played a role in making appointments were usually more concerned with satisfying intraparty factional and ethnic group claims, or with placing individuals to whom they felt personally indebted or who had important family ties or the like.

Most merit systems are potentially manipulable in a variety of ways. Take, for example, the well-known "rule of three" that is used in the federal system and elsewhere. Use of this rule means that when a classified system position is to be filled, the personnel administrator certifies to the appointment authority the top three names on the list (in terms of examination scores); the authority must then appoint one of the three. The Rhode Island legislation of 1939 required that the appointing authority be given the name of *the* person standing highest. In 1941 the Democrats, having returned to power, took their first opportunity to do so and amended the statute to replace "one" with "three." Then in 1955, during the Roberts administration, the act was amended again to replace three with six, which continues as the current law.

The rationale for these changes is, of course, a matter of speculation, but the first shift to three was in line with generally accepted personnel theory of the time. A single certified name on a take-it-or-leave-it basis tied the hands of the appointing authority too tightly. At the same time, the later shift to six may well have occurred in order to increase the chances that among the six certified names there would be one with a special claim on preferment. It also obviously diluted the impact of a high score as the primary appointment criterion.

In 1995 the Rhode Island Public Expenditure Council (RIPEC), a business-supported and highly reputable organization whose staff monitors state government, published a document optimistically titled "The State Merit System Act of 1996." It contained a careful analysis of the current state of the merit system and the legislation on which it is based, and listed a number of recommendations for change along with appropriate draft legislation. The General Assembly did not oblige by passing the proposed act. In fact, it did very little about the merit system during the 1996 session. RIPEC's report, however, provides a useful review of the status of the system.

In addition to the shift to the rule of six, there have been a number of other changes over the years, some of which doubtless were created with similar motivations. The overall result is a state public service system that retains many of the attributes of a merit system but that has been altered and is used as part of the traditional Rhode Island system of using state government to provide group and individual benefits. Few state civil service systems exhibit or make possible the thoroughgoing professionalism inherent in the merit system ideal. Rhode Island's certainly falls short of that ideal.

One of the most useful ways of making such a system permeable for desired appointments is the provision usually made for making temporary appointments. Temporary appointments are, at times, necessary when the office of the personnel director does not have in hand a list of eligible appointees for a particular vacancy that an appointing authority desires to fill. Hundreds of lists have to be maintained to cover the various specialized positions that make up the public service, and the personnel administration can well fall behind in the holding of qualifying examinations.

The 1939 act provides that in such cases the appointing authority may nominate to the director of the civil service administration a person to fill the vacancy temporarily. If the administration finds the candidate qualified, he or she is appointed. The appointee may only hold the office for sixty days and cannot be given a renewal appointment. Successive amendments to this section of the law produced the current state of affairs under which a temporary appointment may last for a year; if the personnel administrator still does not have a list of candidates for the position within a year, the temporary occupant becomes a provisional employee until a list is assembled. If the provisional appointee takes the exam for the position at the end of twelve months or more on the job, five points are added to his or her score for each year of service in the position. If the appointee becomes certifiable for the position, the job shall be given to him or her.

This system sounds complicated, but what it can mean is that, given no list at the time the vacancy occurs, a temporary appointee chosen without the list restrictions might well hang on in the job until it works into a permanent appointment. The RIPEC report urges that the personnel administrator be required to produce a list within three months of any temporary appointment; once the list is available the temporary appointee may serve no more than fifteen days in the job. These tightening changes would, if adopted, return the situation to something that more closely resembles the 1939 provisions.

A couple of other major changes urged by RIPEC's report were the introduction of a fairly strict formalized evaluation system and a graded system of ratings (ranging from excellent to unsatisfactory). The ratings then figure in later promotions or the granting of other benefits. Other recommendations, designed to empower supervisors with more management authority, relate to such things as limiting both the strict use of seniority in filling positions and promotions that are often mandated by labor contracts. A broad provision recommended in the report prohibits including in collective bargaining agreements any language that conflicts or contradicts language used in the revised merit system legislation.

Overall, the RIPEC report recommendations are hardly revolutionary but at the time they were published they were viewed by the state personnel unions as aimed at taking away hard-won promotions and benefits. In light of the fact that the state currently employs approximately fifteen thousand workers (most of them unionized), and that private sector unions and those representing teachers and local employees will rally around, the chances of enacting these major reforms are remote. Nothing short of a major scandal or acute state budgetary difficulties would be likely to improve the prospects of such legislation.

None of this discussion of the Rhode Island state personnel system should be interpreted to mean that the system is dysfunctional. Nonetheless, the state and local governments, and all of that portion of the private economic sector that is union-organized, face the same general set of problems. Union-secured and protected worker benefits and de facto if not *de jure* tenure in many cases have meant the surrender or modification of traditional management prerogatives. These prerogatives are not likely to be recaptured by management at any time soon, especially in the public sector where the union movement is strongest and flourishing far more than it is in the private sector.

Moreover, the historical evolution of the system for staffing the public service in Rhode Island mirrors certain long-standing aspects of the state's political culture. It is inevitably the case that when governmental reforms are put in place in any context they will tend, by definition, to conflict with elements in the prevailing political culture. The resulting interplay between the work of reformers and the defensive efforts of beneficiaries of the traditional ways of doing things is bound to shape the result. Outcomes will be, to some degree, a blend of what reformers want and what the old guard fights to protect.

RECENT ADMINISTRATIVE TRENDS

The mid-1990s saw a growing controversy around some new administrative entities that were brought into being as additions to the roster of line departments already discussed. Although innovative for Rhode Island, these new elements were created to carry out functions and use modes of operation long familiar to the federal government. In a word, a number of boards, commissions, authorities, and public corporations were established by the General Assembly which, like the federal independent regulatory commissions, are best labeled as quasi-legislative or quasi-judicial (or in some cases both).

Three of the most important will illustrate the phenomenon. Each reflects the growing concern with the environment, which has made its mark on all governments at all levels since roughly the late 1960s. Three landmark pieces of environmental legislation were enacted by the General Assembly between 1971 and 1980 in this area: setting up the Coastal Resources Management Council, or CRMC (1971); creating the Solid Waste Management Corporation (1974); and creating the Narragansett Bay Water Quality Management Commission (1980). A fourth established the Department of Environmental

Management to replace and expand upon the responsibilities of the prior Department of Natural Resources.

The council, the corporation, and the commission all fall into the quasi-legislative or quasi-judicial general category. The Department of Environmental Management (familiarly DEM, often uttered with a snarl) acquired new and roughly similar functions to those vested in the first three. The council (CRMC) exercises regulatory jurisdiction over all construction, development, and related activity taking place along the shores and in coastal water areas. Its purpose is to ensure appropriate development and to protect against the despoiling or damaging of these sensitive areas.

The Solid Waste Management Corporation (now known as the Resource Recycling Corporation) was charged with solving the growing problem of trash disposal and, more recently, with salvaging as much as possible for recycling. Its immediate problems center on where and how to dispose of the mountains of trash that are growing at a frightening rate, and dealing with the air pollution problems resulting from the open burning of trash in many city and town dumps. Land scarcity in Rhode Island and population density obviously made both of these problems increasingly serious.

The Bay Water Quality Management Commission focused attention on the state's greatest natural resource and asset, Narragansett Bay. Something approaching a half million people live on the periphery of the bay and on rivers and streams that empty into it. Some of these waterways were sewered, some were not. Some existing sewer treatment plants functioned reasonably well, some did not. Over time much of the bay had effectively been lost for many recreational activities, and for most shell fishing and related uses.

The interrelationship among the problems facing the commission are dramatically illustrated by the Providence wastewater runoff situation. The city has a quite old sewer system that carries off both household and industrial wastes with runoff from storm action in the same set of pipes. The absence of two separate piping systems is often deplored, but the combined arrangement was deliberately chosen in the latter years of the nineteenth century on the seemingly sound theory that storm runoff would be necessary to keep the sewer lines flushed out. This, of course, was during an era when the population adjacent to the bay was much smaller than it was during much of the twentieth century.

During the late 1990s there was an elaborate process of study of how to deal with the resulting pollution problem. Specifically, a sustained heavy rain causes the combined sewer system flow to overwhelm the treatment plants, allowing vast amounts of raw sewage to end up in the bay. Resewering with separated lines is financially out of the question. Variations on an alternative scheme have been advanced. The key would be the installation of some miles of huge tunnels deep underneath Providence in which overflow could be stored and then fed at a manageable rate into the treatment plants—which would also have to be upgraded. The full scheme would cost upwards of half a billion dollars. It seems apparent that a compromise plan will be implemented. Despite these gigantic problems, the commission has succeeded to the point that much of the bay is again open to shell fishing most of the year, recreational use has grown greatly, and the commission itself has won several national awards for its achievements.

The fourth agency, the Department of Environmental Management, has the thankless task of regulating land use for development purposes in terms of approving individual residential septic systems, controlling industrial runoff (such as the acids and other toxic substances produced by the jewelry industry in Providence), enforcing rules and regulations designed to preserve so-called wetlands from development or any other kind of despoilage, and curbing air pollution.

All four of these bodies must exert regulatory authority that affects individuals, households, and most business establishments in often painful ways. The CRMC must frequently say "no" to those who would dredge, build docks, or develop shore property in other ways. The Solid Waste Corporation has forced new and substantial expenses onto local communities. They can no longer burn trash in an isolated corner of town; now they must pay high tipping fees per ton of trash, which must be hauled to the central landfill in the town of Johnston. That town feels much abused by the traffic and other burdens it must bear as it has become the unwilling home to a veritable mountainous landfill that is rapidly becoming the highest hill in the state. The Bay Commission is caught among competing pressures from sewer users who pay increasing sewer charges needed to fund its activities, shell fishermen and other bay users who want the bay cleaned up faster and more thoroughly, and others who feel their interests are being neglected or placed at risk. The DEM has its own complex set of political problems, making it the target of much bitter criticism and anger.

The Rhode Island General Assembly is at a disadvantage in attempting to oversee the operation of the agencies and programs it has created. The assembly is in session only part time, usually between six and seven months of the year, and staffs that could conduct oversight activities for members and committees have always been very limited.

One response to this situation has been to revive an historic practice of having a portion of the members of most boards and commissions appointed by the legislative leaders. Not infrequently the law calls for appointees to be house or senate members. The regulatory bodies discussed above all have some legislators among their members, either three or four of the total. A large number of other current bodies of various sorts have legislator members and one, the lottery commission, has a majority of legislators. Reformers, as well as the office of the governor, have targeted this general practice for reform on the grounds that such memberships represent a violation of the principle of separation of powers. They argue that these appointments represent a "power grab" on the part of a legislature bent on further encroaching on executive turf. Moreover, until the mid-1990s when campaign finance reform and ethics commission regulations barred legislators from taking anything of value from entities with any interests in state government, there was a potential for conflicts of interest, especially in the form of campaign contributions from interested parties to legislators serving on these boards. Although these potential conflicts have been removed, conspiracy theories remain current.

An alternative explanation is that a board or commission with a mixed legislative–executive official–citizen kind of membership is a good way to contrive an administrative instrument that is asked to wield rule-making and adjudicative authority in politically difficult areas with proper sensitivity and awareness of citizen concerns. One could argue that it is a virtue to have regulatory legislation administered by a board rather than by a more remote department head who has an array of competing responsibilities and who answers only to the governor. There may well be advantage in having a multiple-member body responsible for both rule making and adjudication rather than have such functions vested in a single administrative official. Moreover, Rhode Island's regulatory bodies have serving on them both public members (who are not themselves committed professionals) and elected legislators. The latter are directly responsible to their chambers and to their constituents, and are thus a key source of information on how the citizenry is reacting and what it will stand for. In a democratic system no regulatory policy can work without at least the grudging acquiescence of those being regulated. The legislator board members are thus a bridge between the bureaucrats and those being regulated. In short, some evidence suggests that mixed member boards and commissions perform effectively and, at times, as with the bay commission, extraordinarily well.

In the late 1990s various reform groups took as their primary goal the abolition of the system of legislative appointments to and legislator service on state boards and commissions. This prompted the Ethics Commission to pass a regulation barring the practice in the future. In 1998 Governor Almond asked the state supreme court to provide an advisory opinion that would resolve the issue; he had insisted that the doctrine of separation of powers was violated by legislative appointments and legislator service on these bodies.

In 1999 the court issued its advisory opinion upholding the status quo by a four-to-one vote. It accepted the argument that the Rhode Island constitution did not provide for full separation of powers on the federal model and, if there were a problem involved, it could only be solved by constitutional amendment. Thus the court kept in place a system wherein Rhode Island's governor not only shares power with other statewide elected general officers but also with a General Assembly that can exercise some executive powers. As a result, the court left to the people of Rhode Island the task of altering and strengthening, via a constitutional amendment, the role of the chief executive in Rhode Island.

CHAPTER SEVEN

The Courts

The State Court system in Rhode Island is still Valhalla for a lot of pols in this state.

Federal Court Administrator, 1997

It was the celebrated maxim of Montesquieu that . . . there can be no liberty . . . if the power of judging be not separated from the legislative and executive powers.

Taylor v. Place, 1856

It's like Baghdad down there.

An elected official describing traffic court, 1998

Rhode Island's court system, like other institutions of government, is in the midst of significant transition as it evolves from a highly political system—linked to the legislature and the executive through constitutional design, budget authority, and traditional patronage—toward a more professional and independent judiciary. The late 1980s and 1990s began a period of particularly difficult change, given the long-standing political nature of the courts. The benchmarks in this struggle provide a splendid example of the shifting influence of various political elites as the courts move, however haltingly, toward a more modern system.

THE LEGACY OF POLITICAL CONTROL

Since the inception of the colony, the court system in Rhode Island has been a highly political institution linked to and dependent upon the legislature. The original charter of 1663 gave the General Assembly the right to establish courts of law that would "hear and determine disputes." The General Assembly annually elected judges and determined their rate of compensation. Moreover, the General Assembly itself sat above a three-tiered court system and, on occasion, acted as a supreme court in that it heard appeals from other courts and established rules for petitions.[1]

Thus, even before the American Revolution, patterns and themes that recurred throughout the court's history began to play out in the partisan machinations of the Hopkins-Ward party factions of colonial times. In 1761 when the Ward faction captured the assembly, it fired the entire Hopkins court and elected its own partisans to the bench. During subsequent elections the continual turnover of judges reflected the annual electoral fortunes of these two factions. As a result, the court was subjected to frequent and severe criticism as being too political; many decisions were highly suspect; and the character and caliber of judges were sources of continuing reform initiatives.[2]

The character of the court system changed little after statehood was gained because the constitution was a slightly modified version of the royal charter. Essentially the courts remained the creature of the legislature: the General Assembly had the power to elect and remove judges, set salaries, appropriate budgets, and appoint sheriffs and other court administrators. Legislators also routinely served as district judges while sitting in the assembly.

Attempts to create a more independent judiciary through the constitution of 1843 failed. While the main reform issues were the restrictive franchise and legislative apportionment, the Dorrites were also concerned about the complete subjugation of the courts to the legislature. The new constitution, while creating the separation of powers clause, essentially retained the sweeping authority of the legislature over the judiciary. The courts continued to be a rich source of patronage for leaders in the legislature, and judicial decisions supported the agenda of the powerful Republican leaders who controlled state government.[3]

The constitutional link with the judiciary, of course, proved to be a critical factor in the Democratic takeover of state politics in 1935. The state constitution at the time provided that during the annual reorganization session, any sitting judge's place could be "declared vacant by a resolution of the general assembly to that effect."[4] This provision allowed a newly established Democratic majority to declare vacant all seats on the supreme court at the January 1935 reorganization meeting, thus capturing one of the Republicans' bastions of power and preventing the court from striking down the other sweeping changes in government the Democrats had engineered on that January day.

Unfortunately, the Democrats, who had for years been campaigning for constitutional reform, proceeded to use the court as their own patronage system. While Theodore Green persuaded his Irish cohorts to exercise a measure of restraint and appoint a bipartisan and ethnically balanced new court, he did appoint to the court, through the grand committee, his law partner and the ex-mayor of Providence, Joseph H. Gainer, and filled other lower court positions with political allies. Between January and June of that year, in an attempt to head off a fractional dispute within the Democratic party, Green appointed thirty-four legislators to state positions, many of them in the judiciary. In another telling maneuver, Green had Francis Condon appointed to the supreme court in a move designed to head off Condon as a contender for a U.S. Senate seat that Green ran for and won in 1936.[5]

Indeed, as the Democrats solidified their control of state government, the judiciary provided a rich source of patronage for both the legislature and the executive. After 1935 governors gained considerable appointive power for judges and administrators to the superior court and to the lower state courts, and often used this authority for political purposes. Although excellent appointments were not uncommon, appointees were often political supporters or members of the legislature, or both.[6] Governors would also routinely nominate members of their staffs to the bench before leaving office.

The legislature controlled appointments to the supreme court through the grand committee, wherein the senate and the house sat together and elected nominees to that court. While all legislators were free to nominate candidates (and many used this perk to recommend inappropriate constituents), the real power of selection was in the hands of the leadership, especially the House Speaker. The informal influence of the legislature, most clearly exerted through its statutory and budget authority, also gave legislative leaders considerable clout within the court system.

THE ERA OF TRANSITION

The courts under the Democrats maintained reputable judicial standards insofar as the quality of their opinions generally guaranteed due process, protected the rights of defendants, and supported the claims of the poor and working class. Nonetheless the bloated, inefficient, and parochial judicial system remained a bastion of favoritism and patronage in a changing environment—until, that is, some highly visible scandals prompted reform legislation and internal structural and administrative reforms provoked sweeping change.

Early in 1976 the grand committee of the house and senate elected the then-sitting Speaker of the House, Joseph Bevilacqua, to the position of chief justice. Bevilacqua had grown up in the Silver Lake section of Providence, an Italian working-class community; in 1954 he was elected as a state representative from that district. In 1969 he was elected Speaker of the House. During his time in the legislature and as a practicing attorney he was known to have associations with members of the Mafia, he defended some in court, and as Speaker was publicly critical of press coverage of the Mafia, routinely accusing the press of anti-Italian slurs.

Bevilacqua was also an able jurist and administrator who, during his tenure as chief justice, initiated reforms that brought more efficiency into the system—clearing up backlogs of cases, initiating sentencing benchmarks and guidelines to promote uniformity in sentencing, and generally presiding over a court that issued fair and competent decisions. As chief justice, however, he continued his associations with known felons and people connected to organized crime. These associations, as well as reports of the preferential treatment of some court employees, prompted an investigation in 1985 by the Commission of Judicial Tenure and Discipline.[7] The commission voted to censure Bevilacqua on the grounds that he had brought disrepute on his office because he had associated with criminals, took gifts from them, and was alleged to be linked to activities in a motel owned by mobsters connected with gambling and illegal drugs. During this time he was also asked to give testimony before the U.S. President's Commission on Organized Crime in Washington DC.

While Bevilacqua had temporarily stepped down from the bench during the judicial hearings, after the commission voted to censure him for bringing his office "into serious disrepute" he refused to resign and resumed his position on the bench. In the midst of a debate over these actions, his remaining colleagues on the bench, in a 3–1 advisory opinion in late 1985, advised the General Assembly that it could not vacate the chief justice's seat. This ruling set the stage for impeachment proceedings and in May of 1986, after closed-door hearings, the house began open impeachment hearings. During Bevilacqua's tenure on the court, the state police (under the direction of State Police Chief Walter Stone) had been tracking Mafia figures and conducting surveillance operations that documented—by way of the testimony of state troopers and pictures—the alleged activities of the judge. The prospect of this testimony in open hearings prompted Bevilacqua to resign.

The sitting Speaker of the House at this time was Matthew Smith, who had served in the General Assembly since 1973 and as Speaker since 1980. In that capacity Smith presided over the initial impeachment proceedings of Bevilacqua and then maneuvered to have a long-time friend and associate,

Thomas Fay, of the family court, elected chief justice in 1986. Smith, who was not an attorney, was not eligible for the job; he was, however, eligible to be appointed chief state court administrator and clerk of the supreme court. After Fay became chief justice he in turn appointed Smith chief court administrator in 1988.

Together Fay and Smith presided over an expanding court system that was laced with cushy judicial and administrative positions. Smith's political skill and legislative ties enabled him to provide jobs for his allies, particularly his friends in the legislature. This in turn allowed him to influence legislation that affected the courts and to garner generous appropriations from the legislature at budget time. Moreover, while he held this position in the court Smith was also the chair of the unclassified pay board (which set the salaries of high-level political appointees), a position that further enhanced his political influence.

As expectations about professionalism in the courts became more common, the Fay court initiated a number of reforms to streamline and consolidate court functions, provide services to victims of crime, create a courtwide judicial performance evaluation program, and implement professional development programs for judges and attorneys. Generally, Fay and Smith supported organizational and professional reform as long as it did not touch on judicial selection and appointment procedures, which sustained their patronage base.[8]

These arrangements began to unravel in late 1992 and into the summer of 1993 when the *Providence Journal* published a series outlining an increasingly expensive court system and citing some problematic patronage appointments. The exposé honed in on an incident involving Smith's failure to report the petty theft of $4,000 of court funds by the son of a long-time associate. Instead, Smith had engineered the replacement of the money. Finally, the *Journal* had obtained data on and published spending reports from a special fund managed by Smith, which was "off line" in that it was not subject to direct administrative review by state auditors.

Although there were certainly questionable judgments and behaviors in this affair, the incendiary nature of the *Journal*'s reporting produced a classic media feeding frenzy for which the *Journal* received a Pulitzer Prize. In one example the paper published full pages of item-by-item expenditures, which they continued to dub "the secret fund" administered by Smith. In fact, the fund was not secret. Most people associated with the judiciary knew about the account funded by fees from the bar exam which had existed long before Fay and Smith's tenure and which was used at the discretion of the court administrator for extra expenses. The published list included reimbursement for judicial travel to legal conferences, fees for bottled water coolers at the courthouse, special trips to baseball games, deli deliveries, and baskets of fruit and flowers sent for condolences to court employees or their families. Although some of this spending was surely inappropriate, it paled in comparison to the wholesale graft and extortion that was unfolding in other political venues during this period in Rhode Island's history.

Unfortunately for Smith and Fay, it proved to be the last and very visible straw for voters who had grown cynical and incensed over scandals like RISDIC, which had cost the state and its taxpayers millions. The result was that even before the Judicial Tenure and Discipline Board could hold hearings, the legislature began to openly discuss impeachment. Fay pleaded no contest to lesser felony charges, resigned, and was disbarred. Smith, who was later exonerated in a trial, was forced to retire.

Reformers used the momentum associated with Fay's resignation to push for a system of merit selection of judges, which was approved by the voters as a constitutional amendment in 1994. Although few would deny that replacing the grand committee (an anachronism) was a positive move, merit selection has not proved to be the panacea expected by reformers. The system created a nine-member appointed commission that reviews applications and recommendations for all state court judicial appointments; the commission then nominates a list of from three to five potential candidates for gubernatorial selection and confirmation by the General Assembly. A few highly contested and political appointments suggest what political scientists have long known: merit selection "simply substitutes private politics for public politics" insofar as it gives more power to the legal profession, the media, and select interest groups, and also limits accountability. This proved to be the case in Rhode Island. In 1997 the *Providence Journal*'s editorial page, originally a vocal supporter of merit selection, reluctantly acknowledged the impossibility of eliminating politics from what continues to be an "inherently political process."[9]

In addition to judicial selection reform, during this period the legislature, responding in some cases to first-rate investigative reporting by the *Journal*, passed reforms that included revolving-door legislation, which mandated a one-year waiting period between elected service and political appointment. Other reforms or restructuring mandates were aimed at eliminating the more blatant abuses in the system. These included rescinding some excessive perks enjoyed by court employees.

In one case, state statutes allowed state court clerks to receive a yearly bonus for having college degrees. These clerks, depending on level of education and rank, received an *annual bonus* for post-secondary education of from

10 to 16 percent of their annual salaries. In some cases this allowed administrators with salaries of close to $80,000 to get annual bonuses of more than $12,000—because they had college degrees! Clerks with associate degrees received 10 percent of their annual salaries. Similar incentive legislation for police and firefighters was amended in 1979 to give flat stipends of from $2,000 to $3,000 for degrees in their field. But the court clerk's bonus plan was carefully crafted so that it was not linked to availability of funds, it was protected by a labor contract, and it was amended to include clerks who had obtained degrees before 1970.

Most telling here was the time frame of these statutes. While one might certainly expect these types of programs to be initiated during the postwar period—especially in a working-class state where a need for professionalization was developing—the fact that this particular program was *initiated* in 1976 and *enhanced* in 1987 suggests a culture of patronage that has a distinctly nineteenth-century ring to it. Legislative leaders, acknowledging in 1994 that this was not really an incentive program but more an example of "planned greed," amended the legislation to confer a flat stipend for those in the system and eliminating it for new hires.[10]

THE JUDICIARY IN THE TWENTY-FIRST CENTURY

While there remains a legacy of administrative patronage, during the 1990s the judiciary evolved into a more independent and accountable system. Internally it is better organized and more professional; externally it appears to have gained considerable independence from the legislature and the executive as a less political and more autonomous branch of government. Progress, however, has been uneven. Notable examples of reform exist, but remnants of the "old style" politics remain.

Rhode Island now has a unified state court system of six statewide courts (see figure 2). The district, family, and workers' compensation courts are trial courts of limited jurisdiction. The administrative adjudication court hears all noncriminal traffic cases and reviews traffic decisions of the municipal courts. The superior court is the general trial court, and the supreme court is the court of review or "court of last resort." These courts are state funded; below them are probate and municipal courts of limited jurisdiction, which are the responsibility of local cities and towns.

The state supreme court was established in the Rhode Island Constitution of 1843 and redefined by statute in 1905.[11] It is the only court established in the constitution; other courts are established by statute. This court, which hears appeals and rules on points of law only, is the court of last resort.

Figure 2: Rhode Island's Unified Court System

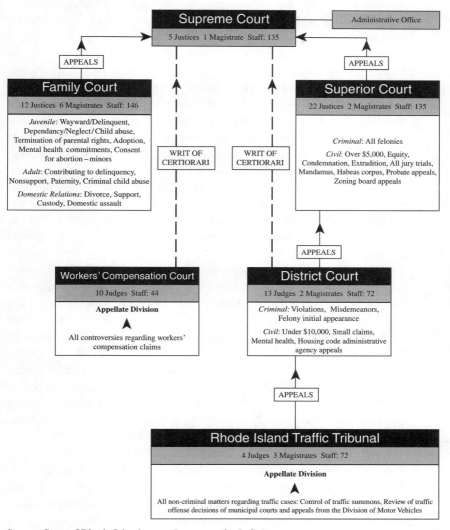

Source: State of Rhode Island, *1999 Report on the Judiciary.*

It is the final jurisdiction for all civil and criminal appellate cases in the state. Five justices preside over an extensive array of cases, because some district court as well as superior court rulings can be appealed directly to the supreme court. District court cases are generally tried first in superior court, but technically the constitution allows all cases from lower courts to be reviewed directly by the supreme court through a *writ of certiorari*. In fact, such direct review rarely happens in cases where the superior court is available to hear a case.

In addition to the adjudicative process, the court oversees an array of boards and commissions, many of them recently created and aimed at increasing professionalism, accountability, and ethical standards in the entire court system. The Supreme Court Disciplinary Board investigates complaints against attorneys accused of unethical behavior, and the Committee on Character and Fitness screens applicants to the Rhode Island bar. In addition, the Ethics Advisory Panel (established in 1986) provides attorneys with confidential advice based on rules of professional conduct, and the Advisory Committee on Judicial Ethics (established in 1983) issues opinions on standards of judicial ethics. The Commission on Judicial Tenure and Discipline reviews the actions of all members of the bench, and the Judicial Performance Evaluation Committee (established in 1993) periodically evaluates the professional competence of judges. In 1993 the court also established the Mandatory Continuing Legal Education Program, which requires annual legal education for all licensed attorneys. Another important role of the court with broad political implications is the constitutionally mandated advisory opinion process whereby justices of the court hand down advisory opinions on questions concerning the constitutionality of pending legislative or executive actions.

The superior court, established by statute in 1905, is the court of general jurisdiction that hears all felony cases and civil cases for claims in excess of $10,000.[12] The five counties in Rhode Island are divided into four superior court jurisdictions: one each in Kent, Washington, and Newport Counties, and the fourth comprising Providence and Bristol Counties. The court holds concurrent jurisdiction with the district court on civil claims from $5,000 to $10,000. The superior court also hears appeals, *de novo*, from district court. The court has appellate jurisdiction over decisions from local municipal and probate courts and also hears appeals from various boards and commissions and the ethics commission. Appeals of decisions from superior court are taken directly to the supreme court. In 1994 the superior court established a special jurisdiction gun court—the first in the nation—designed to expedite firearms-related crimes. This addition has proved particularly successful, reducing the average time of resolution of gun-related crimes from an average of eighteen months to just over four months.

Throughout the 1990s more professional procedures and reforms, including an arbitration office, have resulted in a reduced pending civil and felony caseload, quicker turnaround, and expedited collection of fines. Moreover, a judicial evaluation program initiated in 1992 has encouraged more professional standards among superior court judges and personnel.[13]

Family court hears all petitions for divorce and related proceedings, such as property distribution, alimony, and child support and custody. This court has jurisdiction over all matters related to children as well as adoptions and paternity proceedings. Appeals from this court are also heard in the supreme court. Although the pending caseload in divorce and alimony cases has been reduced, juvenile custody and parental rights cases have increased, largely due to various and contested definitions of appropriate standards for and solutions to child neglect, child abuse, and parental rights. Given the increase in violent juvenile crime in the state, that caseload is increasingly being shifted out of family court as demands increase to try offenders as adults.

District court, which comprises five geographical jurisdictions, is usually the initial venue for most court proceedings. This court hears civil cases for under $10,000, criminal misdemeanor cases, and some initial felony charges. Appeals and requests for jury trial go on to superior court and in some cases directly to the supreme court. Reforms initiated by the General Assembly have mandated more efficient procedures and a case disposition of sixty days. Over the years the courts have made considerable progress in meeting the mandates of the legislature.

Workers' compensation court, formally established by the General Assembly in 1990, adjudicates disputes and claims between employees and employers on matters related to occupational disabilities, hospital and medical bills, and the extent and conditions of disability. The integration of this court into the unified system in 1991 and reforms in legislation passed by the General Assembly provide a success story of court reforms that work.

Before 1954 all workers' compensation complaints were resolved in superior court. In an attempt to alleviate caseloads, the Worker's Compensation Commission was created in 1954. Over the years the system had become bogged down by a bloated and inefficient administration that perpetuated a huge backlog. Existing law and union contracts encouraged large numbers of complaints, expensive insurance settlements, and escalating insurance rates. In an ill-fated attempt to depoliticize the system, a two-tiered system was set up to split litigation from administration by creating a new department with additional procedures, hearing officers, and staffs. These new positions provided an ideal source of patronage in a state system where patronage appointments in other branches of government were drying up. By early 1990 the system was on the verge of collapse. The backlog of cases was over eighteen months and workers' insurance rates were so high that several insurers announced they were withdrawing from the state system.

The governor and General Assembly responded with legislation that revamped the system and mandated a twenty-one-day limit for petitions to be heard. Under the direction of a new chief judge, Robert Arrigan, the system was transformed within a year. The backlog was eliminated, the twenty-one-day mandate was met and, in conjunction with stricter requirement reforms in the workers' compensation law, complaints began to decline steadily. The reforms in the system represent a "reinventing government" example that has been cited as a national model.[14]

Judge Arrigan, with the assistance of three new judicial appointees, was able to transform a lax working culture of late morning starts, long lunches, and brief hearing hours by judges and administrators which had set a tone of indifference and inefficiency. Arrigan held 8:30 A.M. pretrial hearings for judges and staffs, increased judicial caseloads, and demanded more careful scrutiny of legal and case resolutions. In doing so he set a new standard of accountability and professionalism. Although he made some enemies, employees generally came around.[15] As one administrator put it, "when you treat people like slugs, they act like slugs. Now things are different." Indeed, things are so different that lawyers in the state that practice workers' compensation law now regard this branch of litigation as a dying field and supplement their practice with other endeavors. Claims have declined by about 50 percent, lump-sum settlements have decreased by about 60 percent, and, most telling of all, as of 1997 annual fees paid to lawyers have declined from $10 to $4 million.[16]

The administrative adjudication court (established in 1992) is where most Rhode Islanders encounter the state court system in the form of traffic court. Unfortunately it is at this level that the system has remained inefficient, indifferent to the needs of citizens, bloated, and patronage-based.[17] Previously, traffic violations were handled in district court, but after 1974 an administrative adjudication agency was established in the Department of Transportation and was presided over by part-time hearing officers appointed by the governor. Over the ensuing years the budget and staffs of the agency expanded. In 1993 the agency became part of the judicial system under the authority of the supreme court and hearing officers were eventually made into full-time administrative judges with high salaried lifetime appointments and retirement benefits at 100 percent of salary after twenty years of service.

Indications of malfeasance emerged in the late 1990s. In 1997 a lawyer and other employees working in this division were reprimanded and fined for pursuing private client work on state time using state facilities. In that same year a major misdirecting of traffic ticket fines cost the state millions in uncollected revenue. The event suggested a working culture and an administrative system that smacked of "old style" features. This was followed by an excellent investigative series by the *Journal* in 1998 that revealed a system in which judges put in only a few hours on the bench daily, computer records were in shambles, millions were lost in uncollected fines, and citizens endured maddening inefficiencies in dilapidated surroundings.[18] In addition, judges were criticized for denying due process by routinely rendering "boilerplate" decisions without a full review of both sides of a case. Responding to the public uproar that followed the *Journal*'s series, the chief justice of the supreme court appointed a fourteen-member panel to review the court's workings.

In response to the review, the legislature proposed that the existing court be dismantled and made into a division of district court. Judges, as they retired, would be replaced by magistrates, while the court's enforcement division would be relocated to the Registry of Motor Vehicles. Concerns were raised that this arrangement would swamp district court, which hears more than eighty thousand cases a year and has its own difficulties. As one former state representative noted, "District court is just as user-unfriendly as the ACC [traffic court]—in fact more so. It's like going from Sing Sing to Alcatraz, from a motorist's point of view."[19] Ultimately the responsibility for operating the revamped traffic court system was given to the chief judge of the district court. The enabling legislation, however, ran into difficulties insofar as it expanded the number of magistrates and gave appointment authority for these positions to the district court. The governor, in an attempt to bring these appointments within the merit system, threatened to veto the legislation. Unfortunately, the traffic court scandal and the uneasy resolution of the problem have sustained the impression that the court system, despite considerable progress, continues to be influenced by politics. Looking on other fronts, however, one sees a picture of a more autonomous judiciary.

THE POLITICS OF ADVISORY OPINIONS

Advisory opinions, through which the supreme court justices issue opinions on the constitutionality of proposed legislative or executive actions, give the supreme court the potential to carve out an independent position. In the past these opinions tended to closely reflect the interests or perspectives of the dominant political party and the established political elite. Recent decisions, however, suggest more independent interpretations less tied to politics insofar as they do not appear to conform to any pattern that supports the positions of either the governor or the legislature or other interest groups.

Such independence marks a distinctive turn in the history of the court. In 1883, for example, the supreme court blunted an attempt to call a constitutional convention to redress the restrictive franchise and the system of unequal representation to the legislature. Reformers, who had by then solidified under the growing ranks of the Democratic party, pressed for such a convention but the supreme court ruled that, according to the 1843 constitution, a convention could not be called. The decision granted the Yankee elite a reprieve in the face of the growing majority of Democrats. In 1908 it also sustained the interests of GOP leaders by upholding the so-called "Brayton Act" of 1901, wherein the Republicans, faced with the prospect of Democrats winning the statewide elections, essentially transferred the governor's appointive and financial power to the state senate, which at the time was controlled by rural Republicans.

When the Democrats finally took control in 1935, disbanding the existing court was a critical link in sustaining the coup that surely would have been deemed unconstitutional had the Republican-appointed court remained in place. But, as noted earlier, the Democrats continued to use the system for their own advantage and the court remained tied to the interests of the establishment. Patterns changed in the 1990s. A 1993 advisory opinion, unpopular with both the legislature and the executive, upheld revolving-door legislation that considerably stemmed the tide of patronage appointments for politically well-connected elites. In that same year the court also, quite unexpectedly, affirmed the "limited and concurrent power" of the ethics commission to enact substantive ethics regulations for government employees. The court rejected the argument that these powers legitimated a fourth branch of government and violated separation-of-power principles.[20] What surprised many observers was that the court's position affirmed the authority of what, by any standard, is the most powerful state ethics commission in the country. While many states created or reconstituted their state ethics commissions during the past decade, no other state allows its commission to *draft* and *enact* law without at least the ratification of the legislature. In another telling opinion (which resulted from an appeal brought by the executive), the supreme court denied a stay requested by the powerful teachers union to prevent the opening of pension records, thereby allowing public scrutiny of excessive pension awards the General Assembly had made over the years.[21] All of these decisions went a long way toward eroding the old-style system and promoting reform.

In a 1997 debate between the executive and the legislature, though the court affirmed the "plenary power" of the General Assembly it also held that the governor could appoint a lieutenant governor to fill a vacancy created when the sitting officer was elected to Congress.[22] These decisions were merely the prelude to a protracted institutional power struggle among the governor, the legislature, and the ethics commission, a struggle in which the stakes for all parties were extremely high. Responding in fairly broad terms to the judicial support it had received in the 1992 decision, the ethics commission promulgated a regulation that barred all legislators, on the basis of an "inherent" conflict of interest, from sitting on quasi-independent boards and commissions. In response to that regulation the governor requested an advisory opinion from the supreme court regarding the practice of allowing legislators to sit on quasi-independent boards and commissions, arguing against the practice based on a separation-of-powers argument. The governor's advisory request asked the justices to rule on the role of the ethics commission and the linkage between the federal and state constitutions regarding separation of powers, as well as on the constitutionality of limiting the role of legislators on these boards and commissions. The justices, in a four-to-one decision issued in 1999, rejected the ability of the ethics commission to issue such sweeping restrictions. While a majority of justices declined to specifically address separation-of-power issues until they had an actual case before them, they implicitly argued for the broad prerogatives of the legislature under the existing provisions in the Rhode Island constitution. Although this opinion represented a considerable loss for the executive and disappointed reform groups at the same time, it was generally received as the valid interpretation of an autonomous judiciary. A subsequent decision issued in 2000 addressed the specific question of the constitutionality of legislators sitting on and controlling the workings of the lottery commission. The court reaffirmed the prerogatives of the legislature, outraging reform groups which then turned their efforts to calling a constitutional convention to amend the provisions.

JUDICIAL TEMPERANCE AND NEW JUDICIAL FEDERALISM

While the Rhode Island court system appears to be more professional and politically independent, it cannot be considered an "activist" court in the sense that it enters into substantive policy areas or "makes" laws, as is the case in many other states. In light of perceptions of the more conservative nature of the U.S. Supreme Court after the Reagan administration, trends of a new judicial federalism have been documented in many states. This pattern is defined by state court systems assuming a more a activist role in promoting and mandating substantive policy reforms, particularly in areas like education. One application of this pattern is in comparative studies of state court systems that argue that an activist court system would be committed to developing an independent body of state law based on principled—meaning historical and legal—decisions.[23] By these standards the Rhode Island supreme court cannot be considered activist insofar as it is not inclined to make forays into legislative territory or to set new policies.[24]

This traditional position of the court was succinctly underscored in a 1995 decision that affirmed the state constitution's "endorsement of the Legislature's primacy over education" and made crystal clear the Rhode Island court's rejection of an activist role. The justices, in a unanimous opinion, overturned a lower court ruling on the method of financing public education. Rejecting the argument that reliance on the property tax of local communities rendered educational opportunities unequal and hence unconstitutional, the court found that the lower court ruling failed "to recognize the role of the Judiciary in our tripartite system." They argued that the lower court went "far beyond the Judiciary's constitutional powers or institutional capacity." The court then went on to reaffirm that "members of the legislative and executive branches are directly accountable to the electorate, and such responsibilities as the allocation of property-tax burdens and general state revenues are best dealt with through the political process."[25]

Generally speaking, the Rhode Island supreme court has been regarded as "well integrated" in that justices share a similar perception of their role, they issue fewer dissenting opinions, and in comparative state studies they are generally regarded as administrators rather than activists. They are considered to be committed to the ideals of *stare decisis* and, in substantive policy areas, they defer to the legislature.[26]

By the 1990s, however, an increase in split decisions suggests this tradition may be changing. In a 1998 case involving the rights of crime victims under the state constitution, one justice issued a blistering dissent. He noted that the majority of the court was adhering to such extreme principles of judicial restraint that such a posture by the court made the judiciary no more than "liveried footservants to the General Assembly."[27] In another case a majority opinion by members of the court that appeared to contradict a previous ruling of the court prompted the chief justice, in a separate opinion, to warn his colleagues that such a position might create a "crisis of confidence" in the court and implored the justices to adhere to the court's previous rulings. In 1999 sitting Justice Robert Flanders, one of the court's most prolific dissenters, wrote a compelling article that challenged the conventional wisdom about dissents and argued that they promote legal and intellectual "vibrancy" to questions of law and contribute to the integrity in the court.[28]

Another aspect of new judicial federalism sees state supreme courts rather than federal courts as the preferred venue for trying cases on issues of individual rights. Scholars argue that in addition to the perception of federal courts as more conservative on issues of individual and minority rights, there has been a fundamental change in the way most people understand rights, that there has been a marked shift from accepting community standards to recognizing individual rights. This creates a need for stronger civil rights protections.[29] In this sense Rhode Island courts have long been ahead of the curve insofar as concern for the rights of individuals traditionally has been part of the political culture and manifests itself in decisions by both the state and federal district courts.

In one notable decision relating to the famous Sunny von Bulow murder case, the court in 1984 found that Claus von Bulow's constitutional rights of privacy had been violated by the state police and therefore overturned his conviction. In this decision the supreme court set a stricter standard than the federal court's vis-à-vis search and seizure protection.[30] In 1995 the superior court, in a decision that outraged reformers and the public alike, the court also refused to construe as felonious theft—by the somewhat tortured reasoning of the attorney general—the actions of Matthew Smith, chief court administrator, thereby allowing him to keep his pension.

In 1997 a superior court justice threw out the attorney general's bribery and extortion case against former Governor Edward DiPrete on the grounds of extensive prosecutorial misconduct. Given the extent of corruption during that administration, this dismissal caused a huge public outcry and, in a somewhat unexpected turn of events, the supreme court reinstated the charges on appeal. Although the court was compelled to balance the rights of the former governor with the interests of the state and people, the decision's tepid rebuke of the actions of the attorney general's office caused many people to express concern that the protection of an individual defendant's rights, long the tradition in the state, and the discretion of superior court judges were being undermined.

The federal district court in Rhode Island has also staked out a role in the protection of individual and minority rights. In one famous case, the intensely controversial 1981 "crèche case," the U.S. district court found, in this most Catholic of American states, that a public religious crèche display on city property along with other Christmas ornaments violated the establishment clause of the U.S. Constitution. (Although the general principal ultimately stood, the case was overturned by the U.S. Supreme Court.)[31] In a subsequent ruling on church and state, the U.S. district court found that even public nondenominational invocations at events like graduations also violate the establishment clause, setting a strict standard that was later upheld by the U.S. Supreme Court.[32] These and other decisions suggest that, to the extent that one can discern any pattern, the Rhode Island courts have held to a standard of protections for minority and individual rights despite changes in the federal judiciary.

Any attempt to evaluate the contemporary judiciary necessarily comes down to the difficult question of just how much progress has been made. What one can say is that, regardless of the flaws that still exist in the system, the judiciary in Rhode Island has evolved from an old-style political system toward a more professional and autonomous branch of government. It now has the capacity to provide a more independent anchor to the political process and realize Montesquieu's ideal that the power of judging be separate from legislative and executive powers.

CHAPTER EIGHT

Political Parties

> Action on behalf of the underprivileged elements of society is not a common feature of a typical one-party state. More often than not, the dominant political interests of such states are so closely tied in with industrial and business interests that the rank and file of the public gets scant attention from government. This is not the case in Rhode Island.
>
> Duane Lockard, *New England State Politics* (1959)

> We [the Democrats] are not taking money away from poor children.
>
> House Majority Leader George Caroulo,
> 1996 floor debate on welfare reform

Political parties at the turn of the century present something of a paradox.[1] While the vast majority of American states have become politically competitive, Rhode Island is one of the few states still considered a "modified one-party Democratic state." This means that along with states like Arkansas, Louisiana, West Virginia, and Maryland, the Democratic party dominates.[2] Yet, in terms of significance, the role of the parties in Rhode Island's political system has declined dramatically. A majority of the Ocean State's voters no longer identify with the two major parties; party organizations have only limited influence in the political process; and in ideological or political terms, the differences between the Republicans and Democrats at the state level are minor. Yet, absent unusual circumstances, voters continue to reelect Democrats.

The one-party dominance is nothing new. A significant characteristic of politics in the Ocean State since the Civil War has been its one-party status. As noted in other chapters, the Republicans dominated politics until the Green Revolution of 1935 when the Democrats took over state government.

The Democratic takeover was surely dramatic. It involved winning the governorship, the lieutenant-governorship, and the house in the general election of 1934. Then, at the January 1935 organizational meeting, Democrats, with the aid of the Democratic lieutenant-governor who presided over the senate organizational meeting, challenged and invalidated the results of two GOP state senate seats, thus creating a Democratic majority in both houses. To ensure that the reorganization would not be constitutionally challenged, the General Assembly then appointed a completely new supreme court. All in one afternoon.

Yet signs of the erosion of Republican hegemony were evident earlier. Given that the political divisions of the period were along class, ethnic, and religious lines and that the Yankee Protestant Republicans were vastly outnumbered, the GOP strategy was to keep as many ethnic Catholics as possible away from the polls and, failing that, to encourage partisan divisions among the Irish, Italians, and French Catholics.

The first breakthrough for the Democrats occurred in 1888 when the legislature was forced to pass the Bourne amendment, which rescinded the real-property qualification for naturalized citizens in statewide elections.[3] This increased the statewide electorate by about fifteen thousand voters.[4] As a result, gubernatorial races between Democrats and Republicans became more competitive, with Democrats occasionally winning (in 1906 and 1922). But, as we know from other studies on the national political realignment of that period, such changes apparently did not engage the potential Democratic electorate that existed in Rhode Island at the time.[5]

Looking at presidential turnout from 1920 to 1932, table 6 indicates that the Democratic rolls began to expand in the mid-1920s, with the most significant Democratic mobilization occurring around the 1928 presidential candidacy of Al Smith, an Irish Catholic from New York. During that race the Democratic electorate increased by a full 55 percent. Smith, who was the first Democrat to carry the state in a presidential election since the Civil War, may have been a weak candidate nationally but he had a stunning effect on mobilization in the Northeast and in Rhode Island in particular. There was some slight fall off in the Republican vote between 1924 and 1928, suggesting that some Republican voters—perhaps French and Italian Catholics who until then had failed to align with the Democrats—switched to the Democratic party in 1928. But the significant change in the partisan balance was the result of mobilizing new Democratic voters into the system during the 1920s.

One can only assume that because the 1928 election preceded the Depression, the cleavages in 1928 were related mostly to class, religion, and the

Table 6: Changes in Presidential Vote, 1920–1932

Date	Republican	Democrat
1920	107,463	55,062
1924	125,286 (+17%)	76,606 (+39%)
1928	117,522 (−6%)	118,973 (+55%)
1932	115,266 (−2%)	146,604 (+23%)

Source: Congressional Quarterly's *Guide to U.S. Elections*, 3rd ed., 1994.

strengthening labor movement. Thus, the presidential candidacy of a Roman Catholic from a working-class background apparently resonated with large numbers of Rhode Islanders who came into the political system in 1928. By 1932, with only a 2 percent decline in the Republican electorate that held steady during this time, another twenty-five thousand voters were drawn into the system around the candidacy of Franklin D. Roosevelt, apparently for economic reasons. By the following election the Democrats, under T. F. Green, won the governorship and laid plans to effect their organizational "coup" at the opening session of the legislature in 1935.

Although occasionally Republicans were returned to office, the Democrats continued to solidify control and, especially after reapportionment mandated "one man, one vote" representation, they essentially dominated the political system. They honed a finely tuned political machine in the urban areas in and around the city of Providence. But some things did not change. The resentment and bitterness the Democratic voters felt toward the Republican regime ensured a stable and loyal base of voter support and a continuation of the tough, patronage politics that had long characterized the system. As Duane Lockard noted: "Unhappily, the change in control did not greatly alter the dominant political practices. The outgoing Republican organization, based largely on rural machines, was changed for a Democratic organization based on city machines. The corruption that had disfigured the state for so long . . . went on as before."[6]

In the late 1970s the machine began to fall apart. As noted in other chapters, the demands of a modern, professional government and the emerging reform movement rendered the patronage system less acceptable. In addition, generational changes and the impact of suburbanization lessened partisan ties and encouraged voters to be more independent, to move beyond traditional party loyalties, and to hold individual candidates and the parties accountable. These trends were capped by the scandals of the 1980s and early 1990s that created dissonance among voters and upheaval in the partisan system. By the turn of the twenty-first century, however, it appears that the system has stabilized and the status of the parties continues to reflect the dominance of the Democrats in a vastly transformed and hollow party system.

The notion of political parties encompasses a broad range of functions that in academic studies are usually considered in terms of parties as voters, parties as organizations, and parties as coalitions of elected officials. These divisions provide a useful framework within which to assess the status of parties in Rhode Island.

PARTY IN THE ELECTORATE

A fundamental aspect of the parties' strength is the extent to which voters express an enduring identification with them. Generally, contemporary polls of the Rhode Island electorate indicate a large portion of independent identifiers and a Democratic advantage among partisans. One national study indicates that disaffection with the parties in Rhode Island had been developing by the mid-1970s. Using aggregate data from 1976 to 1988, the study found that Rhode Island had the highest percentage of independent voters of any state in the country, with a record 56.4 percent of the electorate claiming independent status.

Statewide polls conducted by Brown University suggest a similar picture. Using data from 1978 on, table 7 shows high levels of independents. This tendency is probably related not only to the softening of party loyalties but also to Rhode Island's open primary system, initiated in 1978, which encourages voters to remain disaffiliated in official registration procedures. This may in turn prompt a number of respondents to claim independent status on polls. But, for whatever reasons, the number of independents remains in the 50 percent range, although overall it appeared to have declined somewhat by the late 1990s.

In terms of loyal partisans, there has been some fluctuation in the respective status of the parties, especially during the 1980s when voter dissonance became evident. (One should note, of course, that these variations are relatively minor, and represent samples of voters that should be interpreted with caution). In the 1980s the GOP made slight gains and, conversely, the Democrats lost some ground while a somewhat higher number of independents became evident. By the mid-1990s GOP support receded slightly, independents declined, and the Democrats continued to hold almost a two-to-one edge over the Republicans. The polls from the late 1990s, which

Table 7: Party Identification in Rhode Island, 1978–1998

Date	Rep	Dem	Ind	Other	DK
1978	9	35	56		
1980	9	33	58		
1982	10	35	55		
1983	9	30	61		
1984	14	29	57		
1986	17	22	61		
1987	16	29	55		
1988	18	28	54		
1990	16	32	52		
1994	13	26	51	7	3
1995	12	28	48	7	5
1996	12	31	46	6	5
1997	11	28	50	5	6
1998	15	26	49	6	4

Source: Years 1978–83, Alpha Research Polls; Years 1984–98, John Hazen White poll, Brown University.

show a slight spike in Republican support, could be the result of increased satisfaction with the status quo in a growing economy under a Republican governor.

Unfortunately, these polls do not ask a follow-up question to assess how many of the voters who consider themselves independent "lean" toward one party or the other. In other polling samples that question reduces the number of "pure" independents to under 15 percent. Selective candidate polls indicate, however, that Democrat "leaners" hold a significant edge among that group.

That assessment is consistent with data that compares the actual distribution of registered Democrats, Republicans, and Independents statewide. These records recently became available and, as of 1998, the distribution of registered voters in Rhode Island was 352,445 unaffiliated, 217,218 Democrats, 52,387 Republicans, and 830 other. While Democrats hold more than a four-to-one advantage over Republicans, the large number of unaffiliated voters creates considerable variation in primary participation. For example, in a 1990 statewide primary for governor, just under 168,000 voted in the Democratic primary, while about 108,000 cast a ballot in the Republican contest. In 1994 the gap widened when about 99,000 voted in the Democratic primary as compared to just over 43,000 in the Republican race. In a 1996 statewide U.S. Senate race over 67,000 votes were recorded in the Democratic contest, while fewer than 15,000 partisans voted in the Republican primary election.

Regardless of the attitudes the electorate holds about the parties, a look at the results of the general elections and the partisan structure of government indicate an electorate that, however nominally independent, is inclined to support Democrats in elections. Although the Republicans made periodic breakthroughs in the 1980s and early 1990s, Democrats continue to dominate federal and state offices.

FEDERAL ELECTIONS

In federal elections support for the GOP is an occasional event. Since Al Smith carried the state in 1928, Rhode Island has voted for Republicans in only three presidential contests. In the 1950s the state backed Dwight D. Eisenhower, and then helped reelect Richard M. Nixon in 1972 and Ronald Reagan in 1984. In all other races they continued to support Democrats by wide margins. Indeed, in recent presidential contests the Rhode Island vote has been considered a "given" for the Democrats. Democratic candidates may stop over in the state on their way to more competitive or electorally rich states, but they can generally count on Rhode Island's four electoral votes. The state supported Mike Dukakis in 1988 by over a two-to-one margin and gave Bill Clinton strong support in both his presidential bids. In 1996 Clinton carried the state by a thirty-three-point margin, receiving 60 percent of the vote to Robert Dole's 27 percent. In the 2000 election, Al Gore received his largest Democratic plurality in Rhode Island winning over 61 percent of the vote.

In contests for the U.S. Senate, only one Republican, John Chafee, had held a U.S. Senate seat since the New Deal. Results of recent Senate elections reflect the strong support for two political icons in the state, John Chafee and Claiborne Pell, whose support, after long years of service, went beyond party loyalties. Pell, who in 1960 was the first candidate to win the primary without an organizational endorsement, was held in high esteem during his political career by the voters for his many national and international accomplishments. His status as one of the old-moneyed families in Newport society and his dignified presence played extremely well in this working-class state where in retirement he remains a revered figure. John Chafee, who died unexpectedly in office in 1999, was another scion of an old Yankee family.

Chafee throughout his career represented the moderate and progressive wing of the Republican party; his policies and political positions resonated with voters in this relatively liberal state. He served in the General Assembly and then during the 1960s served for three terms as a popular and respected governor who was defeated only after he supported an income tax, which was then put in place by his successor, Democrat Frank Licht. Chafee had been in the U.S. Senate from 1976 to 1999. Given his seniority and the majority status of the GOP in that body during the 1990s, he had a significant impact on issues of concern to Rhode Islanders, especially in light of the fact that after Pell retired the rest of Rhode Island's federal delegation were Democrats without much seniority. When Chafee announced in the spring of 1999 that he would not seek another term in the year 2000, his son, Lincoln Chafee, the popular mayor of the city of Warwick, announced he would seek the seat for the GOP. When his father died months later, the Republican governor, Lincoln Almond, appointed the son to fill the term vacancy. Chafee had the benefit of an appointment to the U.S. Senate, the Chafee name—revered in the state—a considerable family fortune, and the potential to secure substantial support from the GOP outside the state. The younger Chafee handily won election to the U.S. Senate seat, defeating congressman Robert Weygand, a former lieutenant governor, who had been severely weakened by a divisive primary in which the Democratic organization backed his opponent.

Races for the two U.S. House seats have shown solid Democratic control followed by Republican success in the 1980s and then a return to Democratic control (see table 8). With the exception of Republican Charles Risk, who was elected to fill a vacancy in 1935, Democrats enjoyed control of U.S. House seats after 1934. By 1980, however, the tendency for the Democrats to support inept or mediocre candidates in the primaries coupled with an emerging reform movement allowed the GOP to break through when an energetic reform candidate, Claudine Schneider, defeated a particularly lackluster sitting representative. Split control of the delegation continued until 1988 when another Republican, Ron Machtley, ousted "the legendary Fernand St. Germain, who had held the seat since 1960 and had managed throughout those years to stay just one step ahead of an indictment."[7] During Machtley's first term the Republicans held both seats. In 1990 Democrat Jack Reed reclaimed one seat and in 1994 Democrat Patrick Kennedy claimed the other.[8]

Absent the unusual circumstances surrounding the Chafee appointment, the Democrats appear to have a lock on the federal delegation. When Pell retired in 1996 the contest for this open seat saw the Republican national committee spend over a half a million dollars to boost the campaign of a

Table 8: Rhode Island Partisan Vote for U.S. House of Representatives, 1968–1998

Year	Winner 1st District	Winner 2nd District
1968	St. Germain—D	Tiernan—D
1970	St. Germain—D	Tiernan—D
1972	St. Germain—D	Tiernan—D
1974	St. Germain—D	Beard—D
1976	St. Germain—D	Beard—D
1978	St. Germain—D	Beard—D
1980	St. Germain—D	Schneider—R
1982	St. Germain—D	Schneider—R
1984	St. Germain—D	Schneider—R
1986	St. Germain—D	Schneider—R
1988	Machtley—R	Schneider—R
1990	Machtley—R	Reed—D
1992	Machtley—R	Reed—D
1994	Kennedy—D	Reed—D
1996	Kennedy—D	Weygand—D
1998	Kennedy—D	Weygand—D

well-known sitting state treasurer, Nancy Mayer, who had a reputation as a popular reformer. She was trounced by three-term Congressman Jack Reed, who received 64 percent of the vote. The open U.S. House seat, vacated by representative Bob Weygand (who ran for the U.S. Senate) passed on to a Democrat, James Langevin.

In the congressional delegation Democrat Patrick Kennedy has emerged as a formidable figure in Rhode Island politics and is likely to remain on the scene over the long haul; his entire life appears to be devoted to politics using Rhode Island as a base. He was elected to the General Assembly while still a student at Providence College. Aided by celebrities from his family, he campaigned hard and won the Democratic primary from an old-line legislator at the age of twenty-one. When he entered the General Assembly he introduced some reform legislation that attempted to give the rank-and-file membership more power. As a result, he was marginalized by the leadership who regarded him as an immature upstart; the running joke among the leaders was that they would all be happy when "Boy Patrick" was old enough to move up and out of the General Assembly and run for the U.S. Congress.

In 1992, however, he joined up with an insurgent group that took control, thus gaining insider status in the legislature. He became a more visible player, sponsored reform legislation, and diligently and successfully used his family connections to court the senior vote. He also mobilized the Portuguese vote, a heretofore untapped base of political support. This positioned him to declare for an open seat for the U.S. Congress in 1994 at the age of 27. It was a tough race insofar as many people took umbrage at the idea that he was using his status and money as a Kennedy to "claim" a seat in Congress. Hence, many voters supported a talented and articulate Republican opponent. At this point Kennedy was not particularly articulate or good on his feet, which forced the Kennedy machine to move into high gear and engage in an expensive and hard-hitting negative campaign that relied heavily on out-of-state money and the star quality of his family.[9] Clearly this election was the beginning of a lifelong quest, which many say includes the presidency. In 1997 he started making personal and nasty partisan attacks on U.S. Senator John Chafee, in what many saw as an attempt to nudge Chafee away from running for reelection in the year 2000. But as polls saw Kennedy's negatives rising, and as the impeachment backlash suggested a possible takeover of the U.S. House by the Democrats, Kennedy backed off. Instead he accepted the chairmanship of the Democratic Congressional Campaign Committee (CCC), vowing to take back the House and make Dick Gephardt Speaker in 2000. While he fell short of that goal, over the long term and with Kennedy's base in Rhode Island time, celebrity, and money are on his side.

Since the time Kennedy won his first race for the U.S. House, subsequent contests have lacked meaningful opposition. Kennedy does little campaigning during election periods and avoids debates with opponents. During the elections of 1996 and 1998 he spent more time on the campaign trail out of state supporting Democratic candidates for the U.S. House around the country. Given his position in the Democratic party and his secure base in the state, the year 2000 has brought more of the same. The Democrats' partisan edge in congressional races, however, goes beyond the obvious star quality of a Kennedy. In the second district when an open seat occurred in 1996, a tough primary race among two Democrats occurred but the victor of that race, Bob Weygand, had no significant challenger in the general election and he, too, made himself scarce. In his next run in 1998 Weygand faced two fringe candidates and kept a low profile during a cakewalk of an election. A tough run in 2000 for the U.S. Senate against Lincoln Chafee caused him to reappear.

One should note, of course, that the edge the federal delegation holds on their seats is also related to their incumbent status, their Washington connections, and the money those allow them to amass. Federal candidates can build campaign war chests that are designed to discourage serious challengers. These officials have access to significant out-of-state contributions, the national parties' soft money, and the ability to draw national leaders to aid in in-state fundraising. In 1998 Congressman Bob Weygand, who faced only token opposition, had Vice President Al Gore come into the state for pricey fundraisers with the stated goal of raising over a million dollars. Although his pitch was "to guard against the prospect of the GOP infusing soft money into the 1998 race," Weygand's efforts were clearly more about shoring up his incumbent status and building up resources for future races.

Although the costs of campaigning for federal elections have escalated in Rhode Island, they still remain low by national standards. Primarily because it is a single media market, a million dollars goes a long way. If running in a race for an open U.S. Senate seat in the year 2000, a serious candidate might spend between two and three million dollars. In a contest for an open U.S. House seat, depending on the name recognition of the person running, a successful candidate would need to spend between one and two million dollars.

STATE ELECTIONS

In statewide elections one can see more volatility. This was especially evident during the 1980s and early 1990s. From the Green Revolution on, Democrats completely dominated the five statewide general offices. Table 9 charts the shifts in control since 1968. In gubernatorial contests, after a long period of Democratic hegemony Edward DiPrete was elected governor in 1984, 1986, and 1988. In 1994 voters elected Republican Lincoln Almond by a slim margin but reelected him in 1998 by a nine-point margin. That victory was probably due in part to good economic times and general satisfaction among the electorate who, after a period of turmoil, felt the state was finally "on the right track." The fact that in 1998 among all the other statewide races the Democrats either were returned to office or reclaimed offices formerly held by the GOP suggests that the normal pattern still favors Democrats.[10]

Nonetheless, statewide races are likely to remain an area of possible volatility insofar as they are visible contests supported by public funds. At this level voters are most likely to "throw the rascals out" when they are dissatisfied. Certainly this was true in the 1980s and early 1990s. As table 9 indicates, after decades of Democratic control the Republicans won not only the governorship but also the secretary of state's office, the general treasurer, and attorney general in selective races during this period. What is fascinating about these wins is that with the exception of the contest for the attorney general in 1992, all other GOP breakthroughs were made by women who would not have found the same structure of opportunity within the Democratic party and opted to run as Republicans. Given the initiation

Table 9: Party Control of Statewide Offices, 1968–1998

Year	Governor	Lt. Gov.	Treas.	Sec. of State	Att. General
1968	D	D	D	D	R
1970	D	D	D	D	R
1972	D	D	D	D	R
1974	D	D	D	D	D
1976	D	D	D	D	D
1978	D	D	D	D	D
1980	D	D	D	D	D
1982	D	D	D	R***	D
1984	R	D	D	R***	R***
1986	R	D	D	R***	D
1988	R	D	D	D	D
1990	D	D	D	D	D
1992	D	D	R***	R***	R
1994*	R	D**	R***	D	R
1998	R	D	D	D	D

*After 1992 terms for all general offices were extended to four years.

** In 1994 voters elected a Democrat to the office of lieutenant governor, who vacated the seat in 1996 to run for Congress. Republican Almond appointed a Republican to finish out the term.

*** Contests in which Republican women took office.

of public financing in 1992, energetic challengers are likely to be readily available in the future, creating the potential for competition for these offices under the right circumstances.

This situation is in sharp counterdistinction to the lock that the Democrats appear to have in the General Assembly. The Democrats have enjoyed solid control in the house since 1940 and, after rural malapportionment was corrected, they stabilized control of the state senate in 1958. Moreover, as indicated in table 10, except for one term in the 1980s when a particularly brazen reapportionment plan was thrown into the courts and resulted in a special election, Democratic majorities have been veto proof. Even the scandals of the 1980s did little to diminish this hold. It is not unusual for more than 40 percent of the races for legislative seats to go uncontested, and even when the political climate encourages competition the Democratic party dominates. In the wake of the credit union scandal, good-government groups encouraged independent candidates to challenge the establishment. In the 1992 election, for example, eighty-five independent candidates ran for various seats in the legislature; not one was elected. In 1998 one legislator won a seat as an independent in the lower house.

These lopsided majorities in the legislature proved especially frustrating for Lincoln Almond, a Republican governor who, because of the weak position of the GOP in the legislature, had limited input on the policy agenda of the time, particularly the budget. Thus in 1996, in order to gain some leverage in the legislative process, Almond headed up "Majority 96." This was a campaign which, while ostensibly touted as a movement for the GOP to take control of the state senate, actually was designed to pick up enough Republican seats in the senate to create a Republican block that could sustain a gubernatorial veto.

The campaign created a political action committee (PAC), raised money, and offered grassroot support for selected Republican challengers. The end result was that the GOP managed to *lose* a seat in the senate and pick up one in the house, leaving the GOP right where it had begun. Adding insult to injury, after the legislative session opened in 1997, one newly elected Republican state senator switched her party affilition to the Democrats. The GOP fared no better in 1998 when they held on to their eight (out of fifty) seats in the senate and lost three seats in the house, leaving the Republicans with only thirteen seats in a hundred-member body.

PARTY ORGANIZATIONS—WANING VESTIGES OF THE PAST

In contrast to the electoral success of the Democrats, party organizations have become peripheral to the statewide political process. The once-powerful machine staffed by a cadre of loyal and enthusiastic supporters created a network of organizations that existed in most local communities on up to the state committee. They screened and nominated candidates, recruited new voters onto the Democratic rolls, campaigned and raised money tirelessly at the local and state levels, and provided core electoral support in primaries for the party's endorsed candidates. While these organizations still can make a difference locally, recent state endorsing conventions have been so obviously staged and peripheral to the electoral action that many party activists wonder "why we do this anymore."

In addition to the declining loyalty of voters, several other factors have encouraged organizational decline. Up to the 1960s Democratic party leaders established a pecking order that limited access to statewide and federal offices to a select few. For one, the number of offices—given the size of the federal delegation—was small; moreover, those who held them tended to stay in office for decades. T. F. Green held a U.S. Senate seat for twenty-

Table 10: Partisan Division of Rhode Island General Assembly, 1978–1998

Year	State Senate Dem–Rep	Uncontested Percent	State Assembly Dem–Rep	Uncontested Percent
1998	42–8	(40)	86–13*	(56)
1996	42–8	(24)	84–16	(48)
1994	40–10	(24)	85–15	(49)
1992	39–11	(22)	85–15	(23)
1990	45–5	(40)	89–11	(41)
1988	41–9	(52)	84–16	(61)
1986	38–12	(24)	80–20	(31)
1984	37–13	(18)	77–22*	(35)
1982	29–21**	(6)	85–15	(39)
1980	43–7	(22)	82–18	(33)
1978	45–5	(48)	84–16	(43)

Source: Office of the Secretary of State, *Rhode Island Manual.*

*Third party or independent elected.

**Election postponed until July 1983 because of a contested redistricting case.

four years, John Pastore for twenty-six, and Fernand St. Germain kept his U.S. House seat for twenty-eight years. "This created a bottleneck in the structure of opportunity monopolized by a parochial and increasingly mediocre elite."[11]

Moreover, Rhode Island's state party organizations were weakened in the early 1970s when national campaign finance reforms made it easier to give money to individual candidates than to parties. Given this weakened party system, breaking into this structure of opportunity became possible because running for federal and statewide office was relatively inexpensive. The relatively low cost allowed capable and talented candidates to contest and win Democratic primaries; Claiborne Pell won a U.S. Senate seat without the endorsement of his party, marking the beginning of a continued trend. In addition, during this period voters, reflecting national trends, no longer voted the straight party line. In 1962 Republican John Chafee's successful gubernatorial bid encouraged split-ticket voting in the state. These factors also allowed women, who had been shut out of consideration for higher office among the Democrats, to seek and win office as Republicans. As noted above, most of the significant breakthroughs in statewide and federal elections for the GOP were made by women.

Another compounding factor was the initiation of the open primary in 1978. A closed primary law, passed in 1947, sustained organizational control insofar as it required that voters who registered with a party had to wait twenty-six months before they could disaffiliate and register with another party. The courts invalidated the twenty-six-month rule, which forced the legislature to create an open system wherein voters, after registering as unaffiliated, can declare a partisan choice at the polls on primary day. Immediately after voting they can then sign a form and disaffiliate, leaving them free to vote in either the Democratic or Republican race in the next primary election. Such provisions no doubt help to further disengage the voter from long-standing ties to the parties.

State campaign reforms initiated in 1992 provide public funding for individuals running for governor as well as for lieutenant-governor, attorney general, secretary of state, and general treasurer. This encourages a range of individuals to enter the primaries and the general election races. Candidates must declare if they will take public financing by the late-June filing date. To qualify for matching funds they agree to spending limits, which in 1998 dollars was set at $1.6 million. The matching formula favors small donations, in that contributions up to $500 yield a two-to-one dollar match while contributions at $500 and up to $2000 bring a dollar-for-dollar match. Candidates who face a primary may spend an additional $500,000 of nonmatched funds.[12] The growth of television and polling operations has shifted the focus of statewide and federal campaigns from retail to wholesale politics involving more money. In statewide races about two-thirds of campaign money is spent on television ads that flood the networks as the general election nears.[13] While most statewide races are publicly financed and hence capped, federal races, into which the national organizations can funnel soft money, can escalate into the millions, which is very big money by Rhode Island standards.

Given these developments, the role of party organizations has become insignificant in statewide and federal elections. For the Democrats, statewide conventions at which the state committee gives an endorsement to a slate are hollow events. The state committee consists of a man and a woman from each of the one hundred house legislative districts who meet and vote for a slate. In fact, the endorsements are controlled by the legislative leadership who line up votes for their candidates. Endorsements have come to mean little to candidates and in some instances can be seen as a detriment because, in certain contexts, the label of "insider" can work against the candidate.[14] This became increasingly apparent in the 1990s when, in a series of high-visibility races, unendorsed candidates trounced the party-backed opponents.

In 1990 the former mayor of Providence, Joseph Paolino, won the Democratic endorsement for governor but came in last in a three-way primary race won by Bruce Sundlun; Sundlun then won the general election. In 1994, however, as sitting governor Sundlun was endorsed by the party but was handily defeated in a three-way primary by an outsider, Myrth York. In 1996 Paolino, after spending time as ambassador to Malta, returned to Rhode Island, reentered the electoral arena, and received the party's endorsement for an open U.S. House seat. Paolino was handily defeated in the primary by a candidate who, with labor's backing, won the primary and the general election. In a 1998 highly visible race for attorney general, the Democratic leadership in the General Assembly pushed the state committee to endorse a candidate with ties to the legislature even though polls showed him running behind the other contenders. With the leadership looking on their candidate received the unanimous endorsement of the convention but victory went to the unendorsed candidate, Sheldon Whitehouse, who won in a landslide; the endorsed candidate came in third.[15]

The same situation holds true for Republicans. Their state committee is constructed somewhat differently in that representatives from the city and town organizations join members who are appointed by the state chair, which gives that party's leadership more control. Still, endorsements have little weight and candidates who fail to receive their party's endorsement routinely go on to win in the primaries.

At the local and legislative level, however, retail politics is alive and well. In this context the backing of the city and town party organizations can, in selective contests, be critical.

In races for the state legislature and other local elections, big money is not an issue. An average legislative race can be mounted for ten to fifteen thousand dollars for a contested seat. Long-time incumbents spend much less. Most of the effort is put toward grassroots activities like mailings and campaigning door to door; very little is spent on radio and virtually nothing on television. One woman who was running for an open state senate seat, when asked about campaign costs noted, "Buying my stationery was *really* expensive." In this context the help of local party organizations can be important, as can the financial and political support of the legislative leadership. 1992 campaign reforms banned the use of campaign funds for personal use by individuals, but the law does allow politicians to spend campaign funds for any expenses related to "gaining and holding" public office. This gives key individuals, especially legislative leaders who can generate higher contributions, considerable discretion and leverage in supporting other legislative candidates for office. This type of grassroots support can also be critical in city and town elections.

INDEPENDENTS AND THIRD PARTY CANDIDATES

Given the weakened loyalties of the voters and the declining position of party organizations, one might expect that independent or third party candidates would be successful, especially during the recent past. Generally speaking this is not the case. In the 1998 legislative races alone, over six different parties, as well as a range of independents, were on the ballot. Only one independent—a former legislator—was elected to the lower house.

A third party candidate who did make a mark on electoral politics was Robert Healey of the Cool Moose party. In the 1994 race for governor he received nine percent of the vote, a showing that entitled him to matching public funds. Consequently, he entered the race again in 1998. Perhaps as a sign of the settling down of the electorate, Healy only received six percent of the vote in that election. Although that was enough to keep him eligible for public funds and allow him to draw a paycheck as the head of a recognized third party, records indicate that as of 1998 only 759 voters are registered with the Cool Moose party. In 1998 the Reform Party fielded candidates for the general offices. Although these candidates have only a small registered following, their ability to engage disgruntled voters and to eventually access public funds allows them a visible place in elections and the opportunity to indirectly influence the outcome of competitive contests.

The notable exception to this pattern is the ability of the legendary Vincent "Buddy" Cianci, mayor of Providence, to be able to win reelection under *any* party label. He was first elected mayor in 1974 as a Republican after a divisive and bitter Democratic primary had weakened the ticket. In that election he devised a mercurial strategy that garnered him the votes of Italians on Federal Hill (an Italian section of Providence). This block, which normally would support a Democrat, proved to be critical to his victory.[16] He was reelected as a Republican in 1978 and then as an independent in 1982. During that term he was forced to resign for a felony conviction for assaulting his wife's alleged lover. Much to most everyone's surprise, later he was able to reclaim office as an independent with a narrow victory in a three-way race in 1990.

Since that time his popularity has soared and he has won the grudging approval of a range of voting blocks in the city for his enthusiastic and shrewd management of the city and the "Providence Renaissance" that came together during his tenure. In 1994 city registration records indicate that of 74,669 registered voters, more than 43,000 were Democrats, almost 29,000 were unaffiliated, and just under 2,500 were Republicans. In that year Cianci won in a landslide with *no Democrat* on the ticket. In 1998 he ran unopposed. Most political folk concede that the Democratic party organization in Providence is "on ice" until Cianci moves on.[17] Given his popularity and his political base in Providence, he posed a threat to statewide candidates, especially Democrats who, after a tough primary could face the prospect that Cianci could jump into a contest as an independent and in a three-way race quite possibly win. In 1999, however, a federal investigation into the workings of Providence City Hall dramatically changed the picture.

THE FUTURE OF TWO-PARTY RULE

Given the class and generational changes that have eroded strong party ties, the range of independents across the political spectrum, and the ability of candidates to run outside the once-powerful Democrat establishment, should we expect more partisan competition in the future? Or will the Democrats continue to dominate? Several factors suggest, at least in the short term, continued Democratic dominance.

One explanation for Democratic success, quoted at the beginning of this chapter, was offered by Duane Lockard when he last observed party politics in Rhode Island in his insightful 1959 study. Lockard noted that although the extent of patronage and corruption in the system at the time should have encouraged competition, the Democrats in Rhode Island exhibited a tendency, unusual in one-party states, that has helped sustain their position. That is, whatever else they did they took care of the needs of the poor and the working class who, in turn, continued to support them. That analysis appears to hold true today in that whatever else the Democrats have done, they have remained "on the side of the angels" insofar as they continue to protect the interests of these large constituencies and promote fairly progressive legislation.

Although the ideological range between the parties has narrowed considerably, at times traces of former class divisions emerge. In 1996, as welfare reform was taking shape across the nation, coalitions concerned with protecting the benefits of welfare clients knew that their interests would be best served by forging an alliance with the Democratic leadership in the legislature. In so doing they prevented the cuts in welfare benefits and the elimination of food stamps for legal immigrants that had been proposed by the Republican governor and his administration. In remarks tinged with the resentments of the past, Democratic Majority Leader George Caroulo made it strikingly clear in a speech on the house floor that—even during a lingering recession—such actions (the reduction in welfare benefits) were completely untenable.

In terms of the legacy of corruption, as the scandals of the past recede the Democrats have either supported or acquiesced to most political reforms.

Moreover, the fallout from scandals has proved to be bipartisan in nature. In a highly visible and memorable episode, former Republican Governor Ed DiPrete plea-bargained to multiple counts of bribery and extortion and began serving a reduced sentence in the state prison in 1999. In that same year allegations of misuse of state funds by the Economic Development Corporation under a Republican administration, forced a state audit. Whatever the outcome, the GOP can no longer campaign on Democratic waste or corruption.

Moreover, on the ideological front it is increasingly hard to tell who is who. Characterizing New England politics generally, former U.S. Senator Warren Rudman from New Hampshire noted, "Democrats are essentially where moderate Republicans used to be."[18] This is certainly true in Rhode Island. The Republicans in the state continue to represent the moderate, progressive wing of the party, in sharp contrast to the national GOP which is dominated by southern conservatives. Conversely, the Democrats have moved away from the big-spending liberal largesse of the past. While there remain some partisan debates on the margins, with Republicans keeping a keen eye on the interests of business and Democrats being mindful of the needs of union constituencies, distinctions are increasingly muted.

During negotiations for the 1999 budget it was the Democratic leadership that resisted the Republican governor's attempts to fund more programs. The Democrats instead opted for broad-based tax cuts. In the 1998 election the unions refused to back the Democratic candidate, who opposed several large capital expansion projects that would have created more union jobs. The unions remained neutral, which was a backhand way of endorsing the Republican candidate. These events prompted observers to quip about "role reversals" in the two parties' positions.

These changes should provide opportunities for the GOP. But, however capable the selected individuals may be, Republicans still lack the structure of opportunity that produces depth and experience in a pool of electable candidates. In the year 1999 the entire elected federal delegation had all served stints in the General Assembly, as did three of the four Democratic general officers. Given the weak presence of Republicans at the statehouse, and the understandable reluctance of Republicans to run and serve as part of a weak minority in a General Assembly that pays a salary of ten thousand dollars a year, the eligible pool remains small. Of course this does provide selected opportunities to energetic and capable members of the GOP, especially women, in their efforts to avoid costly primaries and secure a place on the ticket. But in the general election and under usual circumstances these candidates remain at a disadvantage.

Hence, as the state moves into the twenty-first century, the Democrats are likely to continue to dominate in a weakened and altered party system. Other paths to power, of course, can be found through interest groups, which also play a critical role in Rhode Island's representative system. It is to these groups that we now turn.

CHAPTER NINE

Interest and Group Representation

This bill is about unions . . . anyone who doesn't think it's about unions is denying reality. . . . The real worry about this bill is that it is going to open up low-cost alternatives and provide better results. This [bill] has to do with protecting a [unionized] system that has become indefensible.

  House Majority Leader George Caroulo, in a floor debate about authorizing charter schools, 1998

The so-called captains of industry in Rhode Island have proposed something which they feel is a jobs bill. . . . They're going to have to come in and do a heck of a selling job.

    State Senator Charles Walton, commenting on a proposal to cut the state income tax for upper-bracket wage earners, 1999

In addition to the influence exerted by the parties, the primary means by which various groups and interests in the state express their policy concerns is through lobbying. This supplement to the formal electoral-representational process involves a variety of methods of making contact with legislators and other state and local officials to influence their decisions. Lobbying is as old as the republic, probably older. Not until the twentieth century, however, did it become a matter of official concern. Reformers see these backdoor approaches and informal pressure tactics as a threat to democratic processes, threats that should be exposed to public view and regulated by law.

As early as 1912 Rhode Island had enacted a lobbying regulation. It called for registration of lobbyists, a listing of the bill or bills with which the registrant was concerned, a post-session filing of expenses incurred during the session, and it specified penalties for violating the law. This act was obviously passed in response to national reform impulses of the Progressive

Table 11: Registered Lobbyists in Rhode Island, 1997

Category	Number of Lobbyists
Government units and agencies	212
Organized labor	45
Reform groups	38
Social welfare and advocacy groups	37
Insurance, including health insurance	27
Utilities	25
Professional groups and organizations	25
General business organizations	23
Individual business corporations	23
Builders and contractors	21

Source: Secretary of State, tabulated by authors.

Era.[1] Then in 1975 in the wake of Watergate the 1912 statute was amended to tighten and detail its provisions.

In 1988 the current legislation was passed to replace earlier enactments.[2] This legislation is considerably more detailed and, among other things, requires that individuals lobbying on behalf of any federal, state, or local government agency also must register with the state but are exempt from most other provisions of the act.

The list of registered lobbyists published by the secretary of state as of March 1997 contains 554 entries. One hundred of the names listed appear twice or more, indicating representation of two or more agencies or clients. All the rest appear only once. As table 11 shows, representatives from government units and agencies, as per the 1988 legislation, are by far the largest group shown, at 39 percent of the total. The next largest group is that containing labor lobbyists, who amount to 8 percent. The table lists categories of lobbyists that contain twenty or more entries. Falling into the twenty-or-less registrant category one finds beverages, banking, transportation and automobiles, and nonprofit organizations like health and education groups. The remaining seventy-five registrants are scattered across policy interests.

The extraordinarily large number of government lobbyists is in part the result of insistence by private lobbyists that these government spokespersons be acknowledged. Obviously this group frequently ends up in adversarial relationships with the privates on any number of issues. One could argue that lobbyists who represent state government agencies are only filling the traditional lobbying role in a very general sense. Usually they are in the statehouse in order to explain to legislators who are designated to manage bills on the floor what the bill will accomplish, or to advise on what the impact of a proposed floor amendment might be. In many cases their role is in connection with a bill proposed by the agency for which they work.

The fact that Rhode Island is a "labor state" accounts for the reality that the second largest number of registered lobbyists represent unions. The additional prominence of reform-group representatives reflects the reform phase the state went through in the 1990s. Most of these lobbyists are unpaid, and their numbers are explained in part by citizens' attraction to reform causes. These are generally people who have not been involved in party politics or run for partisan office.

The social welfare and advocacy cluster is also explainable in part by the questions that were salient during this period. Following federal welfare-reform legislation in 1996, concerned groups brought as much pressure to bear on the legislature as they could, and quite successfully persuaded the assembly that it must find state money to replace the federal cuts and prevent the stoppage of benefits to various categories of recipients. Most of the other categories listed in table 11 are typical of what one would find on lobbying lists almost anywhere.

THE IMPACT OF LOBBYING

Some illustrations of lobbying from the 1997 session of the General Assembly will suggest the importance of that kind of activity in Rhode Island's political process. First, a vivid example of the potency of highly focused lobbying on a specific and rather low-visibility issue. At stake was a minor piece of legislation that would have shifted responsibility for payment of increases in life insurance costs incurred by retired teachers from the city or town taxpayers to the retirees themselves. As explained, if passed the bill would actually have left up to collective bargaining the issue of who paid. The bill passed the House of Representatives fifty-two to twenty.

Three hours later the teachers' unions weighed in on a quest for reversal, having realized that their members might have to pay a bit more. The press account says that after heavy lobbying by union representatives, the previous vote was reconsidered and the bill lost on a vote of forty-two to forty-one. Supporters of the legislation, the reporter noted, "were not happy with lawmakers who switched, particularly those from Providence who regularly complain about not receiving enough state school aid money but refused to make a modest step to save money."[3] Among the switchers were five

Providence Democrats, two of whom candidly admitted that they changed their votes due to the teachers' union lobbying.

Even in this marginally important case one can see the impact of focused lobbying and can imagine the mixed feelings of legislator targets like the Providence Democrats. Their voting is generally liberal and pro-union, but their constituents are burdened with high property taxes driven to a considerable extent by school budget costs. One of the bill's supporters, who was critical of the "switchers," was the house finance committee chairman who has the thankless task of trying to meet the unrelenting demands on state spending priorities in the face of, in this case, insatiable school needs and mounting taxpayer resistance.

In this instance, as in many others like it, it would be pointless to try to divine the "correct" or most popular decision. In other instances, where the issues are more weighty and the potential impact on the citizenry is much greater, one often does find that the representational system works reasonably well. One example that also came up in the 1997 session had to do with hospitals. Up to then Rhode Island had never had a for-profit hospital. All were nonprofits, with either religious or secular sponsorship. It became known that the giant national corporation, Columbia/HCA, was negotiating to buy Roger Williams Hospital, a large Providence institution that was having financial difficulties.

The news aroused widespread concern. State legislators concluded that action was called for, and many groups were galvanized into feverish activity. Opponents of various stripes sought each other out and joined forces with the union movement, which feared that jobs and unions would be jeopardized in purchased for-profit hospitals. Columbia sent in its lobbyists, and as time went on spent more and more money for television and newspaper advertising. It became a kind of David and Goliath fight, with the "pickup" team of local interests fighting a gigantic national corporation. As the *Providence Journal* wrote: "It became the most heavily lobbied bill of this year's legislative session, pitting an amalgam of labor union and community groups organized as the Not For Profit Coalition against Columbia lobbyists."[4]

The issues involved were unprecedented for Rhode Island, and thus difficult to deal with. The Columbia proposal appeared to many opponents to open the door to truly major and unsettling changes in the delivery of health care. Advocates for the poor feared cutbacks in the free care that hospitals provided for the indigent, especially care in emergency rooms. For many the linking of "for profit" with health care in general grated. Others, including the governor, felt that competition might be a good thing or questioned the right of the state to keep Columbia and other such organizations out.

The house Democratic leadership, responding to what seemed to be the public's fears and concerns, crafted legislation that would allow an outside corporation like Columbia to purchase no more than one nonprofit hospital. The bill also included other provisions, such as language to ensure no cutbacks on emergency room care. This passed the house with a wide majority but met resistance in the senate. The bill that finally passed both houses had a compromise three-year mandatory delay before a corporation that had purchased a Rhode Island institution could negotiate for a second one. The governor vetoed the legislation, but it was repassed over his veto by a wide margin in the house and a narrow one in the senate.

Time will tell whether the legislature or the governor read the public mood correctly. An opinion poll taken during the debate by Brown University found widespread knowledge of the issue, and a two-to-one majority of those who expressed an opinion favored limits on such hospital purchases. There are thus some tenuous grounds for arguing that the General Assembly had crafted a compromise that matched public attitudes. Arguably the system was appropriately responsive. Also one might say that the system had worked, in that "Goliath's" lavish use of its corporate resources had not been able to prevail over "David," the ad hoc coalition of local interests. The feverish lobbying by both sides had helped to educate the public about the tangled issues involved. It will be a long while, however, before anyone should venture a firm opinion on which side was right, although increasing concern about the activities of for-profit hospital conglomerates and general problems with managed care suggest the legislature's caution was well placed.

Whatever the policy outcomes, lobbying remains a critical aspect of politics and representation in Rhode Island. Campaign finance reforms initiated in the early 1990s and subsequent rulings by the ethics commission bar state officials from taking "anything of value" from anyone having any interest in state government. This ruling just about eliminated the extensive wining and dining by lobbyists that regularly occurred at various bars and restaurants around the city of Providence. Indeed, many felt these restrictions, which included a "no cup of coffee" rule were, in fact, counterproductive. In one telling example, Brown University conducted a one-day policy symposium on key state issues for state legislators at the beginning of the 1999 session. The event included lunch. The ethics commission, however, ruled that because Brown has "interests" at the statehouse, legislators could not accept the lunch, which the legislative leadership ultimately paid for. By 2000 the ethics commission rescinded the strict rule and settled instead for a more moderate standard, which angered the reform groups.

The exception to all restrictions is the provision in campaign finance law that allows officeholders to accept campaign contributions and to use these monies for "the gaining and keeping of office." Thus lobbyists are usually ubiquitous supporters of campaign events that legislators, especially the leadership, routinely hold to replenish their campaign coffers. However, these sums by any standard are minimal: most fundraisers are low-ticket events and backbenchers in the legislature might host fifty dollar events while the leadership might request one hundred to two hundred dollars per ticket.

These limitations put an additional premium on "being there." The major responsibility of a good lobbyist is to work the halls of the legislature during the session, attend and testify at committee hearings, and contact individual legislators and the leaders with reliable information whenever possible. The extent to which teachers' representatives, organized labor in general, and representatives of the tourist industry are a constant presence at the statehouse during the session goes a long way toward explaining the success of their agendas. Conversely, groups that do not make a constant effort to work the halls of the legislature often come up short when their interests are at stake. The rule is that a good lobbyist needs to "show face" during the legislative session to be successful. One lobbyist noted, "[I]n this business, politics is process and you need to respect the process."

THE INTEREST GROUP LANDSCAPE IN RHODE ISLAND

The kinds of entities tabulated earlier in this chapter are what political scientists usually refer to as interest groups. They are the subject of a substantial literature and, as in other states, Rhode Island displays a range of conventional interest groups. In addition there are important sources of pressure and influence on the Rhode Island political system that do not fit easily under the traditional interest group heading. This is doubtless true of any state's politics, but seems especially true in Rhode Island. Both types are very much a part of the political landscape, and the most significant of these warrant some discussion.

Fifty-state rankings of the influence of various interest groups put school-teachers' organizations first in most states, general business organizations like the chamber of commerce second, and traditional labor associations fifth.[5] The rankings in Rhode Island are somewhat different. While the teachers' union is certainly one of the most influential organizations in the state, the relationship between business and labor presents a different, more uneven picture. Certainly labor has remained a dominant force in the state since the early 1940s; business associations have been less influential. However, during the late 1990s the "we-they" distinction that so long characterized the labor-business relationship in the state has been altered as forces of economic development have created mutual interests and a new politics of accommodation.

LABOR

Rhode Island is known as a "labor state." This reputation fit better in earlier years when manufacturing was the predominant form of employment. Manufacturing employment, however, has declined with the loss of the textile industry and, in more recent years, with the steady decline in other forms of manufacturing. As a result, employment in service industries has become increasingly important. Table 12 illustrates these patterns. Note that manufacturing employment has declined both as a percentage of the total and in absolute terms, while wholesale and retail and the service sector have gone up proportionally and absolutely. Along with the loss of manufacturing came a steady decline in the portion of the workforce that was unionized. This has obviously caused some loss of political clout for organized labor, though labor remains an important force both organizationally and as a political point of reference for low-income workers, whether or not they belong to unions.

Much of the loss of membership by unions representing workers in the private sector has been made up through the rapid increase in union membership in the public sector. The basic legislation guaranteeing the right to organize was first passed in 1941, not long after federal legislation (the Wagner Act) was put on the books. From 1959 to 1967 a series of enactments granted the right to organize employees in the public sector. The first act, in 1958, covered state employees. Subsequent legislation covered firemen, policemen, teachers, and other municipal employees, in 1961, 1963, 1966, and 1967, respectively.

The public employee unions have been the strong growth area in the labor sector. Virtually all of the categories of public employees are currently covered by unions, with some exceptions in state service: employees of the General Assembly and of the statewide elected officials. Significantly, the president of the steelworkers was made president of the united AFL-CIO when it was formed in the 1950s and served until 1978, when the office went to the president of the R.I. Federation of Teachers. Then, when that individual went to Washington to take a position in the national labor movement, the head of the firefighters union took over as president of the AFL-CIO in Rhode Island. Public unions have become a major force in the labor movement.

Generally, union power has gone through a number of phases. Jay Good-

Table 12: Employment Trends in Rhode Island (in thousands)

	1955	1975	1995
Total Employment	227	290	374
Manufacturing	130	113	85
(Textile Manufacturing)	(40)	(12)	(8)
Wholesale & Retail	47	71	98
Services	13	61	136
Finance, insurance, etc.	11	18	24
Transportation, utilities, etc.	14	13	14
Miscellaneous	12	14	17

Note: Public employees not included in data.

man, in his study of the relations between labor and the Democratic Party from the early 1950s to the early 1960s, concludes that, "Labor-party relations were excellent during the administration of Governor Dennis J. Roberts (1950–1958); they were strained under Governor Christopher Del Sesto (1958–1960); and they were disrupted under Governor John A. Notte Jr., (1960–1962)."[6] Roberts had obviously presided over a period during which the relation of labor to the political system was developing and some of the basic legislative objectives of labor were being achieved. The administration of John Notte was followed by Governor John Chafee's six years in office. Republicans Del Sesto and Chafee obviously disrupted the close relationship labor had enjoyed when both executive and legislative branches were Democratic.

It is probably fair to say that by the 1970s a reasonably stable relationship prevailed between labor and government. This was due, in part, to the fact that the major legislation that labor wanted was already in place. Another key factor was that after the court-mandated reapportionment of the General Assembly in the mid-1960s, the Democratic Party enjoyed overwhelming majorities in both legislative chambers.

This realignment had the effect of ensuring that if labor, as well as other groups with liberal agendas, could convince a substantial part of the Democratic majority of their position, they would be successful. The record in the last couple of decades has shown that labor could indeed count on solid support in the General Assembly when it needed it.

On a few occasions the willingness of the assembly to go along with labor requests was a little too enthusiastic. One example, which severely damaged labor's image in the eyes of the public, came with a piece of pension legislation passed at the end of the 1987 legislative session. It allowed full-time employees of unions representing state and local employees (many of whom had never worked for the state) to buy credit for their time as union employees and apply it toward state pensions and early retirement incentives. When news of this became public a loud outcry ensued. The act was repealed at the next session.[7] Lengthy litigation followed as the state tried to take back benefits that some union leaders had hastened to claim while the legislation was on the books. Ultimately the federal courts rescinded the pensions.

This unsavory deal was by no means typical of relations between the unions and the legislature. Two years earlier, in 1985, labor lost a hard-fought battle on a much more important issue. For years Rhode Island was one of only two states (New York was the other) that allowed strikers to claim unemployment compensation payments when on strike. This benefit became one of the most glaring examples to the business community, in and outside of Rhode Island, of the pro-labor and anti-business climate of the state.

After repeated efforts to overturn the law, in 1985 the legislature repealed the law over the bitter objections of organized labor.[8] This particular issue became a major turning point between labor and those concerned with economic development in the state. With the decline in manufacturing employment and the recession of the late 1980s and early 1990s, the pressure on the state to do all in its power to ensure the preservation of jobs and to help create or bring in new ones is strong and continuous.

Most recently, labor has fought on the side of those seeking to stimulate Rhode Island's economy. The construction of a state-funded convention center in Providence (completed in 1996) was strongly supported by labor because it provided many good construction jobs as well as staff jobs at the center. The same was generally true of the alignment of forces brought about by a proposal for the construction of a mega shopping mall in Providence on state-owned land adjacent to the statehouse. Although privately funded, it required major tax concessions by both the state and the city. Again labor saw jobs and economic stimulation. Opposition from existing malls and some who saw the project as another state taxpayer-funded boondoggle was overcome, and construction began. Perhaps the most striking sign of the times was the fact that during the gubernatorial election of 1998, the Democratic candidate, Myrth York, who had at best been tepid in her support of the megamall construction project, was not endorsed by the unions. The unions remained neutral, which was a subtle endorsement of the Republican incumbent who favored it and other state-supported construction projects.

THE BUSINESS COMMUNITY

Although the era of the dominance of textile mill owners is long gone, the influence of the business community as a proactive force for change can be formidable. During 1978 a group of influential business elites, which included Bruce Sundlun (then-president of the Outlet company), Michael Metcalf (owner and editor of the *Providence Journal*), and G. William Miller (CEO of Textron corporation), formed the Capital Center project, an offshoot of the Greater Providence Chamber of Commerce.[9] The group provided the initiative to promote massive infrastructure relocations and commenced several redevelopment projects with public-private investment, which ultimately resulted in the downtown urban renewal that became the centerpiece of the Providence Renaissance. Working with U.S. Senators Claiborne Pell and John Chafee and Governor J. Joseph Garrahy, they secured federal money and state support for relocation of the railroads and demolition of the "Chinese wall" of railroad tracks that ran through the city, and ultimately the relocation of the rivers. These massive infrastructure improvements became the backdrop for corporate investment by members of the Capital Center group that included, among other projects, the purchase and renovation of the Biltmore Hotel in the center of the city, the purchase and restoration of two old theaters that were transformed into performing arts centers, and the refurbishing of several abandoned buildings into retail centers. During this period corporate ownership was locally based and the costs of private redevelopment projects were more feasible. These types of partnerships are now less common because, first, corporate ownership is increasingly nationally or globally based, and second, the cost of infrastructure projects are massive. Thus, except for giving to foundations and other nonprofits, the business influence in community development and change has declined.[10]

But when it comes to trade-offs or concessions with labor, by the early 1990s both business and labor understood that the need to work together was critical to economic recovery and economic development and a new modus operandi emerged. After the repeal of the strikers' unemployment compensation provisions in 1985 (over the objections of organized labor), two benchmarks suggest a more cooperative dynamic. In 1992 the insurance rates for the workers' compensation program escalated to the extent that a request from the trade association for a 123 percent increase caused twelve insurance companies to announce they were leaving the state. As a result, a task force that included representatives from labor, state government, the insurance industry, business, and the worker's compensation court fashioned reform legislation that restructured the program and revamped the court system that adjudicated disputes. The program is considered a national model: costs to business have dramatically declined, more workers are covered, and injured workers get timely adjudication of their claims.

The second benchmark came in 1998 when labor and business supported legislation that revamped the costly unemployment compensation program, long a point of contention between labor and business. The reforms considerably lowered the base rate of employer contributions, saving employers throughout the state what were considered onerous contributions to the unemployment compensation fund. In addition, since the late 1990s both the legislature and the governor have supported targeted tax incentives that have greatly enhanced the business-friendly image of the state.

While these examples represent a changing dynamic in labor-business relations, business can still encounter resistance in the legislature. In 1999 some of the top CEOs in the state caucused privately with the governor and legislative leaders, requesting a tax cut for the 1 percent of wage earners in the state with incomes over $200,000 per year. Instead of a flat state income tax rate, as is the case in neighboring Connecticut and Massachusetts, Rhode Island provides for a lower rate for low- and middle-income wage earners and a progressive escalation, based on the federal tax structure, for high-end earners. The argument of the CEOs was that this tax structure inhibits top executives from relocating themselves and their businesses in the state. While there is probably some merit to the argument, the proposal did not sit well with many of the rank-and-file legislators and some legislative leaders. First they objected to the manner by which the proposal was made, which bypassed the normal lobbying and legislative process. As one legislator noted, "if they want consideration, let them submit a bill like everybody else." Second, peeved legislators noted that these very corporate leaders who were pleading on behalf of wealthy executives were opposing a hike in the minimum wage at the same time. At the end of the 1999 session the minimum wage hike passed and, given the perceptions of the opposition, the business community will probably have to wait for another session. Some argue that a complete revamping of the state income tax structure (detaching it from the federal tax) would provide the political cover to adjust the tax for top executives at a flat rate.

THE PROVIDENCE JOURNAL

From a political perspective probably the most influential "interest group" in the state is *The Providence Journal*. As the only major statewide paper, its circulation far outstrips any combination of more localized papers. The paper provides a number of regional editions that specialize in covering local area news and it prides itself on its thorough coverage of state political and governmental affairs.

Founded in 1829, the *Journal* is one of the oldest daily newspapers in the United States. During its early history it was closely allied with the textile mill owners and the Whig Party, and thus represented a bastion of Yankee conservatism. These links were epitomized by the tenure of Henry "Boss" Anthony, an editor whose nativism and anti-Catholic propaganda filled the *Journal's* pages. Anthony went on to become governor under the Whig–Law and Order Party (1849–1851) and Republican U.S. Senator (1859–1884).

For a long time in the nineteenth century the *Journal* was virtually the official mouthpiece of the Republican party, operating as an adjunct to it. In 1889 at an official meeting it was read out of the party for its attacks on the Republican machine, and specifically for refusing to endorse one of the chosen party candidates in the 1888 election.[11]

It went on to become a first-rate publication, providing thorough coverage of national and international news as well as detailed state news. Throughout, however, it retained close ties with the business community and generally supported Republican candidates for office. In 1937 the *Journal* bought out its statewide competitor, the Democratic *Star-Tribune*, and since then has been the only statewide daily in Rhode Island. Currently about two-thirds of the people of the state report that they read the *Journal* regularly.[12] Certainly everyone in public life reads it thoroughly.

It has been said that there are really two *Journals*. One is the editorial board with its enduring Republican perspective, salted from time to time with a (token?) Democratic endorsement. The other is the reportorial staff whose members resemble their counterparts in the rest of the country insofar as they tend to be politically liberal and reform oriented. At times there is a confluence of perspectives as when, during revelations of the scandals of the late 1980s, the Democrats, who represented the political establishment, became the object of critical journalistic scrutiny. The resulting critical news accounts obviously tended to serve the preferences of the Republican-leaning editorial board.

At times these two perspectives conflict. Shortly before the 1988 election, at which Edward DiPrete was seeking a third term, hints of political scandal led reporters to investigate a land deal wherein the governor and his son acquired a parcel of property, obtained a development variance, and the day after the variance was granted sold the property for a substantial profit. The paper broke the story just before the election, but despite these revelations the editorial board endorsed DiPrete over Democrat Bruce Sundlun. The latter campaigned, among other things, on ethics and reform of government.

DiPrete won that election narrowly but was overwhelmingly defeated by Sundlun in 1990. Shortly after leaving office DiPrete was indicted on charges of extortion and bribery. By the end of the decade, however, the newsroom versus editorial distinction seems less pronounced and the partisan leanings of the paper appear less obvious.

Polls indicate the direct and indirect influence of the *Journal* on the general public's perceptions of politics. A 1986 poll found that over 70 percent of the population claimed to get a lot or quite a bit of information about politics from the *Journal,* while 58 percent claimed the same for TV.[13] While it is true that more recent polls have shown a reversal (with television pulling ahead), people indicate that they receive most of their information about specific public questions, like the 1984 Greenhouse Compact economic development plan and the work of the 1986 constitutional convention, from the *Journal.* In a statewide poll during the 1998 election period, 61 percent of the respondents claimed they received most of their information about the candidates from newspapers, while only 31 percent claimed they got more information from television.[14]

Certainly the most important influence of the *Journal* relates to its role in setting the political agenda. Any cursory review of the electronic media in the state reveals that television stations essentially "rip and read" political news stories from the *Journal*; they take most of their cues from the morning paper and build their political reporting on them in the evening news. Moreover, the thoroughness with which the *Journal* covers stories and the slant it gives them clearly seems to have retained for the paper its opinion and agenda leadership role, albeit somewhat less directly than in the past. If the *Journal* seizes a major scandal and prints story after story about it, the television news directors have little choice but to follow its lead. One TV producer, speaking about the frenzied reporting around the Fay-Smith supreme court scandal, noted, "I tried for a few days not to lead with the Court story but the *Journal* kept hammering away at it from all angles and the networks just followed suit. I was getting a lot of heat and was afraid I'd get clobbered in the ratings, so I put it back as the lead story." Even when the networks "break" a story and lead with it on the evening news, the coverage it gets in the next day's *Journal* pretty much determines the way the story will play out.

THE CATHOLIC CHURCH

Given the overwhelming Roman Catholic majority in Rhode Island, and the interest the church has had in a number of important political issues over the years, it was bound to become a significant force in politics of the state. The centralized governance structure of the church reinforced its clout, particularly in the 1940s and up through the 1980s. In recent years its political influence has declined due in part to the reforms instituted by the Vatican II Council, and in part for other reasons as well, the church's hold over its own people and politics has weakened considerably.

Catholics were virtually nonexistent in the colony during the eighteenth century; a traveling priest from Boston found only eight participants in a service he held in 1820. The first Catholic church was founded in Newport in 1829. The flood of largely Catholic immigrants into the state during the 1840s brought the Catholic population in Providence, for example, from 1 percent in 1830 to 16 percent in 1850.[15]

This rapid change in the religious composition of the state's population spawned an intense Know-Nothing movement, which was nativist and anti-Catholic. The franchise restrictions discussed earlier in relation to constitutional development doubtless had, among other objectives, the aim of blunting the political influence of the church. Governor William Hoppin, first elected in 1854, was openly sympathetic to the nativist elements. He was overwhelmingly reelected on a joint Whig–Know-Nothing ticket along with Know-Nothing majorities in the General Assembly. As the slavery issue heated up thereafter, and as the Republican party gained strength, Know-Nothing influence rapidly declined.

For some time the Catholic Church did not gain the organizational strength that its numbers would have led one to expect. The Catholic portion of the population was divided ethnically, and various groups had quite different views on parish life. The Irish supported an institutional hierarchy which, being the state's earliest arrivals, they tended to dominate. The French and later the Italians saw "their" church more as a local community affair, and eschewed the traditional organizational structure. Language differences were divisive as well.

By the time the Democrats took over the statehouse with the Green Revolution in 1935, the church had grown in strength. Networks of schools, orphanages, and hospitals were serving the growing Catholic population. With the arrival of the new Democratic political majority, Catholics took over more and more offices from their Yankee predecessors. Well-qualified candidates for office had become plentiful as the sons and daughters of the immigrants had moved up the economic and status ladders. The vehicles for this upward mobility were usually a Catholic education in a parish elementary school, on to one of the many proliferating Catholic high schools, and then to Providence College.

The latter had been founded in 1917 by Dominican fathers. The University of Rhode Island, established in 1892 as the state's land grant institution, displayed blatant anti-Catholic tendencies in its early years. As a result, Providence College became the spawning ground from which Democratic officeholders were recruited and, until the late 1980s, graduates from Providence College represented the largest group among college graduates in the General Assembly. Although precise religious data on General Assembly members are difficult to come by, the overwhelming number of Democrats are clearly Catholic, and up to the 1980s the political influence of the Catholic Church at the statehouse was considerable. The church certainly supported the economic liberalism of the Democratic legislative majorities, which fostered welfare and labor legislation. In turn, the relative conservatism of the Democratic party on social issues paralleled the conservative stance of the church on such issues as abortion and gay rights. The state provided as much support for parochial schools as could be managed constitutionally, within the structures of U.S. Supreme Court rulings, in the form of school bus transportation and textbooks for science and mathematics.[16]

This pattern of church influence began to decline during the 1980s. The impact of Vatican II meant a general internal liberalization of the church, which in turn led to significant changes in the attitudes of Catholics themselves. Mass attendance declined, and more and more Catholics displayed a growing independence in their adherence to church teachings. Poll results have shown, for example, little difference between Catholics and non-Catholics on questions of birth control and abortion.

After extensive debate, the constitutional convention that met in 1986 placed before the voters, among its other proposals, an advisory amendment on the right to life designed to limit abortions as much as possible. The Catholic diocese provided strong support for the amendment; yet, significantly, in a state that remains almost two-thirds Catholic, it was defeated by nearly a two-to-one margin (102,633 for, 197,520 against). With the exceptions of the mill city of Central Falls and the heavily French Canadian city of Woonsocket, the amendment was defeated in every city and town.

In 1995 the General Assembly passed a gay rights bill over the strenuous opposition of the Catholic Church and conservative Protestant groups. This legislation had been before the assembly for a number of years but had failed, usually at the committee level. A majority might have emerged a bit sooner but for very noisy and angry demonstrations in the corridors of the statehouse by pro-gay groups.

In addition to these defeats, the church and other religious groups had to accept two unpalatable federal court decisions that originated in Rhode Island. In 1984 one of the earliest challenges to the constitutionality of a

Christmas crèche on city property was upheld.[17] More recently, a challenge to the inclusion of a nondenominational invocation at public school graduation ceremonies was also upheld by the U.S. Supreme Court. Also damaging to the Catholic Church, and doubtless another factor that has weakened the allegiance and support of many Catholics, have been recent accusations of sexual assaults by priests and jury trials of a number of parish priests in the state.

An attempt in 1992 to terminate district-supported busing for Catholic school children where busing exists for public schools was successfully quashed by parents who rallied for the issue; out of that came a new group called the Rhode Island Catholic School Parents Federation that was formed in 1997 to lobby legislators and policymakers on behalf of the eighteen thousand children who attend parochial schools in the state. Insofar as the primary focus of their efforts is linked to regulatory and economic issues related to the school population, the interests of this group are likely to be successful. In electoral terms, while the overall influence of the church is minimal, in a contested primary among Democrats it can provide a critical margin of support at the local, grassroots parish level for candidates who are perceived as good Catholics and who adhere to the church's official position on issues like abortion and right-to-die questions.

THE MAFIA

There is little hard evidence on which to base a judgment as to the political influence of organized crime in Rhode Island. As noted, Federal Hill in Providence until the 1990s was the central command point for southern New England Mafia's activities. Federal imprisonment of the head of the Patriarca family and other successful federal prosecutions have curtailed its influence. That there long existed, and probably still does to an extent, a substantial underground pattern of mob activity involving book making, loan sharking, protections selling, and the like seems apparent. For the most part state police and prosecutors have left it up to federal authorities to deal with these activities. They in turn have had considerable success in securing mob leader convictions in Rhode Island, Boston, and elsewhere in the region.

It is probably accurate to say that while conspiracy theories about political influence of the Mafia abound, there is little evidence that the mob has directly influenced the course of politics or public policy in the state in any significant way. Links of association probably exist between mob figures and leaders of organized labor, but attempts at lobbying by the former have been limited, indirect, and narrowly focused. The Patriarca family had a vending machine business. Thus, it would not be surprising if, when an increase in the cigarette tax was a prospect, the Mafia joined legitimate business interests in opposition. This, however, is the kind of activity that represents the extent of Mafia influence on the policymaking process.

PUBLIC INTEREST GROUPS

Several public interest groups deserve mention in part because they are of quite recent vintage, but also because they illustrate the impact focused group activity can have on the policymaking process. They also illustrate new concerns that are becoming important to Rhode Island voters.

Save the Bay was formed as the first major environmental organization in the state. It was created to fight the construction of an oil refinery at Tiverton, on the upper east side of Narragansett Bay. The group succeeded in its immediate aim and has remained a vigorous advocate for measures to clean up and make widely available for public use this vital and beautiful state asset. As of 1998 the telephone yellow pages list no less than nine organizations under the heading of "Environmental, Conservation, and Ecological." Prominent and vocal among these are the Audubon Society, Clean Water Action, the Environmental Council of Rhode Island, and the Sierra Club.

These groups have worked hard and successfully to deal with pollution of the bay from urban sewage systems and industrial enterprises. Often they work along parallel lines with organized groups of commercial fishermen of various kinds. Issues related to proposed channel deepening by dredging, for example, find a confluence of interests involved. Dredging disturbs shellfishing beds and also poses problems relating to the disposal of dredged material, which can blanket fishing areas and lessen or destroy their productivity.

In 1998 a major bay issue arose which mobilized all of the environmental and fishing groups. A large abandoned naval air station at Quonset Point on the bay contained air strips and dockage areas that had been dredged to accommodate aircraft carriers. When the facility reverted to the state it became the subject of various economic development proposals. The most ambitious was a scheme to fill some five hundred acres of the bay to secure more land space to accommodate the largest container and other ships designed to transport large numbers of new cars for distribution to dealers.

Not surprisingly, the idea of a five hundred-acre fill caused loud outcries. The resulting clash between environmental protection and economic development dramatized what likely will continue to be a chronic source of political conflict in the state. It was not long before Governor Almond back-peddled on the project, promised no filling of bay acreage, and also undertook to set up a formal machinery, known as the "stakeholders" process, to give environmental interests a seat at the table as plans for Quonset development were reworked and refined. Polls have shown that a large majority of Rhode Islanders are in favor of environmental protection, but the vocal groups probably represent a relatively small number of citizens who are truly active in this cause. Nonetheless and particularly in good economic times, the stakeholders give environmental and fishing interests considerable leverage to limit, and perhaps even thwart, plans for the redevelopment of the Quonset Point area.

Another cluster of public interest entities that have flourished over the past decade are devoted to good-government causes and bent on fighting corruption, promoting and enforcing codes of ethics for public officials, and pushing for structural reform that promotes these objectives. The archetypal and, to an extent, umbrella organization in this sphere of concern is Common Cause of Rhode Island. This group, in conjunction with other reform groups like Operation Clean Government, became very visible during the scandals of the late 1980s and very successful in promoting reforms. The resignation of two chief justices, the pattern of improper exploitation of the state pension system, and the collapse of the credit unions have certainly fueled the reform drive. Building on this momentum these groups have played a significant role in promoting the structural changes that included amending the constitution to provide for a powerful ethics commission, revamping the selection system for state judges, and eliminating pension abuses. Presently they are involved in pushing for an extension of the open-records law.

One concern is that these groups became "politicized" insofar as they were vocal and ardent supporters of an effort by the governor to prevent legislators from sitting on state regulatory boards and commissions, and making appointments to these entities. This battle was essentially less about ethics or reform and more about shifting power from the legislature to the executive. The extent to which they became embroiled in a power struggle between two branches of government may have somewhat marginalized their credibility for the future.

One unique public interest group that has long functioned in Rhode Island and has the respect of groups across the political spectrum is the Rhode Island Public Expenditure Council (RIPEC), a business-backed study and advocacy group. The focus and orientation of this group goes far beyond the narrow concerns of taxes and spending that one traditionally tends to associate with business-backed groups. RIPEC has been at the forefront in promoting state aid to education, urban renewal projects, property tax relief based on need, housing and infrastructure improvements, as well as debt reduction and economic development. As a result, it has done much to strengthen the structure and policy orientation of state government. Thanks largely to its long-time and highly respected executive director, Gary Sasse, it has conducted studies as an outside critic and been a source of expertise; it has also at times been called upon by government to do research and provide assistance for various policy issues and initiatives. It is nonpartisan, neither liberal nor conservative, and genuinely bent on serving the public interest.

In summary, the pattern of interest group activity in Rhode Island is rich and varied. It contains both highly organized groups and broad segments of the population that share common feelings. The reformers of the 1990s insisted that the system was too closed and inaccessible and had to be opened up. The impact various interest groups have may well indicate that the system is actually quite open and permeable to those seeking access to policymaking. The small size and compactness of the state and a single major newspaper have the effect of making information relatively easy to acquire and putting public persons and offices within easy reach. Many citizens know their legislators personally or live but a few streets from them. Perhaps the paradox is that Rhode Islanders are so close to their governmental system that its flaws loom a bit larger than they would in a typical large state.

CHAPTER TEN

Budget Politics and Policy

If he [the governor] wants authorization for specific [spending] reasons, he should come to the legislature; the legislature will either give him that authorization or give him an explanation as to why not.

> Antonio J. Pires, Chair, House Finance Committee, 1996

Follow the money.

> Political strategist, 1998

We'll reconvene the House tomorrow for our veto-override party.

House Majority Leader George Caroulo, during the 1996 budget negotiations

Exploring the politics of taxing and spending provides a perspective from which one can assess the enduring as well as emerging priorities and policy choices that face state leaders as Rhode Island moves into the twenty-first century.[1] A strong tradition of support for programs that protect the interests of poor and working-class constituencies continues to be evident in policy debates. Emerging priorities, however, reflect a need to hold the line on taxes, invest in programs linked to expanding the economy, and achieve higher levels of efficiency and accountability in state and local government.

Viewing the process through the lens of the annual machinations over the budget gives additional insight into the institutional and political rivalries that have developed over the past decade. It also brings into focus the institutional, political, and economic forces that set the parameters of the debate, allowing one to evaluate the role of the key players who ultimately determine fiscal policy in the Ocean State.

The state constitution charges the governor to "prepare and present to the general assembly an annual, consolidated operating and capital improvement state budget."[2] However, the legislature, most particularly the house, enjoys considerable constitutional and statutory authority over the process and, depending on the political circumstances, the house leadership can exercise enormous influence in setting fiscal policy. Absent unusual conditions, the governor, who can garner public and press support, takes the lead, strikes deals with legislative leaders, and forges a general agreement. Generally, by the time the budget package reaches the floors of the assembly, debate, although increasingly long-winded and contentious (given the tight constraints of the recent past), is largely *pro forma*. Legislators ultimately endorse the agreements made by legislative leaders, finance-committee chairs, and the governor. Increasingly, though, the legislature has taken to flexing its constitutional and political muscle in dominating the process.

HISTORY OF BUDGET POLITICS

Prior to 1935 the governor played only a marginal role in fiscal policy. Under the authority granted to it in the 1843 constitution, the assembly mandated by statute that the state's elected general treasurer compile a budget and present it for approval to the General Assembly. In 1926 the Republicans, realizing that their time was running out in statewide elections, created a powerful state commissioner of finance under the authority of the General Assembly.[3] The commissioner was charged with preparing an annual appropriations bill and presenting it to the assembly. The commissioner was also to transmit a copy of this bill to the governor, who then had ten days to comment on it to the General Assembly. In addition to the power of the veto over final appropriations, these were the extent of the governor's influence on the budget process.

After the Green Revolution in 1935 the Democrats, more amenable to gubernatorial participation, abolished the finance commissioner's office, gave the governor a budget director and staff, and created an executive budget system. The governor, therefore, originates the budget, submitting it first to the house and then to the senate for amendment and passage. Given that the governor does not have a line-item veto, he or she can either sign the final budget package into law or veto the entire package and face the prospect of a legislative override by a three-fifths vote.

The system worked fairly well as the Democrats supported liberal welfare policies for the poor, better wages and working conditions for union members, and generous benefits and working conditions for expanding and expensive state and municipal bureaucracies. To pay the bills taxes were raised, and in 1971 the state was forced to initiate an income tax linked to the federal tax code.[4] Taxes continued to escalate until the boom of the early 1980s. During most of the administration of Republican Edward DiPrete (1984–1990), the state's economy was fairly prosperous. As a result, the annual revenue from state taxes tended to grow without concurrent tax increases. This made budget-making relatively easy, and agreement between the executive and the legislative branches was achieved without much difficulty. Most often, new initiatives by the governor were accepted by the legislative leadership in exchange for his acceptance of programs they proposed. On some occasions the assembly prepared its set of initiatives as their own legislative program to join the governor's program on the budget agenda.

By the beginning of the 1990s the state was in the midst of a deep recession. The costs of a liberal social welfare tradition, an expensive public sector workforce, and the loss of federal defense projects came home to roost during a period when the regional economy and most particularly Rhode Island's had stagnated.[5] By 1994 other parts of the country were on the road to economic recovery, but New England and Rhode Island remained fiscally distressed as manufacturing operations continued either to close or to move south, and the service sectors of the economy were still emerging.

When Bruce Sundlun succeeded Edward DiPrete in 1991, in addition to the economic downturn he inherited a large unanticipated deficit. Hence, cutting rather than innovating became the order of the day as revenues leveled off and actually declined. It was during this grim economic cycle that the credit unions failed. Their failure forced the newly elected governor to temporarily raise the income tax from 22.96 to 27.5 percent of federal liability. He also had to dedicate a fixed portion of the sales tax proceeds to the Depositors Economic Protection Corporation (DEPCO) in order to defease the debt the state had incurred in paying back the more than three hundred thousand depositors who had lost their savings when the credit unions failed. That same year Sundlun was also forced to reduce state aid to education, reversing a trend whereby the state had been moving toward assuming a greater share of spending for local education. This, in turn, caused increases in local property taxes.

These rather desperate events created an extremely cooperative working relationship between the legislature and the governor during the first few budget cycles of Sundlun's administration (1991–1994). The governor provided decisive, albeit tough, fiscal proposals, and legislative leaders and the rest of the members were relieved to go along with the proposed solutions. Legislators let the governor take the lead, the light, and the heat in resolving the crisis—getting the legislators, many of whom who did not run for reelection, off the hook.

Table 13: Tax Effort and Tax Capacity in New England States

State	Tax Effort	Rank	Tax Capacity	Rank
Connecticut	99%	17	130%	4
Maine	102%	10	95%	23
Massachusetts	101%	12	117%	8
New Hampshire	84%	42	110%	10
Rhode Island	**115%**	**4**	**89%**	**37**
Vermont	97%	20	105%	14

Source: Kendra and Harold Hovey, *State Fact Finder, 1998*, Congressional Quarterly Press.

As expenses escalated and economic growth stagnated, the state maxed out on taxes insofar as the existing structure was widely perceived as detrimental to expanding the economy. Looking beyond simple national rankings, standard national measures that attempt to indicate the capacity or ability of states to generate tax revenue confirms this view. As table 13 indicates, the state's tax capacity—that is, the ability of the state to raise revenue based on a national average of 100 percent—remained the lowest in New England and was thirty-seventh in the nation. In contrast to capacity, the state's tax effort was the highest in New England and fourth highest in the country. Another standard measure, fiscal "comfort," which looks at the relationship between fiscal capacity and need, found Rhode Island ranked below the mean comfort line.[6]

Thus, the major goals of fiscal policy were reducing taxes and debt, creating tax incentives for economic development, and continuing to provide for the social and educational needs of the population.[7] This made for some tough political choices and political jockeying as political elites attempted to implement workable fiscal policies.

TAXING AND SPENDING IN RHODE ISLAND

During the past decade there have been attempts to assess and reform the state's tax structure. In 1993, at the direction of the General Assembly, the administration completed a major analysis of the state tax structure.[8] The study concluded that Rhode Island has a relatively balanced tax system based on its predominant use of sales, income, and property taxes. It noted that the total state-local tax burden was higher than the national average when measured on a per capita basis and as a percentage of personal income. It concluded that reliance on the personal income tax was close to the national

Table 14: Major State and Local Taxes in Rhode Island

	Per Capita			Per $1,000 of Income		
	Amount	R	Index	Amount	R	Index
Individual Income Taxes						
United States	$495		100.0%	$24.03		100.0%
New England						
Maine	496	24	100.2%	26.41	18	109.9%
New Hampshire	32	42	6.4%	1.44	42	6.0%
Vermont	493	25	99.7%	25.56	21	106.4%
Massachusetts	942	3	190.4%	38.67	4	160.9%
Rhode Island	**530**	**19**	**107.1%**	**24.91**	**25**	**103.6%**
Connecticut	683	9	138.0%	24.41	27	101.6%
Property Taxes						
United States	$757		100.0%	$36.78		100.0%
New England						
Maine	945	12	124.8%	50.35	6	136.9%
New Hampshire	1,442	2	190.5%	65.74	1	178.7%
Vermont	1,052	6	138.9%	54.50	3	148.2%
Massachusetts	985	10	130.0%	40.43	18	109.9%
Rhode Island	**1,052**	**7**	**138.9%**	**49.45**	**8**	**134.4%**
Connecticut	1,337	3	176.6%	47.80	11	129.9%
General Sales and Gross Receipts Taxes						
United States	$572		100.0%	$27.81		100.0%
New England						
Maine	498	28	86.9%	26.51	29	95.3%
New Hampshire	—	—	—	—	—	—
Vermont	303	45	53.0%	15.72	43	56.5%
Massachusetts	381	42	66.6%	15.65	44	56.3%
Rhode Island	**414**	**39**	**72.3%**	**19.47**	**40**	**70.0%**
Connecticut	667	9	116.5%	23.84	35	85.7%

Source: Census Bureau data as cited in *Tax and Spending Data Book: How Rhode Island Compares*, Rhode Island Public Expenditure Council, 1997.

average, reliance on the property tax was above average, and reliance on the sales tax was somewhat below average. The overall structure was found to be somewhat regressive. While the income tax is highly progressive, the analysis showed that sales and property tax incidences are regressive.

Looking at straight comparisons, table 14 supports these evaluations. It outlines the overall tax structure in Rhode Island, and compares taxes in the Ocean State to the fifty-state average and to other New England states. In Rhode Island the individual income tax falls in the middle range for the country; it nearly equals the national average and is the third highest in New England. Individual income taxes, however, are calculated as a piggyback percentage of federal tax payments. Although the effective tax rate is at the national average, the actual rate is defined as 27.5 percent of federal tax liability, which makes Rhode Island appear to have the highest tax *rate* in the country. (Most states tie the tax rate to a percentage of adjusted gross income.) Beginning in 1998, the rate has been reduced a half percentage point per year to 25 percent of the federal tax, addressing the complaint that this provision discouraged high-end executives from relocating in the state.

Nonetheless, as long as the tax structure is calculated on the basis of an already progressive federal tax, individuals who earn over $200,000 a year (about one percent of the population) continue to pay a hefty additional amount. Taking advantage of flush economic times, a group of high-powered executives sought relief from the legislature in 1999, arguing that the change would affect fewer than five thousand taxpayers and bring more executives into the state. But political leaders, acknowledging that it was something of a perception issue in this "working-class" state, are unlikely to pass such specific legislation. The most likely solution is a complete overhaul of the state tax system that would uncouple the state structure from the federal system and provide for a flat rate of between five and six percent of income (as is the case in Massachusetts and Connecticut). That change, however, is off in the future.[9]

In terms of the sales tax, the state has one of the highest *rates* in the country at 7 percent. The tax, however, is applied to many fewer items than in most other states, lessening the comparative effective tax burden. Food, clothing, prescription and patent medicines, and most services are exempt. This selectivity reduces the tax burden on individuals and creates a ranking for Rhode Island that is fortieth in the country and third lowest in New England.

Administration initiatives that were promoted early in the decade to broaden the tax base by removing exemptions and applying the sales tax to services have not advanced. The issue of taxation of services is a serious one facing all states. As the United States has moved from a goods-consuming to a service-consuming economy (a trend since the end of World War II), the portion of consumption that is subject to state and local sales taxes has decreased. Additionally, court decisions and the growth of internet sales further exacerbates the problem of the shrinking tax base. The U.S. Supreme Court ruled that states and local governments cannot force mail order retailers to collect and remit sales taxes on goods sold to residents of states in which the retailer did not have a physical nexus. While state and local governments have sought relief from the U.S. Congress for over fifteen years, relief has been stymied by large mail order retailers and by disagreements between state and local governments about how to collect local sales taxes.

Internet sales pose a similar problem for the sales tax base, and Congress has placed a moratorium on individual state taxation of the internet. A leading economic forecasting firm recently predicted that internet retailing would make up four percent of non-auto retail sales by 2003, which would be roughly 1.2 percent of Rhode Island's total sales tax revenues.

Property taxes are the critical issue in the state; they raise problems regarding general equity and have profound implications for quality and equity in education because a significant portion of local property taxes goes to fund public school education (see chapter 11). As table 14 indicates, property taxes are generally high in New England because of a strong tradition of local control. But the combined impact of income taxes and property taxes, given the rate of all taxes and the capacity of these states to produce revenue, puts Rhode Island at the highest tax effort in New England. Thus a critical issue state leaders faced from 1994 on was to reduce taxes to ensure long-term growth and stability as the state pulled out of its recession.

In an effort to give local communities some property tax relief, the 1998 General Assembly grappled with the property tax issue through a number of measures that substitute state general-tax revenues for local property taxes. The single largest measure is the seven-year phaseout of the motor vehicle excise tax. The law mandates that local governments freeze the tax rates at FY 1999 levels and provide increased levels of exemptions until the tax is eliminated in FY 2006. The state in turn will reimburse communities for both the lost property tax revenues resulting from the exemptions and the frozen tax rates. The final impact will be the substitution of $195.4 million of state general tax revenues (in 1998 constant dollars) for local property taxes.

A second measure adopted by the 1998 assembly provides for a ten-year phaseout of local inventory taxes, with local governments receiving increased state general revenue sharing to compensate for the loss. The state would move from providing 1 percent of state tax revenue to 4.7 percent. This would substitute $69 million (in 1998 constant dollars) for local property taxes.

During that same legislative session the state increased the portion of the $1.40 per $500 paid for the purchase of property that is retained by local governments from 25 cents to $1.10. This change had the impact of providing an additional $5 million to local governments.

Table 15: Sources of Revenue in Rhode Island, FY 2000

All Funds	FY 2000
Federal Grants	$1,356.9
Personal Income Tax	787.5
Sales Tax	649.1
Other General Revenues	627.5
University & College Funds	315.1
Employment & Training Funds	274.7
Lottery	146.4
Gas Tax Revenues	129.9
Restricted Receipts	83.9
Other Funds	56.9
Total	$4,427.9 billion

Source: Budget as Enacted, Executive Summary, State of Rhode Island.

Note: Figures based on 1999 budget estimates.

Table 15 and table 16 give a broad picture of the revenues and expenditures from all sources in Rhode Island in the post-recession years. Total estimated revenues for fiscal year 2000 were just over $4 billion, with about $2.5 billion derived from general revenues (as contrasted with federal funds, restricted receipts, and other sources). Sources of general revenues have remained fairly stable during the recent past. In 1994, for example, the income tax, the largest single source of general revenues, represented 37 percent of general revenues, while for the year 2000 it represented approximately 36.3 percent of monies the state took in. Likewise, sales and use taxes constituted 36 percent of general revenues in 1994 and 38.5 percent in the year 2000. One growth area is in lottery funds: in 1995 lotteries brought in $45.6 million dollars, in 1997, $96 million, and in 2000, $146 million, which now represents 3.3 percent of total revenues. This is especially significant in light of the debate about allowing casino gambling run by the state's Native American populations. The idea that Rhode Islanders do not approve of gambling becomes a bit strained in light of the escalation of these revenues.

As to how revenues are spent, table 16 indicates 2000 spending by category from all funds and from general revenues. Human services and education represent the largest categories from both federal and general revenue funds. Human services include all programs for medical assistance, supplemental social security, cash assistance, daycare, elderly services, youth, and mental health; expenditures for education include elementary and secondary programs as well as public higher education. Spending for these have remained

Table 16: Spending from All Funds and General Revenues, 2000

	All Funds	General Revenues
Human Services	1,734.1	807.6
Education	1,200.4	776.8
General Government	879.4	352.5
Transportation	297.2	—
Public Safety	276.2	236.5
Natural Resources	73.9	33.9

Source: Budget as Enacted, State of Rhode Island, 1999.

fairly stable over the past decade. Spending from general revenues for human services was 36 percent of the budget in 1989, 38 percent in 1994, and 37 percent in 2000. Education spending took a slight dip during those years, going from 36 percent in 1989, to 37 percent in 1994, to 35 percent in 2000. In terms of all expenditures for 2000 (including federal funds), spending for human services represented 38.9 percent of spending, education accounted for 26.9 percent of spending, general government was 19.7, and public safety and natural resources were 6.2 percent and 1.6 percent, respectively, of the budget. Transportation spending, which essentially is a federally funded enterprise, represented 6.7 percent of expenditures from all funds. Public safety spending (which supports about 85 percent of public safety programs) accounted for 11 percent of general revenue expenditures. Beyond these very broad categories of expenditures, many of which are dedicated through federal funds, budgetary politics is found in the details on which programs do or do not make the cut at budget negotiation time.

BUDGET POLITICS IN THE 1990S

The budget process at the turn of the twenty-first century provides a fascinating picture of the politics and priorities of a state coping with federal mandates, more responsibility for programs like welfare and health care for the poor and elderly, and long-term systemic problems in taxing and spending. The nature of political coalitions, rooted in an individualistic culture that sees politics in terms of group gains, and the structure of government institutions, which gives a particularly strong hand to a constituent-based legislature, can make for particularly difficult negotiations at budget time as well as a quotient of comic relief.

It also results in the politics of delay as sessions of this part-time non-professional legislature drag on into the summer. During the 1990s sessions often extended well into July, and the end of the 1995 session was the latest to date in Rhode Island history. Delay is itself a tactic the leadership employs as it attempts to create a sense of urgency whereby the legislature, after a bit of posturing, is pressed to go along with a deal. As one seasoned legislative leader observed, after we've "indulged everyone's mania for delay, analysis, and reflection" it finally becomes time to approve the budget. The July heat also adds to the urgency. Another long-time participant observed, "Long ago, I advised the leadership *never* to air-condition the senate or house chambers or we'd never get out of here."

Beneath the surface, however, the budget process is hardball politics requiring strong leadership from both the executive and the legislature. Since the beginning of the administration of Republican Lincoln Almond (1995–2002), the influence of the executive appears to have diminished considerably. New and particularly savvy leadership came to power in the house in 1992 and these leaders, together with capable and respected finance chairs in both houses, tend to dominate the budget process. The governor does not have a particularly strong constitutional hand over the budget, and in 1996 the legislature passed statutory changes that further limited the governor's fiscal authority.

The professionalization that is becoming evident in other aspects of state government also manifests itself in the budget process. Since 1990 a Consensus Review Estimating Committee, composed of the governor's budget officer and the senate and house fiscal advisors, is required to meet in November and May to provide revenue estimates that inform the budget for the upcoming fiscal year. Votes are not taken and the committee must, in sometimes heated sessions, ultimately agree on its forecast. The committee's fiscal staff is increasingly knowledgeable and, if knowledge is power, these experts play an important role in increasing the ability of the respective institutions and the legislative leadership (particularly in the house) to influence policy.[10]

In addition, the assembly enacted a "rainy-day fund" in the early part of the decade and placed it on the ballot to be added to the constitution. The fund maintains a balance equal to three percent of general fund revenues; it is funded annually by two percent of annual revenues. When the fund reaches three percent the excess is transferred to a capital improvements account. This, in conjunction with a statutory balanced budget provision and a constitutionally mandated provision that most deficit borrowing must be approved by the voters, provides the framework for crafting the budget.

As a newly elected Republican governor and the first chief executive to serve a four-year term, in 1995 Almond experienced rocky encounters with the Democratic legislature and generally came up short. While the state was still grappling with shortfalls he proposed a budget designed to cut some expenditures and provide funds for economic growth. Revised budget estimates, however, projected a larger deficit. In response the governor proposed major cuts in pensions and benefits for state and municipal workers. There were political and constitutional problems with his proposal. Politically the idea of such a major and contentious reform—almost as an afterthought—took away from the proposal's credibility. The constitutional glitch was that the plan was to apply retroactively to workers already in the system. This created a firestorm of protest from representatives of the public service unions who work the halls of the legislature daily and threatened to seek remedy in the courts. Workers from the private sector, however, were in no mood to tolerate increased taxes. They overwhelmingly supported various proposals to trim state workers' salaries and benefits, particularly those at the high end of the scale.[11]

The legislature countered with an offer to table the pension reform plan until it could be studied carefully. The General Assembly instead sought to raise the state's public employee pension contribution by one percent, to make no cuts in programs, and to make up the deficit difference with one-time revenue sources and new gambling revenues. After long nights of negotiating with legislative leaders, the governor agreed to their package. No one was satisfied. Business and reform groups criticized the governor and the legislature for missing the opportunity to effect structural change. The media and the public at large criticized the governor for a lack of leadership. The unions howled that the budget was being balanced on the backs of state employees (who essentially got a good deal because an annual 3 percent compound increase in place essentially realized a 2 percent gain). Reform groups complained that the budget process continued to rely on one-time scrambles to close the budget gap rather than on developing stable expenditures in line with revenues.

The political reality was that legislative leaders held veto-proof majorities. Unless the governor could strike a deal beforehand, he had to be prepared to veto their budget and face an override, which is exactly what happened the following year.

The debate that structured budget talks in 1996 was again the need to downsize state government and cut spending. The centerpiece of Governor Almond's budget was an ambitious early retirement plan that would have encouraged retirement for about forty-eight hundred state workers, a doubling of the hospital tax, and reductions in spending for local education. The legislature's response was to "just say no." They argued that a similar retirement plan initiated in the 1980s was a fiscal disaster and that a more prudent course of action would be through attrition-driven downsizing.[12] After extended negotiations the governor refused to concede, and the legislature submitted and passed its own budget which raised no taxes, sustained social services, and implemented a plan of state workforce reduction through attrition. In addition it raised, albeit by small margins, spending for all the state's school districts. For the first time in Rhode Island's history the governor vetoed the budget, and the legislature overrode the veto the very next day.

The legislative-executive confrontation over dollars and programs did not stop there but quickly escalated into a tug of war over the distribution of power between the two branches. As noted previously, over the years the legislature had acquiesced to the development of an executive budget system. A number of factors probably contributed to the 1996 effort by the General Assembly to recapture some of its budgetary authority. The immediate motive was no doubt to counter the threat represented by a Republican governor bent on major government shrinking of cherished Democratic programs. Moreover, the governor in question was at the middle of a four-year term. He would not have to face the voters until 1998, whereas the legislature was up for election a few months later. One wonders, too, if there was not some memory of the happy DiPrete days when legislators could propose and adopt their own policy initiatives instead of contemplating painful cuts.

Whatever the reasons, the legislature decided to tighten the reins and assert its budgetary authority. While the governor does not have a line-item veto, previous statutes had allowed the chief executive to move funds within fairly broad allocations and to defer spending under certain circumstances. This authority was rescinded insofar as when the budget package finally became law, new checks on budget implementation were part of the package.

In two separate pieces of legislation the assembly sought to place further restrictions on the governor's budget authority by repealing his ability to suspend appropriations for budget-balancing purposes and to tap a reserve fund to deal with revenue shortfalls. The two proposed changes were obviously intended to ensure the legislature's input in these initiatives. The governor vetoed both bills. Although the votes were certainly available to do so, the leadership decided not to attempt an override.

One inside observer noted that the overall purpose of these actions was to send a message to the governor that even though the legislative leadership realized they could not "micromanage the budget process," they wanted to communicate to the executive that the legislature still had plenary power over budgetary matters.

The budget process for 1997 was less contentious, and it put in place some innovative tax-credit programs to lure business and encourage economic development. By 1998 the state faced the happy prospect of a projected budget surplus for 1999. Nonetheless, the partisan and institutional jockeying continued. The governor, who was facing reelection, proposed several spending projects including using projected surpluses from DEPCO collections to implement a one-time five-year property tax rebate. Again, the Democratic legislature—looking more like tightfisted conservatives—refused.[13] The powerful house finance committee chair, Antonio Pires, argued that DEPCO funds should be used to defease the debt as soon as possible and that property tax relief should be part of long-term systemic change.

As estimates of a budget surplus for 1999 increased, the legislature rejected the governor's key budget proposals and passed its own, which the governor signed. The legislative package included the provisions, discussed above, to phase out hefty local auto taxes over seven years, to eliminate a burdensome business-inventory tax over the next ten years, and to provide local property tax relief.[14] It also included increased spending for urban schools and a large increase in an innovative health insurance program for the working poor. The legislature rejected other key spending proposals from the governor, prompting one expert on Rhode Island politics to comment, "It is extraordinary that, given the large surplus, the Assembly Democrats are cutting taxes and paying down debt. . . . These are Republican principles."[15] The political dynamic during the summer of 1999, which set the framework for the FY 2000 and FY 2001 budget was much the same: while the legislature gave significant consideration to Governor Almond's proposals, in the end the governor accepted a budget that reflected legislative priorities.

But budget politics is less about Republican and Democratic ideology and more about institutional and leadership differences. As noted in chapter 8, when it comes to ideology and issues the political parties in Rhode Island over the past decade have moved closer together. Democrats are no longer the supporters of big spending and big government. Republicans in Rhode Island, and in New England generally, represent the older, more progressive and moderate wing of the national party that has been eclipsed by more conservative, hard-line GOP leaders primarily from the South. In the recent past the legislative budget agenda has reflected a relatively prudent, long-term approach less tied to partisan politics. Given the constitutional and partisan clout of the General Assembly, it will take particularly strong leadership from the executive to get into the game, let alone dominate it. Whether a different executive leader will change this dynamic remains to be seen.

ISSUES DOWN THE ROAD

In the short term the most significant issues facing the state revolve around meeting the existing debt obligations and sustaining entitlements—most of which relate to social welfare programs and to education—in light of recent tax-cutting efforts. Rhode Island maintains strong support for its poor and working-class constituents. Expanded medical assistance programs (like RIte Care and discount prescription programs for seniors), and food stamps for legal immigrants will require continued hefty outlays. For example, in 1998 the Rhode Island Public Expenditure Council (RIPEC) estimated that because the state expanded medical insurance coverage for all children up to age eighteen in families with incomes less that 250 percent of the poverty level, three-fourths of the children who were eligible were not yet enrolled.[16] Their concern was well placed: by the year 2000 enrollments soared (due, to some extent, on some clients "gaming the system" by dropping their available private insurance and signing on to the public system). These additional enrollments, as well as projections of future enrollments, resulted in budget estimating projections that would have absorbed much of the surplus and pushed the state toward a deficit in a few years. A stakeholder committee was formed and adjustments were made in the program that it is hoped will continue to serve the needy and remain within the bounds of budget realities.

Several other long-term issues loom on the horizon if the state is to "manage prosperity" and provide for any slowdowns in the economy.[17] Clearly one of the most significant fiscal problems is restructuring the property tax system, providing "guaranteed, sustainable property tax relief" while continuing to address school financing reform.[18] As noted in chapter 11, a logical strategy would be for the state to assume a greater share of funding for local education, thereby relieving the stress on the property tax and allowing the state to equalize spending for local education, especially in poorer urban communities. This challenge also includes creating a tax structure that provides more property tax stabilization through noneducation revenue-sharing programs, especially in communities where tax-exempt, nonprofit institutions diminish the property tax base. The state also needs to play a larger role in linking state aid to tighter accounting and spending controls at the local level, and to encourage need-based property tax relief to individuals like the elderly and others with the greatest needs.

As detailed by RIPEC's report, the state also must assume a larger role in assisting "fiscally distressed" urban areas where a number of factors warrant targeted state aid. RIPEC argues that an urban strategy must include not only education and property tax relief in these areas but also programs that encourage stronger neighborhoods, home ownership programs, job-training initiatives, and urban incubator centers for small business. Tackling these problems will require not only additional money but also the political will to buck the issue of local control (see chapter 12), and convince a legislature that is dominated by suburban representatives, that urban strategies are high budget priorities. Other budget priorities related to the urban-suburban split center on underwriting and expanding mass transit, mostly in the form of bus transportation, to facilitate transportation for an expanding workforce while stemming continued congestion and parking problems evident in downtown Providence.

The good news is that in a state like Rhode Island, a little change can go along way. In this small state moderate restructuring and reform coupled with some imaginative economic development projects could enhance the economy and lessen the political strain at budget time. It appears that key interest groups have come to understand that certain reforms are not only inevitable but also necessary for economic growth. For example, an unusual alliance in 1998 between business and labor produced reforms in the unemployment compensation system that reduced unemployment tax costs to employers of up to 30 percent. The effect will be to save companies millions in unemployment taxes and lower the rate in Rhode Island— which once was the highest in New England.[19] Such adjustments can have a significant impact on the economic climate and tax revenues in the future. In this sense the advantage a small state has is that committed leadership can make a difference; skilled leaders can command political attention, forge compromise, and build public support for innovative and responsible fiscal choices that would keep the state heading in the right direction.

CHAPTER ELEVEN

The Politics of Education

[I]t shall be the duty of the general assembly to promote public schools and public libraries, and to adopt all means which it may deem necessary and proper to secure to the people the advantages and opportunities of education and public library services.

Article XII, section 1, Rhode Island Constitution

I don't blame the teachers and the teachers unions for all the wrongs in the public schools. . . . I do blame them for refusing to be part of the solution.

House Majority Leader George Caroulo, during a 1998 floor debate on charter schools

Elementary and secondary education is a vital service.[1] Though most education concerns have traditionally focused on local communities, as the link between the quality of public education and a growing technological economy becomes clearer, policymakers, educators, and politicians statewide are working toward reform. Education policy is one of the critical issues facing the state, and the intersection between state and local politics make it an ideal policy case.

The core issues relate to promoting a quality education for all public school students, grappling with the escalating costs of public education, and monitoring problems related to education standards and performance. Significant obstacles include an over-reliance on local property taxes for funding, bureaucratic inertia related to the strong Rhode Island tradition of local control and accountability, and personnel and policy mandates promoted by the powerful teachers unions. Reforms initiated in the late 1990s, however, suggest that policies and priorities—increasingly mandated by state government—have the potential to produce a more effective system.

Table 17: Comparative Enrollments in Rhode Island, FY 1995

New England	High School Diploma	State Rank	Private School Enrollment	State Rank
Connecticut	85.3	17	12.4	12
Maine	84.7	20	7.3	33
Massachusetts	84.9	18	12.6	11
New Hampshire	85.4	15	9.0	22
Rhode Island	**78.6**	**39**	**13.7**	**8**
Vermont	86.9	12	8.1	26
US Average	81.7		10.0	

Source: Kendra and Harold Hover, *State Fact Finder, 1998: Rankings across America*, Congressional Quarterly Press.

Note: FY 1995.

Rhode Island's primary and secondary public school system consists of thirty-six districts with four hundred schools and a student population of about 154,000 pupils serviced by just over 11,000 full-time teachers.[2] Looking at the general education picture indicates the legacy of a strong tradition of local support and control in a working-class state with a large Catholic and ethnically diverse population.

Cultural and demographic factors influence the general picture of education in the state. Reflecting long-standing traditions in New England, where local support and control of education is the norm, about 55 percent of spending for primary and secondary education is funded by local taxpayers. Rhode Island ranks twelfth in the nation in terms of local as opposed to state support for education, in a region where all six New England states are well above the national average for the same. The working-class roots of the population manifest themselves insofar as the percentage of the population over twenty-five with a high school diploma is just under 80 percent. In this regard Rhode Island resembles a southern state in that it ranks thirty-ninth in the country.[3] The state is eighth highest in the nation in terms of private school enrollments because more than 13 percent of the school-age population attends either private schools or a network of Catholic parochial schools.

In the broadest sense spending per se is not the issue; Rhode Island spends over a third of its general revenues in support of public education. By national standards and among the New England states—where support for education has always been strong—funding for primary and secondary education is generous. As noted in table 18, spending per pupil in Rhode Island is the

Table 18: Per Pupil Spending, Teacher Salary and Student-Teacher Ratio

New England	Spending Per Pupil	State Rank	Teacher Salary*	State Rank	Public Teacher-Pupil Ratio**	State Rank
Connecticut	$8,376	4	50,426	2	14.4	4
Maine	6,369	14	33,800	30	13.8	1
Massachusetts	7,069	7	43,806	7	14.8	9
New Hampshire	5,974	16	36,867	21	15.6	17
Rhode Island	**7,284**	**5**	**43,019**	**9**	**14.7**	**8**
Vermont	6,503	13	37,200	20	13.8	1
U.S. Average	5,885		38,509		17.3	

Source: Kendra and Harold Hover, *State Fact Finder, 1998: Rankings across America*, Congressional Quarterly Press.

* FY 1997.

** FY 1994.

fifth highest in the country. Among New England states it ranks second only to Connecticut, with per pupil spending at $7,284. Average teacher salaries rank ninth highest among all the states in actual dollars and are sixteenth highest when adjusted by the cost of living index.[4] The state also scores extremely well on teacher-student ratios, which are eighth highest in the nation.

Most of the critical debates in education relate to the distribution of funds and performance standards. Although statewide averages are generous, severe disparities exist in where, how, and on whom monies are spent. As is the case in many other states, to the extent that funding for education is locally based, per pupil spending varies by community. Poorer communities have a smaller tax base. They also tend to have greater expenditure demands insofar as these schools have less-educated populations, high minority and non-English-speaking enrollments, and more students with special needs.

The other particularly contentious issue related to education expenditures concerns return on investment. Despite the considerable money spent on education, performance scores on national tests at the elementary level are disappointing, and it is generally conceded that Rhode Island's performance is wanting. At the secondary level, while high school teachers are among the highest paid in the nation, the state consistently ranks below the national average on SAT scores. Even allowing that the statewide averages mask concentrations of low-income students having demographic and socioeconomic factors that create disparities, studies that control for these factors indicate that the state should be doing better.[5]

Public education had its beginnings in Rhode Island in 1640 in Newport, where it is thought that the first public school in English colonial America was established.[6] By 1800 the General Assembly had enacted "An Act to Establish Free Schools," but it was not until 1828 that the assembly appropriated $10,000 to fund a public school system and empowered local governments to raise money for public schools through taxes. In 1839 the assembly raised the appropriation to $25,000 annually and also allocated interest on deposits of federal funds to support public education. Article XII of the Constitution of 1843 (and amendments of 1986) established the constitutional prerogative of the assembly in matters of education. In 1882 the assembly mandated town support of public schools, thereby establishing a statewide system.

Throughout the first half of the twentieth century the assembly continued to increase state support to communities, established a statewide education bureaucracy, and set minimum benefits and pensions for teachers. During this period in this heavily Catholic state, the burdens of public education were considerably alleviated by an extensive system of parochial schools that provided primary and secondary education for a sizable portion of the school population.

After the Democratic takeover of the state government in the late 1930s and early 1940s, the General Assembly had a history of providing generous aid packages to parochial and private schools, including bus transportation and school books, health and nursing staff, and state tutoring support. Closer scrutiny by the courts of church-state relations in the early 1970s, however, rendered some of these links unconstitutional.[7] In addition, the loss of aid, the high cost of education, and increasing secularization of the population— wherein the cadre of nuns and priests that staffed these institutions declined dramatically—resulted in diminished enrollment in the Catholic schools and an increase in the public school population. The drop in private enrollments began in the early 1970s insofar as nonpublic school enrollment in 1969 was about 25 percent of the total elementary and secondary school population; by 1996 it had receded to about 14 percent.[8]

By the 1960s the legislature began to grapple with the inherent inequities in town-based support by requiring a per pupil minimal level of funding and establishing an operations aid program wherein the state share of funding was inversely related to the wealth of the community. The 1960 statute, however,

Table 19: Education Revenue by Source, 1990–1997

State	1990			1997		
	Local	State	Federal	Local	State	Federal
Connecticut	51.5%	44.8%	3.7%	57.0%	38.6%	4.4%
Maine	40.1%	53.2%	6.7%	46.4%	46.8%	6.8%
Massachusetts	58.8%	35.8%	5.4%	58.7%	36.0%	5.4%
New Hampshire	88.6%	8.5%	2.9%	90.0%	7.0%	3.0%
Rhode Island	**51.8%**	**43.8%**	**4.4%**	**54.7%**	**41.7%**	**3.6%**
Vermont	58.2%	36.5%	5.3%	66.1%	28.9%	5.0%
National Average	45.0%	48.7%	6.3%	45.0%	47.9%	7.1%

Source: Rhode Island Public Expenditure Council, *Results: Education in Rhode Island, 1999.*

included a minimum-share provision of 25 percent that resulted in continuing inequalities insofar as wealthy townships were still entitled to 25 percent of their education budgets from the state. By the late 1980s several wealthy communities, entitled to under 5 percent state funding by the operations aid standard, received 28 percent under the existing minimum-share standard.

An overreliance on property tax for education is a common problem in many states. A number of critical overviews and national reform proposals recommended that state governments assume more of the burden, encouraging a goal of 40 percent local to 60 percent state split. As a result, Rhode Island state support increased to a high of over 52 percent in 1991. But a lingering recession and the severe fiscal constraints imposed by the banking crisis forced the legislature to cap the aid formula at 38 percent in 1992. Thus, as table 19 indicates, state support for education in 1990 was on the upswing, when the state ranked thirty-first in the country. By 1996 the state share of support dropped to 41 percent of total spending and was just under 42 percent in 1997.

The caps and funding formulas proved especially burdensome for urban and poorer communities. These districts not only get the short shrift in terms of the cumulative effects of funding formulas linked to taxable property, but also require more resources (given the limited language proficiency and other remedial factors associated with poverty). The city of Providence, for example, has 15 percent of the state's total school population but 60 percent of the minority student population. In Providence growth has come in the nonprofit sector; employment in tax-exempt professions of health, education, and government has grown by fifteen thousand positions. The value of tax-exempt property over the three-year period of 1992 to 1995 increased by $240 million. Conversely, over the same period taxable property values declined by $100 million. By 1995 half of the city's property tax base became tax exempt.[9]

As table 20 indicates, as the tax base shrank remedial education problems grew worse over the same period. While public school enrollments increased by just over 10 percent, special education needs increased by 33 percent. From 1990 to 1998 there was a 21 percent increase in the limited English-speaking population, and the free- or reduced-lunch student population increased by over 55 percent.

Underlying these increases in special needs programs is the fact that most of these students are concentrated in urban areas, which have a declining property tax base. Five urban communities account for about 87 percent of all limited English proficiency students, and a majority of students eligible for reduced or free lunches are concentrated in the state's urban districts. As RIPEC reports, over 90 percent of Central Falls students and 70 percent of Providence students are eligible for reduced or free lunch programs.[10]

PERFORMANCE AND ACCOUNTABILITY

Another contentious issue relates to measures of student performance, which have recently been more carefully scrutinized and found wanting. Many states are developing their own measures of performance, making current comparative data across states difficult to come by, but results from one standard assessment suggest that Rhode Island elementary school students perform poorly on math and reading tests. As table 21 indicates, while there has been some improvement in fourth and eighth grade math scores, those improvements tend to be lower than the national average and well below those of other New England states. On reading assessments, fourth grade reading scores actually declined from 1993 to 1998, creating an increase (of from 34 to 37 percent) of the students considered "at risk" by the Rhode Island Department of Education.

Differentials in test performance are known to be linked to demographics. There is a confirmed relationship between an average student's test scores and the median income and education of his or her community; this relationship certainly exists in Rhode Island, where average scores are much higher in wealthier and more-educated school districts. While Rhode Island has a significant number of poor and disadvantaged communities, a national RAND study indicates that even controlling for these demographic factors, performance in the schools is wanting.[11]

The secondary school level scores from the Scholastic Assessment Test

Table 20: Rhode Island Fall Enrollment (School year 1990–91 through 1997–98)

Year	Fall Enrollment	% Change	Special Education	% of Total Enrollment	Limited English	% of Total Enrollment	Free/Reduced Lunch	% of Total Enrollment
1990–91	137,907	1.9%	21,460	15.6%	7,632	5.5%	31,719	23.0%
1991–92	140,915	2.2%	22,195	15.8%	7,645	5.4%	33,856	24.0%
1992–93	143,029	1.5%	23,208	16.2%	7,840	5.5%	40,477	28.3%
1993–94	144,931	1.3%	23,932	16.5%	8,079	5.6%	42,861	29.6%
1994–95	146,604	1.2%	25,144	17.2%	8,646	5.9%	47,961	32.7%
1995–96	148,978	1.6%	26,427	17.7%	8,974	6.0%	49,782	33.4%
1996–97	150,470	1.0%	25,579	17.0%	9,239	6.1%	52,246	34.7%
1997–98*	152,377	1.3%	28,558	18.7%	9,248	6.1%	49,218	32.3%
Change		% Change		% Change		% Change		% Change
1990–1997	14,470	10.5%	7,098	33.1%	1,616	21.2%	17,499	55.2%

Source: Rhode Island Public Expenditure Council, Results: Education in Rhode Island, 1999.

Table 21: Fourth and Eighth Grade Assessment Tests, 1990–1996

NAEP Mathematics Assessment Fourth Grade—1992 and 1996			NAEP Mathematics Assessment Eight Grade—1990, 1992, and 1996			
	Percentage at or Above Proficient			Percentage at or Above Proficient		
State	1992	1996	State	1990	1992	1996
Rhode Island	13%	17%	Rhode Island	15%	16%	20%
Connecticut	24%	31%	Connecticut	22%	26%	31%
Maine	27%	27%	Maine	—	25%	31%
Massachusetts	23%	24%	Massachusetts	—	23%	28%
New Hampshire	25%		New Hampshire	20%	25%	—
Vermont		23%	Vermont	—	—	27%
U.S. Average	18%	21%	U.S. Average	15%	21%	24%

Source: Rhode Island Public Expenditure Council, *Results: Education in Rhode Island, 1999.*

also indicate poor performance rates for Rhode Island schools. Looking at table 22 one can see that Rhode Island students perform below the national average and have the lowest average scores among New England states. While the national average is not necessarily comparable because nationally less than half of the high school population even takes the test, in New England states where a strong tradition of higher education endures, about 70 percent or more of that population takes the test. Although the state's average score improved by 10 points from 1990 to 1998, the state's average score remains the lowest in New England.

Again, these statewide averages mask demographic variations. Students who come from households earning less than $10,000 score at around 725, while scores for students from households earning over $50,000 are above 950. One hopeful sign is that the rate of improvement during the period from 1990 to 1998 is due to increases in minority scores. The increase among white students over these years was 1 percentage point, among blacks it was 18 points, and for Hispanic-Latino students the increase was 13 points.[12] While the overall test results continue to concern policymakers, these rankings do provide a baseline from which they can monitor and assess improvements as they move to reform the system.

THE POLITICS OF REFORM

The capping of state school operations aid by the Sundlun administration

Table 22: Scholastic Assessment Test—Combined Scores, 1990–1998

Year	RI	CT	ME	MA	NH	VT	US
1990	986	1,002	991	1,001	1,015	1,000	1,001
1991	984	999	984	997	1,006	995	999
1992	985	1,002	988	1,002	1,014	1,001	1,001
1993	986	1,004	989	1,003	1,016	996	1,003
1994	984	999	987	1,002	1,013	1,002	1,003
1995	992	1,009	1,003	1,007	1,035	1,005	1,010
1996	992	1,011	1,005	1,011	1,034	1,006	1,013
1997	992	1,016	1,011	1,016	1,039	1,010	1,016
1998	996	1,019	1,007	1,016	1,043	1,012	1,017
			1998 Participation Rate				
	72%	80%	68%	77%	74%	71%	43%
			1998 Regional Rank				
	6	2	4	2	1	5	

Source: Rhode Island Public Expenditure Council, *Results: Education in Rhode Island, 1999.*

prompted a court challenge in 1992. In many other states over the past few decades, educational reform groups have attempted to bypass state legislatures, which have become increasingly influenced by suburban interests that resist demands for a redistribution of state funds to urban districts. In Rhode Island a reform group of plaintiffs argued in *Sundlun v Pawtucket* that existing financing formulas violated the education clause and the equal protection guarantees established in the Rhode Island constitution. A superior court found for the plaintiffs, ordered the governor to formulate a state-based system of finance consistent with the court's decision, and retained the jurisdiction of the court for the purpose of monitoring and enforcement.

In a stunning reversal in 1995, the state supreme court on appeal issued a unanimous opinion that spoke volumes not only about education policy but also about the political character of the state. In terms of policy the court quashed the ruling of the superior court and rejected all the arguments contained in the lower court's decision. The justices refuted the interpretation that each child had a constitutional right to an equal education. Noting that the constitution charged the legislature with "promoting the benefits of education," the justices then went on to refute the idea that spending per se ensured a quality education and argued that the General Assembly had done a fairly good job of fulfilling its constitutional mandate. The court concluded that on the question of on which standards the right to an education is based, the legislature "is endowed with virtually unreviewable discretion in this area."

In terms of process the justices cited the New Jersey courts' activities as an example of ill-advised judicial intrusion. They noted that the Rhode Island court refused to become involved in a "morass comparable to the decades-long struggle of the Supreme Court of New Jersey that has attempted to define what constitutes the 'thorough and efficient' education specified in that state's constitution." The opinion concluded that the New Jersey case provides "a chilling example of the thickets that can entrap a court that takes on the duties of a Legislature" and advised the plaintiffs to seek a remedy through that branch of government.[13]

As a result of *Sundlun v. Pawtucket,* the legislature and particularly individual legislators long concerned with education issues felt empowered to push for sweeping action and, working with reform groups, began to develop a plan of reform. During the summer of 1996 institutional and political factors created an ideal opportunity for the General Assembly to implement a strategy. The institutional and political rivalry that existed between the executive and the legislature over the budget, coupled with the frustration with the existing public system felt by taxpayers, parents, and reform groups, prompted the assembly to take complete control of the process. It bypassed the executive bureaucracy of the Department of Education and the state board of regents and established a ten-member commission composed exclusively of legislators who were charged with overhauling the administration and monitoring of the system. The initial step was part of budget activities in that year, wherein the legislature raised spending levels in every community in direct opposition to the governor's plan of budget cuts for education. In so doing the assembly crafted an aid formula more closely aligned with poverty levels in each district.[14]

By 1997 the outlines of the reform proposals took shape in the form of the sweeping mandates of Article 31 which created, by statute, a more uniform and accountable system among the state's thirty-six school districts. The article mandated a tracking system whereby each district is compelled to adopt uniform accounting and expenditure systems so that the state can assess, in comparable terms, how monies in the districts are spent and what results are achieved. In order to facilitate this system the legislature empowered the state Department of Education to administer a series of detailed statewide tests to assess student performance and general school environments. Schools that fail to meet goals are subject to state intervention, and schools that continue to fail to improve can be taken over by the state.[15] In terms of the education budget, the legislature continued to increase spending generally for education but with carefully crafted packages that provided more aid to the poorer cities. During the 1999 budget negotiations suburban legislators banded together in an unsuccessful attempt to curtail the escalating state aid to urban districts. Although they failed, this issue will continue to be a nettlesome problem for the legislative leadership given the large suburban contingent in the assembly. Late in 1999 a group of representatives from some of the less-affluent nonurban districts brought suit in the courts to force a reconsideration of the existing funding formulas.

THE TEACHERS AND REFORM

The reform initiative also attempted to impose ongoing standards of teacher accountability. On that issue the legislative commission locked horns with the powerful teachers unions and in many respects came up short. Public schoolteachers in Rhode Island enjoy a Lifetime Teacher Certificate whereby, after teaching for six years and obtaining a Master's degree, they gain lifetime certification without the need to be reevaluated or recertified. Although the reform commission never expected to eliminate the guarantee altogether, it proposed grandfathering teachers who had lifetime certification but attempted to initiate reevaluation procedures for the more than four thousand teachers already in the system who had not yet gained lifetime certification as well as for all new hires. The unions won this battle, essentially grandfathering the entire already-existing teaching population; only new teachers hired after 1997 are subject to recertification mandates.

The teacher certification debate is symptomatic of the tremendous clout enjoyed by the teachers unions of Rhode Island—the National Education Association/Rhode Island and the Rhode Island Federation of Teachers. As one respected educational writer noted, "They are one of—if not the most—powerful forces in determining what does and what does not become state law."[16] Certainly this was not always the case. During the 1940s and early 1950s teachers, most of whom were women, were treated shabbily; they were very poorly paid, subjected to arbitrary rules and assignments passed down by the school committees, and faced arbitrary firings. Moreover, in response to periodic local strikes and walkouts in which their demands were relatively meager, the Rhode Island Supreme Court ruled in 1958 that teacher strikes were illegal.[17]

By 1966 teachers won the right to bargain collectively and unions organized in every district in the state. Since that time teachers unions have become a force in state politics, using strikes that disrupt communities.[18] Their influence comes from maintaining a strong presence at the statehouse and from the sheer number of active constituents the unions represent in every district in the state, as well as the hefty campaign contributions the union leadership directs at candidates who support them. Moreover, significant numbers of teachers, retired teachers, and union members serve in the General Assembly.

Teachers unions have been a force for positive change in many areas. Union representatives point out that smaller class size, which some argue is one of the most significant factors in classroom learning (after parental income and parental education), was achieved as a result of union demands. In addition, to the extent that the urban schools have any decent learning environments it is due to the union's bargaining. And, as noted above, teachers in the public school system are, by national standards, very well paid. In addition to pay, teachers enjoy extremely generous contract perks associated with sick pay, rigid work rules that limit hours and duties, and extra compensation for any extracurricular activities. Once retired they enjoy comfortable pension and health insurance benefits.

The charter school initiative in Rhode Island may prove to be a turning point in the unchallenged clout of the teachers unions. By 1998 more than seven hundred charter schools were operating in twenty-seven states and the District of Columbia. Rhode Island implemented charter school legislation in 1995 but, given union influence, the legislation was so restrictive that Rhode Island charter schools were not eligible for federal funds. In 1998 the state had only one charter school in Providence, the Textron Chamber of Commerce Academy, where policy is set by a board of directors of parents, educators, and business persons. A second school, Times2 School, opened in 1999. In 1998 the governor, supported by groups of parents, the business community, and education reformers proposed legislation to allow more charter partnerships not only with business but also with other nonprofit groups and institutions of higher learning, hoping to create more charter schools, particularly in the inner cities. The unions opposed the legislation because it disengaged the charter schools from local district control and, more important, eliminated the requirement that teachers belong to the unions. In a surprising turn of events a few key legislators unexpectedly backed the proposal. The bill passed the house by one vote, made it through the senate and was ultimately signed into law by the governor.[19]

Beyond the outcome of the vote, the significance of the debate reflects shifting attitudes about public education in the state. In Massachusetts, where charter schools are flourishing, lifetime teacher certification has been eliminated for all teachers, and U.S. Senator John Kerry advocated the elimination of tenure for public schoolteachers across the country. In that sense the unions in Rhode Island may have to learn to live with trends that in the long term may diminish their influence. As one long-time observer of statehouse politics noted, "It used to be when the teacher unions lobbyists arrived at the statehouse, it was like the parting of the Red Sea. I see that changing. What they [teacher unions] don't get is that their eye[s] may be on the wrong ball. School vouchers are coming down the road."

For whatever reasons, accommodation by the unions is increasingly apparent. In 1999 the teachers unions and the school committee in a local school district agreed to a new contract that included a bonus package for individual teachers based on classroom performance. This package is a first in Rhode Island and is considered fairly progressive by national standards. This same community also approved a bonus package for the school superintendent that was linked to improvement in students' scores on statewide reference tests.[20]

REFORM AND LOCAL CONTROL

In order to monitor and assess improvement and performance, Article 31 mandated that the Department of Education use performance results and uniform accounting standards to track performance. For the most part the efforts of the state bureaucracy have been well received insofar as they create measurable standards for parents and school committees as well as policymakers. But inevitably these directions in education diminish the ability of local school committees to monitor their own educational affairs. This creates political difficulties in a state with a strong tradition of local control.

Local education policy is normally the responsibility of members of school committees who are elected for either two- or staggered four-year terms by the voters in each city or town. The primary task of the school committee is to monitor school activities and draw up the district's yearly operating budget, which it then passes on to the town council for funding. (Capital projects are subject to local bond referenda.) The town council cannot cut items from the budget, only from the overall bottom line. This arrangement gives the school committees considerable leverage. Increasingly, however, as noted in chapter 12, statewide mandates are creating political and fiscal pressures at the local level while centralizing the process at the state level. This has a tendency to create initial dissonance between state and local participants.

For example, in 1998 as part of its information-gathering mandate created by Article 31, the Department of Education introduced a School Accountability for Learning and Teaching (SALT) survey for administration in all school districts. In addition to a series of state-mandated achievement tests, the

SALT survey sought to learn from teachers and students their attitudes about education and contained probes about a student's home environment. Some parents found the survey intrusive and one community's school committee refused to administer the survey until the Department of Education threatened to rescind federal aid for the district. However, because administering the test required parental consent and given the opposition of the school board, many parents did not agree to allow their children to take the test, which diminished the number of returns in that district. In 1999, however, that same school committee dropped its opposition to the project.

Another aspect of the SALT program requires teams of parents, teachers, and administrators from outside a given school district to perform on-site evaluations of a selected number of schools each year and to compile evaluations. Release of the first reports in 1999 caused some local consternation, especially when two of the state's most highly regarded high schools were the subject of critical reports. Nonetheless, one school grudgingly acknowledged internal problems and outlined plans to correct them. Such tensions are likely to continue as state government moves toward playing a larger role in public education and attempts to improve the overall quality in the public system.

Although the pace of change is slow, progress seems real. In 1999 *Education Week*, in an annual report on the state of the nation's schools, noted the innovative and ambitious efforts of Rhode Island to evaluate the quality of school programs beyond mere test scores. Moreover, a series of internal state standard-reference exams indicate that between the 1996–97 and 1997–98 school years, students' math scores improved in thirty of thirty-three school districts and there was a 25 percent decline in student scores that fell below standard. In addition, another survey indicated that as of 1996 more than 65 percent of high school graduates enrolled in college, placing Rhode island fifth in the nation and above all other New England states except Massachusetts.[21]

POLITICS OF HIGHER EDUCATION

Rhode Island has a relatively small system of state-supported institutions of higher learning, which includes a community college network on various campuses (Rhode Island Community College), a state college (Rhode Island College), and the University of Rhode Island (with four campus locations). A board of governors for higher education, appointed by the governor, with two additional representatives from the legislature, and a commission of higher education oversee the system and negotiate the budget with the legislature.

As is the case in other New England states, the historical development of an outstanding array of elite private colleges clustered in a region puts the public system, and most particularly the state university, at a disadvantage. State universities in the New England region generally have neither the standing nor the visibility enjoyed by most other state public universities across the country.

Consequently, higher education's share of state operating budgets in all New England states is well below the national average. In fact Maine, Rhode Island, Massachusetts, Connecticut, New Hampshire, and Vermont rank fortieth, forty-third, forty-sixth, forty-seventh, forty-eighth, and fiftieth, respectively, among states in terms of budget appropriations for higher education as a share of state general revenues. In Rhode Island spending from general revenues on public higher education for 1999 was just over $150 million, which is allocated among the three networks and the office of the board of governors and the commission of higher education.

In Rhode Island traditional patterns of support for public higher education, particularly for the state university, have been influenced by several historical and demographic developments. For one, the university was and to some extent continues to be in the shadow of Brown University, a nationally renowned Ivy League institution located in the heart of Providence. This venerable institution has long and deep historical roots in the city, and remains the institution of choice for the children of the economic and social elite (when they can gain admission, that is). Moreover, as ethnic groups (who were overwhelmingly Catholic and urban) began to make their way up the socioeconomic ladder, access to a lower-cost public university education was inhibited by an anti-Catholic bias that existed at the university during the first half of the twentieth century. The alternative, particularly among Catholics, was Providence College, a Catholic institution also located in the city of Providence. Many of the sons and then daughters of Irish, French, and Italian working-class families used their degrees from Providence College as a bridge into the middle class.

As these populations moved up the economic ladder they also moved into politics and, through the 1980s a significant number of elected and appointed officials were graduates of Providence College. Indeed, as noted earlier, in the 1980s Providence College had the largest contingent of graduates in the state legislature, which controls spending for public education.

In addition, the culture of this tiny state regards distance in relative terms, so that a drive of twenty minutes is considered a trek and the main campus of the URI system located at Kingston—a full thirty-five minutes from center city—was considered the boondocks. The notion of having public events at the university or getting politicians to travel "way down to Kingston" further isolated the university.

Two antidotes suggest the attitudes of that time. In 1978 both URI and Providence College made the playoffs in post-season NCAA basketball tournaments. As a sendoff the General Assembly approved a special resolution wishing the Providence College Friars success. No mention or resolution was even proposed for URI.[22] In 1989 the *Rhode Island State Manual*, the "blue book" of state government, listed under significant events for the year the inauguration of a new president of Brown University, Vartan Gregorian. In 1991 URI also inaugurated a new president, Robert Carothers but that event was not included in the listings.

Given these general proclivities, the tight money of the early 1990s further disadvantaged the statewide system insofar as budgets for higher education were drastically cut, causing tuition to escalate and facilities to deteriorate. As one executive budget analyst suggested, in difficult fiscal times higher education "is one of the first places we cut."

Patterns have changed. As the cost of private education escalated, Providence College became more of a regional college and increasing numbers of children of working- and middle-class backgrounds came into the state public system, particularly to the university. Many of these graduates then found their way into public life. In fact, by the late 1990s the largest representation in the state legislature was from the University of Rhode Island; in 1994 Republican Lincoln Almond was the first graduate of the university to be elected governor.

As the recession receded more generous appropriations were given to higher education. This, combined with some strong leadership at the university, resulted in improved SAT scores, more research grants, an improved campus infrastructure, and a more serious academic environment in a college long known as a "party school." In tandem with these changes the university became more visible in state events. In 1996 voters supported a generous bond referendum to rebuild the infrastructure of the state system. During this same period national recognition of key research programs, particularly related to the environment and marine studies, as well as some big basketball wins—and a championship bid—helped promote the university as a source of pride throughout the state. This prompted the governor to push for a proposed new indoor sports facility which the legislature, although generally inclined to support it, had initially not considered as part of the 1999 budget package. A groundswell of public support for the project as well as strong and unexpected lobbying from alumni from all parts of the state caused the legislature to approve an initial funding package for the arena. The cumulative effect of these events was a changed recognition about the place and role of the university and the state college network in the state.

This change, however, caught some members of the political establishment by surprise. The office of the board of governors and the commissioner of higher education, considered by many to be expensive patronage boondoggles, attempted to fire the president of the state university, Robert Carothers. Apparently miffed by his aggressive posture toward budget appropriations for higher education and his lack of respect for individuals on the board of governors, board leaders indicated they would not renew his contract. When this attempt became public, the outcry was so overwhelming that it caused a stunning reversal. The governor and the board backed down and, in an unprecedented move, were forced to renew Carothers's contract. Indeed, in addition to statewide solidification of support for the university, the most likely result of this confrontation will probably be a closer scrutiny of the political governance of an education system that has come to be regarded as a key public resource. Public higher education, like every other interest, does not always get what it wants from state government. But after these events there is a much more favorable perception of the place of higher education in the system.

FUTURE PROSPECTS

In the long term, prospects for public education in the state look bright. Changes in the economic structure continue to reinforce the idea that economic prosperity is linked to the quality of public education. This puts issues of education in the forefront of the public agenda. The budget for 1999 again upped state spending for primary and secondary education with a formula that gave a full 75 percent of the increases to poorer urban communities. The board of regents has provisionally approved two more charter schools, which should provide some examples of innovation and competition for the public system. Although performance in the public school system has a way to go, initial results of tracking indicate the trend is in the right direction.

In addition to the results of statewide testing, a respected trade publication released *Quality Counts '98* which, for the second year issued a "report card" on the condition of education in all of the fifty states.[23] Although Rhode Island's grades were less than stellar, they had improved in the categories of standards, assessment, and accountability, mostly as a result of the tracking and yearly assessment tests of performance instituted by the state. The ratings for school climate improved, as did grades for the adequacy and equity of the allocation of resources. In only one area did grades go down—the category of quality of teaching; this, however, was a result of the lack of ongoing requirements in assessments of teachers, which has since been put into place. While the goal of delivering a quality education to all students, especially to poor, minority, urban ones, is still in the future, the reforms at the turn of this century have the potential to dramatically change the landscape of public education in the Ocean State. These trends, however, pose a threat to local autonomy and to the traditional patterns of local government, a topic to which we now turn.

CHAPTER TWELVE

Local Government

> It is the intention of this article to grant and confirm to the people of every city
> and town in this state the right of self government in all local matters.
>
> Article XIII, Rhode Island Constitution

More than once in recent decades the phrase "city-state" has been applied
to Rhode Island. The state's very small size, compactness, high population
density, and high degree of urbanization around a core formed by Providence
suggest that nothing but city-state organization makes sense. Why not one
school district, one fire department, one police department, and so on? To
Rhode Islanders, however, any such city-state would be unimaginable and
violently opposed. Despite encouragement, off and on over many years only
a handful of the smallest among the state's thirty-nine cities and towns have
joined in combined school districts. In all other spheres local autonomy has
been guarded fiercely.

PROVIDENCE AS THE CORE OF THE STATE

There is, in other words, a kind of schizophrenia in Rhode Island about
local government. In part it is a clash between sentiment (devotion to local
autonomy) and reality: the state, by all appearances, is virtually a city-state.
Rhode Island's size and compactness seem to belie the strength of Rhode
Islanders' emotional parochialism. Part of the problem lies in the fact that in
Rhode Island, unlike in Delaware or other small states, Providence is at one
and the same time the state's metropolis, economic center, and capital. It is
easy, therefore, to see the rest of the state as little more than a ring of suburbs
around the core city. (Newport is a partial exception to this perception.)

Providence was not the only or even the preeminent original settlement.

In 1708 Newport had half again as many people. By the Revolution Newport was still in the lead, and Providence had only 8 percent of the state's population. Newport's misfortunes during that war (British occupation, primarily) lost for it the position it had enjoyed as a major Atlantic coastal port and the economic center of the state. By 1800 Providence had pulled ahead in population, and by 1850 Providence had four times the former's population and 28 percent of the people in the state.

By then Providence had become the economic hub of Rhode Island. The Brown brothers (whose family name is borne by the state's Ivy League university) had taken the lead in the pre- and post-Revolutionary development of Providence as the center of a vigorous shipping and commercial economy.[1] When those ventures began to flag, the brothers took the lead in making Rhode Island the cradle of the American Industrial Revolution. The city reoriented itself from the bay and its carrying trade to manufacturing, ultimately to feed the needs of the rapidly growing and westward-moving American population. To make this possible the Browns also pioneered the building of a web of toll turnpikes that radiated from Providence, connecting it with Boston, western Massachusetts, Connecticut, and other points south. Soon the railroads came, and Providence became a key hub and transit point for this new transportation web.

Obviously other communities in the state played roles in this economic development. Textile mills sprang up on a number of rivers in the state. Much of the entrepreneurial spirit, however, was supplied by risk takers based in Providence. The city also became the banking center of the state and even beyond the state's borders. Machine building and machine tool manufacturing also became important industries. To a large extent they, too, were centered in Providence.

The decades that preceded the Great Depression, and that cataclysmic event itself, brought economic decline and hardship to Rhode Island. The textile industry moved south, and other industries fell on hard times. World War I brought a shot of prosperity, as did World War II in the wake of the Depression of the 1930s. But, ever since, the economic prosperity and future of the state have been tenuous. No new winning formula has been found that can do for Rhode Island and for Providence what the carrying trade and then industrialization did in the past.

The fact remains that Providence has long been the center and fulcrum of the economy of the state throughout its various phases. From its earliest days, dating perhaps from the success the citizens of Providence achieved in persuading Rhode Island College (soon to be Brown University) to locate there, the city has been the institutional and cultural hub of the state as well.

Although this has given Providence unrivaled status, with its incomparable array of educational, cultural, religious, and similar institutions, it has been a burden as well as a blessing. About half of the landed property in the city is tax exempt. (The property owned by state government, of course, figures into that astonishing total.) The impact on the tax base is serious and is a progressively more difficult problem for the city.

In short, the role Providence plays in the development and life of Rhode Island has been and continues to be uniquely important and critical. This importance has, not surprisingly, caused observers to insist that the only sensible arrangement for "Little Rhody" is to recognize the obvious and make itself into a city-state with a matching centralized governing structure. Which leads us to seek out the roots of the state's persistent local parochialism.

ROOTS OF LOCAL PAROCHIALISM

The jealous guarding of local government and its prerogatives as a mindset and a creed is older than the state itself. Each of the colony's four original settlements was the result of a separatist movement of some sort.[2] Roger Williams and a small group fled from Massachusetts to the head of Narragansett Bay and founded Providence in 1636. They sought the freedom of worship denied them in the Bay Colony. Another group of dissenters settled Portsmouth in 1638 at the north end of "Rhode Island" (Acquidnick Island). A schismatic group from Portsmouth moved to the south end of the island and founded Newport in 1639. Still another group established what later became Warwick on the west side of the bay in 1642.

Thanks to Roger Williams's liberal views on religious toleration, Rhode Island is often cited as a cradle of religious liberty. As noted earlier, this very toleration led to fragmented settlements which long defied all efforts to establish any kind of unified central authority. In the long run only the vigorous efforts of the colony's surrounding neighbors to divide up this small slice of intervening territory forced cooperation among the rival settlements. Massachusetts, and Plymouth in particular, saw Williams's group and the others as dangerous heretics whose subjugation was highly desirable. Greed for land was very much involved, as well.

When it became apparent that local efforts to develop cooperative arrangements among the settlements would not work, Williams was sent to England to obtain a charter. During that period the king had been deposed and Parliament under the Puritans ruled. Parliament granted Williams a patent in 1644 that formally joined the settlements into one colony but left the design of the central institutions up to the settlements themselves. As Sidney James wrote, localism steadily subverted the intent of the patent. Although the new document became the basis for some successes in fending off predatory neighbors, within the colony, "At every occasion the towns kept asserting their importance . . . [and] were left to handle their own affairs with little interference from above."[3]

Under the 1644 patent the colony did pass legislation that prescribed the election of town councils. But internal confusion continued and worsened, along with the achievement of some progress. By 1658 the central government *had* extended its limited authority over all four of the original settlements. Adding to the confusion was the fact that the Civil War between King Charles I and Parliament was raging in the mother country while the first charter had been secured from a parliamentary commission; after the restoration of the monarchy a new charter was obtained from King Charles II. This charter did much to firm up the colony's boundaries (though they were not finally settled in all respects until 1862). More important, however, was the fact that this new document did prescribe the frame of government to be set up for the colony.

The result was the establishment on firmer foundations of the colony government, and especially the authority of the General Assembly. It became more than a legislature. It also became an elected body that chose most civil and military officials, and was to serve as a court of appeals. None of this, seemingly, was done at the expense of the towns. Indeed, their importance was elevated, wrote James. One result was the curious practice of having the meetings of the assembly and of the Court of Trials rotate among four or five of the towns, rather than holding all meetings in Newport, which for the most part served as the capital.

Many acts of the assembly actually transferred to or confirmed important powers within the towns. Not infrequently the towns simply ignored assembly acts that they chose not to follow; there was no penalty for doing so. The result, as James noted, was that "If the new government of the colony under the charter turned out to be more of a federal structure than the centralized regime . . . prescribed by the document, the alteration at least stemmed from important realities. The towns had come first, obviously . . . they cherished localism and, far from parting with it in accord with the charter, insisted that it be further honored by the central government."[4] So each town proceeded on its own, conducting public business of many kinds. The colony government tried to manage what was left over.

This spirit of local autonomy has persisted down through the years. Since the 1930s the centralization of many functions in the state, which the towns had formerly handled, has brought major changes. It is still true, however, that the towns jealously guard many historic prerogatives. This has always been true, given that the members of the assembly are elected from small districts and that the legislators are closely tied to the local units and thus feel a keen responsibility to represent local interests. The state government really cannot do anything against the determined opposition of the local communities; the representatives of the towns *are* the state government.

LOCAL STATE RELATIONS, THE EVOLVING PATTERN

As the eighteenth century progressed the dynamics of this relationship between the towns and the state changed. James made the point this way: "Burgeoning population and spreading settlement inevitably wrought a transformation in the towns, a transformation that exposed them to uniform regulation by the General Assembly."[5] His suggestion is that many towns ceased to be central village clusters with outlying adjacent farms. As populations grew, town territories began to fill with new settlements. Rhode Island towns, unlike those in Massachusetts, did not have a town common as their geographic focus. Increasingly they came to have more than one "village" or built-up area. The sense of community became fragmented. Distances people had to travel to the center of town government increased. Attendance at town meetings declined. James wrote that "As towns ceased to be communities in a traditional sense, they became simply units of local government."[6]

These trends led to increased legislative activity by the assembly in specifying local responsibilities and authority, regulating the conduct of town meetings, and so on. As town-meeting activity declined more officials were appointed to carry out laws passed by the legislature. Town councils became more important in the governance process, in part because town meetings called on them more and more to draft laws, make appointments, and serve as town executives. In short, town government as it has existed and functioned in recent decades was emerging prior to the Revolution.

What, one might ask at this point, was the emerging pattern of local government? As has become clear already, the town always was and continues to be the basic unit. The original settlements like Providence made land purchases from the Indians to the extent that the town of Providence once encompassed much of what is now the northern third of the state. Gradually pieces of territory were lopped off and set apart as new towns. Under the 1663 charter each of these towns gained representation in the state assembly. From earliest times there was little or no land over which one or more of the settlements could claim jurisdiction that was not already part of that settlement or part of one of the later-created towns. There has never been, in other words, any unincorporated land in the state. In the long run five counties were established, but the only function such designations ever served was as districts for court decentralization.

Until 1832, when Providence was chartered as the state's first city, the form of town government prescribed in the General Laws (as those laws gradually accumulated through assembly action), with slight modifications in the larger communities like Providence and Newport, was the norm for all.

In title 45 of the current General Laws, chapter 5, entitled "Councils and Governing Bodies" (title 45 deals with towns and cities), section 1 reads: "The Town Council of each town shall have full power to manage the affairs and interests of the town and to determine all matters and things as shall by law come within their jurisdiction." This phrasing unquestionably dates back to the eighteenth if not the seventeenth century! Much of the language found in the early chapters of title 45 today has equally ancient origins, though is larded with revised and new language of countless dates in between (which also makes interpretation of portions of these chapters complex and problematical).

Actually the quoted passage rather overstates the situation that exists today. Over time the "creature theory" of local government replaced the substantial autonomy Rhode Island's towns had enjoyed in the early days.[7] According to this principle all local government units are the creation and thus creatures of the state and can exercise only the power explicitly conferred upon them by the legislature. Some states adopted "home rule" in this century, and by doing so moved away from the strict creature theory toward a more permissive conception of local powers. This did not happen in Rhode Island, although it became nominally a home-rule state.

During the nineteenth century the town meetings lost some of their powers to the town councils, retaining only jurisdiction over appropriations and the tax levy. From time to time the General Assembly did pass special acts for individual towns relating to their powers or structures of government.

THE EMERGING CITIES

The first exception to the situation that existed in the early 1800s was the granting of a city charter to Providence. By the third decade of the nineteenth century Providence was by far the largest town in population in the state and was growing rapidly. In 1800 she had 7,614 people. By 1830 that number had more than doubled to 16,836. The town meeting–town council system of government was feeling the strain, and after a false start the assembly enacted a charter to create a city government, which was approved by the voters in 1832. The charter provided for what was then the accepted city government structure: a strong bicameral council and a weak mayor. In effect it set up a board of aldermen with the mayor as its presiding officer; the board essentially took over the role of the town council. A considerably larger common council more or less replaced the role of the town meeting.

The administrative structure was composed of commissions whose members were elected by the council. Commissions were charged with the various administrative responsibilities, and each was responsible to a council committee with oversight in its area. Although considerable revisions were incorporated over the years, with substantial ones in 1866, the basic charter remained in place until it was superseded by a modern strong mayor, weak (unicameral) council legislative charter in 1940.

The other old cities (in other words, those with nineteenth-century incorporation dates) are Newport (1853), Pawtucket (1885), Woonsocket (1888), and Central Falls (1895). With the exception of Newport these cities, along with Providence, gained city status in the course of the state's transformation by industrialization and urbanization. They were the major centers in which the textile industry and other industries grew and flourished. Central Falls represents this development in perhaps its purest form. Located on the Blackstone River, which also powered Woonsocket and Pawtucket mills, Central Falls was made up of a square mile carved out of the southern end of the Town of Lincoln. In reality it was a very large "mill town" with housing for the workers provided by the mills that lined the west bank of the river. At its peak nearly 26,000 people crowded into its tiny territory. As an industrial center in an era of very limited public transportation, the situation made sense.

These cities also became destinations for many of the immigrants who flowed or were recruited into the state to work in the mills. However, their experiences did not mirror the experiences of other American cities with similar characteristics during the last third of the nineteenth century. Elsewhere the urban political machine, rooted in the Democratic party and drawing its strength from the votes of the urban immigrant masses, became the norm. Not so in Rhode Island. The largely WASP, old-stock elite, which had shifted its capital from trading and commerce to the new industries, were also the dominant political elite thanks to property qualifications for voting.

As such, the elite saw to it that Rhode Island's city dwellers could vote for mayor but not for council members unless they owned property. Instead, propertyholders controlled council elections, and because virtually all government powers (administrative as well as legislative) were concentrated in the council, they controlled the government of the city as well. James Q. Dealey, writing in the first decade of the twentieth century, found that from 1886 to 1906 an average of 20,435 votes were cast for mayor, while an average total of only 8,163 were cast for aldermen. "The political effect of this limitation is to place the control of municipal government in the hands of the Republicans," Dealey wrote.[8] The Democrats had great potential voting strength but they couldn't tap it. Rhode Island did not avoid machine rule; it was ruled by a state Republican machine.

Thus the story of Rhode Island's local government during the nineteenth century and into the first decades of the twentieth was that of a limited shift to the forms of city-versus-town institutions, but with a continuation of the traditional elite control despite massive demographic changes. In the towns, until the 1960s, non-propertyholders could not vote on financial or tax matters in town meetings. Moreover, malapportionment of the assembly ensured that the staunchly Republican small towns, each of which sent one senator to the upper house and were also overrepresented in the lower, continued to control the legislative branch.

The state constitution of 1843, which finally supplanted the royal charter, resembled (in terms of power distribution) the pattern of city government that it granted: weak governor and most of the real power residing in the assembly. As under the charter, the General Assembly branches meeting jointly in grand committee elected most administrative personnel. The upshot was that despite the massive changes in the economy of the state, and despite the distribution and composition of the population, little had changed so far as local government was concerned. The town and now the city units functioned much as they always had, with propertyholders now in the place of the freemen of the past and very much in control. The state government had gained considerable nominal authority over the local units as the creature theory gained ascendancy, but it was still as true as ever that the towns, and to a considerable extent the small towns with a very limited fraction of the total population, remained in a dominant position. As noted earlier, one must read the theory of state government supremacy in light of political realities: the all-powerful assembly was a congress of small-town representatives beholden to the dominant economic elite.

THE TWENTIETH CENTURY

The twentieth century saw the addition of three more cities to the list: Cranston in 1910, Warwick in 1931, and East Providence in 1954. These were cities of a different sort, however. None of them has a typical "downtown" business-shopping district; rather, each is a cluster of residential neighborhoods to which the granting of the label "city" is rather arbitrary. They are far more the product of suburbanization and urban sprawl than are the state's older cities.

In 1928 the constitution was amended to eliminate the property qualification for voting in city council elections.[9] Thus two of these newer cities (Warwick and East Providence) were chartered following that change, and Cranston's charter only preceded this franchise liberalization by two decades. It is probably the case that in all three the residential quality of the communities with high percentages of single-family owner-occupied houses meant that the property qualification would have made far less difference than it made in the older cities with their large populations of blue-collar tenement residents.

In general the twentieth century was to see far more massive changes in both the role and structure of local government in Rhode Island, starting in the 1930s, than had occurred during the preceding three centuries. Even before the Depression changes had been under way in a number of sorts. The automobile, together with improved highways, had begun to make possible a move to the suburbs with longer and easier commutes to work. It is not accidental that the population of Providence peaked in 1925 at nearly 268,000 and declined quite steadily from then on. By 1950, right after World War II, it had fallen to 243,674. By 1965 it was under 200,000, and it reached its lowest point in 1980 with 156,421. It climbed a bit thereafter with renewed immigration. To cite one more example, Central Falls's population peaked about the same time, at nearly 26,000. By 1980 it was just under 17,000.

Another major development that again affected the older cities in particular was the decline, starting in the 1920s, of the textile industry.[10] By the 1950s and 1960s most of it had closed or fled south. Much of the rest of the manufacturing part of the economy, save for light manufacture like jewelry, also declined. Again, the loss of jobs affected the older cities hardest. The long-term results of these and other factors brought increasingly difficult budgetary problems to the old cities which, because their boundaries are tightly drawn with little area left for new development, faced stagnating tax bases. The newer cities and the expanding suburban towns have tended to suffer less. The plight of Central Falls became so desperate that in 1991 the state was forced to take over the city's school system.[11] The continuing appeal of local autonomy was illustrated again when a referendum to merge the Pawtucket school system with that of adjacent Central Falls was defeated by voters.

Paralleling these developments were major shifts in the role of local governments in Rhode Island and, indeed, throughout the country. The Depression of the early 1930s quickly strained the efforts of local communities to perform their traditional role in supporting the poor and needy. States were forced to take over; the federal government had to step in with short-term measures to provide relief and jobs with the Works Progress Administration, Public Works Administration, and the like. With the adoption in 1935 of the Social Security legislation Washington assumed the responsibility for helping to deal with problems of this kind in the future. The social welfare roles left to the local communities were marginal at best. Rhode Island had been hard hit and welcomed the New Deal with enthusiasm. Town poor farms to which the indigent had been sent to receive local public support became relics of the past.

HOME RULE

The next major development for local government was of quite a different sort—the adoption of "home rule."[12] In theory but also increasingly in practice the state had conformed to the creature theory, or Dillon's Rule concept of the relationship between state and local government. Home rule as a reform took shape and gained support nationally during the Progressive Era as one of several responses to the sorry and often corrupt state into which municipal government had fallen in many instances.

Specifically, home rule was a response to the efforts that were often made by legislatures in states with large urban centers to curb or root out political machine practices and the corruption they brought with them. Legislative charters were altered and legislation passed taking elements of local authority and vesting it in the hands of state officials or local officials appointed by the governor. Providence had a police commission appointed by the governor up to 1935, for example.[13] Local citizens who had watched helplessly the machinations of the bosses in their cities were also forced to watch local powers taken away entirely to be exercised by state fiat.

Home rule in general promised greater local autonomy. It also targeted these kinds of practices and was intended to give local reform and citizen groups a means of wresting control from the bosses and setting up reformed systems that they hoped would guarantee good, honest government. The home-rule movement in the state owes much to Dennis J. Roberts, who served as mayor of Providence from 1941 to 1950 and then as governor until 1958. He was elected mayor just in time to implement the new city charter, which had been enacted by the General Assembly and approved by the voters. As noted, this was a strong-mayor charter with a small unicameral council.[14] Roberts did a great deal to professionalize the city administration and to establish a management machinery that modernized the running of the city.

The new Providence charter and the innovations installed by Roberts led logically to a movement to adopt home rule for the state. This required amending the constitution. Such an amendment was formulated and adopted by the voters in 1951. Its first section reads: "It is the intention of this article to grant and confirm to the people of every city and town in this state the right to self-government in all local matters." The process by which a community was to take advantage of this new provision began with the circulation of a petition calling for a referendum on the question of preparing a new charter, and the election of a charter commission of nine members by nonpartisan ballot to prepare a draft. The commission, if the vote is favorable, has a year to produce a charter, which must then go to the voters at a general election for approval.

If the charter is approved the community from then on operates under it and is bound only by state legislation that is of general application to all cities and towns. The assembly can no longer legislate specifically for that community unless the act is subsequently approved by a local referendum. The home-rule amendment, since 1986 incorporated into the body of the Constitution as Article XIII, despite the apparent granting of power over all local matters explicitly exempts the levying of taxes, the borrowing of money, and the judicial power of the state from the sphere of local action.

In addition to these areas of policy the courts over the years have identified other powers that are deemed to be part of the sovereignty of the state and thus reserved. One of the earliest identified had to do with elections. Pawtucket was told that it did not have the authority by charter to adopt nonpartisan odd-number year elections.[15] It was forced to secure General Assembly validation for that scheme. Matters pertaining to education and to the creation of crimes and setting of penalties for them, among others, were also found to be beyond the pale of home rule. In overall terms, the result of the collective action of the courts in relation to home rule is that cities and towns have quite free rein regarding the structure of their charter governments. What they cannot do is co-opt areas of substantive governmental power. The courts, in other words, have in effect reconfirmed Dillon's Rule by forbidding home-rule communities from exercising powers not explicitly granted, save over institutional arrangements.

The earliest communities to avail themselves of home rule were four of the old cities.[16] They had had experience with Democratic machine rule during the years between the lifting of the property qualification in 1930 and the adoption of the amendment. (Providence's experience was similar, but its new 1940 charter promised improvement. As a result it did not go for home rule until 1980.) These cities, following Pawtucket's lead, all sought to bypass the troublesome local parties by adopting nonpartisan elections, and to focus exclusive attention on local issues by scheduling municipal elections in odd-numbered years. To a considerable extent the aspirations of the reformers were realized.

The later history of home rule was somewhat different. One cannot encompass all of the local concerns and motives that fueled home-rule aspirations in the various towns with one or two sweeping generalizations. However, some patterns are discernible. For example, growing suburban towns with large populations often turned to the new option. In such communities the appropriateness of the town meeting came to be questioned as smaller and smaller percentages of voters attended them. Rhode Island never experimented with the "representative town meeting" that was being tried in Massachusetts. More important, however, was the growing realization that town councils, made up of citizens with other full-time occupations, were struggling to do their increasingly demanding jobs.

More and more reports were required by the state and federal governments; grant applications multiplied to tap available supplementary resources; and perhaps most demanding of all was the unionization of municipal employees and the burden on the councils to negotiate contracts, deal with grievances, and the rest.[17] The greatest felt need in the face of these mounting pressures was for a full-time person, either as a town manager or an elected administrator, who could take over the essentially executive and administrative roles that councils had first assumed centuries earlier, thus leaving those bodies free to make general policy and enact ordinances.

A succession of larger towns elected charter commissions that produced documents variously containing some full-time executive official to serve as chief administrator; a finance department to centralize budget preparation, tax levying and collection, purchasing, and other financial operations; and a replacement of the town meeting with council authority over appropriations and taxes. This last was often a very sensitive issue. Given the history of town government in Rhode Island, its closeness to the people, and its jealously guarded prerogatives, this element of direct democracy was hard to give up.

Rhode Island charters are often quite detailed documents. None followed the National Municipal League's Model Charter by, for example, making general provision for the creation of administrative departments by the council as needed. Rhode Island charters almost invariably spell out in detail what departments will exist, their duties and functions, the qualifications and selection of their directors, and so forth. This obviously means that charter amendments are frequently needed to make adjustments to meet new situations.

Charters also, interestingly, include quite elaborate conflict-of-interest and, in certain instances, open-government provisions. The early ones written for the old cities went into great detail on prohibited practices (both conflict of interest and political involvement), and penalties for infractions. In this respect they long predated state actions along these lines. One might compare the role of the towns and cities vis-à-vis the state to the innovative laboratory role that has been attributed to the states as precursors of national legislation. In recent years Rhode Island has put in place quite elaborate ethics codes, open-meetings and open-records laws, and other similar safeguards that preempt the earlier charter provisions.

THE TREND TOWARD CENTRALIZATION

There is some irony connected with this pattern of progressive modernization of city and town governing institutions and management capacity. The most recent general trend in the state affecting the role and responsibilities of local government is seen in a number of assembly enactments that have taken from the communities and placed under state control several of the major traditional local functions. This trend, regardless of its other benefits and justifications, has left local governments with just as much to do in most cases but with a good deal less leeway for doing it.

A sampling of policy areas and major enactments by the assembly affecting the role of local government and changing its relations with state government follows. Education may well be the outstanding example, both historically and in terms of the high proportion of state and local budgets that it consumes. Early in the history of the state education was provided at the initiative of the town with no state role. Over time the state role in imposing mandates, and later in providing a portion of the funding, grew enormously. In recent decades, though, the cities and towns must provide a major portion of the funding for public education. Only the local school committee has any voice in education policy, and that occurs within and is limited by a vast network of state rules, regulations, and restrictions. Indeed, by law school committee members are considered essentially state instruments.

Care of the needy and social welfare have already been mentioned. Though towns still have "welfare directors," those individuals and the town governments have little role left in this policy realm. What the state role will be in the future might well be affected by the current changes in federal welfare policy that give creative latitude to the states.

For a very long time public health was largely the responsibility of the towns and the health officers they appointed. In 1964 legislation shifted that whole responsibility to the state Department of Health, so that it might do centrally and more professionally what the towns had long done.[18]

The 1970s were an important decade. In 1977 the Department of Natural Resources was renamed the Department of Environmental Management (DEM) and given enhanced powers and authority in response to growing concern for the environment.[19] The DEM is mandated to deal with all questions regarding the approval of domestic and commercial septic systems and related matters. It also enforces legislation regulating the use of wetlands. In these and a number of other ways its activities impinge on the affairs of towns and their citizens. Legislation was also passed during the 1970s allowing the state to take over from local communities the whole area of building codes and their enforcement. Towns still issue building permits, but the code is now uniform statewide and ultimate control has passed into the hands of the state.[20]

In 1988 the state passed legislation requiring every local community to prepare a comprehensive plan covering land use and development of all kinds within the city or town. Elaborate criteria are provided. Prior to this law cities and towns did have plans, but now they are locked into a far more elaborate planning process which requires, among other things, that the resulting draft plan be submitted to the state for review. State approval is required before a plan is final, and the state can return a plan to a town with instructions for revision.[21] Land use has always been a matter of intense local concern. Until 1988 the planning process represented a largely local prerogative, along with the enactment of zoning ordinances to implement a plan. Now state control is much more direct and tighter. The law requires that each town revise its zoning ordinance to conform to the finally approved comprehensive plan.

In 1992 legislation was passed dealing with an area of local government activity which previously had been exclusively local: purchasing, and the letting of contracts. Under this new legislation each city and town must designate an official to serve as purchasing agent, and must follow state-prescribed guidelines related to the bidding process, selecting the successful bidder, using alternative procedures when required by special circumstances, and following a number of other regulations.[22]

All of these cumulative interventions by the state in what had been local affairs have deprived local officials and councils of much of their authority. In some cases the state has relieved them of responsibilities, but in many other cases it has left them with continuing responsibilities, though increasingly as de facto agents of the state. A far more centralized, professionalized, and uniform pattern of policy has resulted. These changes have not come without local friction, resistance, and frustration, however. Some changes and takeovers of responsibility have been welcomed, but others have aroused the centuries-old demand for local autonomy and freedom to do things as the town citizens desire.

One of the most serious causes of friction and resentment has been the chronic tendency of the state to enact mandates that must be carried out by the local communities without providing state money to pay for them. This has been most evident in education. Such mandates and collective bargaining agreements with teachers and other personnel have caused the cost of public education to rise steadily, often outstripping, as in the case of Central Falls, the local willingness and even ability to pay. Communities perceive the situation as one in which the local education establishment, with the strong support of state law and the state Department of Education, sets the bottom-line figure for the annual budget. The city or town then must find the money.

STATE-CITY COOPERATION

Despite the fact that much of the relationship between the cities and towns and the state in recent years has been tinged with rancor and created a local sense of victimization by an overbearing state government, this is not the whole story. By no means have all state "takeovers" and mandates been resisted or resented. There has also been cooperation and welcome acceptances at times, which can be well illustrated by Providence's story, where a couple of recent joint state-city projects should be noted.

The first of the two state-city cooperative projects was the construction of a convention center downtown, complete with a new major hotel. Very substantial state funding went into this project motivated by the expectation that while it would help to continue the rejuvenation of the city's central core, it would also boost the influx of tourists and therefore the state's as well as the city's economy.[23]

Another is the capital center project. Covering a large area of land between the statehouse and the downtown business district, a large railroad freight yard had long been adjacent to the tracks of the Boston–New York rail route that passes through Providence. By the early 1980s the freight yard had fallen largely into disuse and was occupying a tract of land strategically placed for other development. A plan was devised to take over this area, move the through tracks to provide still more space, and construct a new railroad station. The land thus made available would then be developed carefully under the supervision and control of a Capital Center Commission composed of appointees of the governor, of the mayor, and representatives of private historic preservation concerns and other interests.[24]

The most important project launched under the supervision of the commission is variously referred to as Providence Place Mall, or the Mall of New England. It is to be a massive downtown shopping mall with over a hundred shops plus restaurants, movie theaters, and anchor department stores. The city and the state have worked closely together on this project, particularly to provide financial support to the private interests committed to building it.[25] Both levels of government are providing portions of the funding. The city, for example, will give up some claims on property taxes in the expectation that the jobs created and the shoppers lured to the city will more than offset that loss. The state, of course, sees the project also as a major shot in the arm for the state's economy.

In summary, local government in Rhode Island has over the centuries—in terms of its form and shape, powers and responsibilities, and relation to the state—been one of the most important and persistent public issues. In a sense local control has been the master issue, and has affected and been affected by the development of policy in just about every other area of concern. The local government pattern at of the end of the twentieth century has moved very far from the almost chaotic pattern in the early days of colonial settlement. In many respects local government is a kind of branch office of the state government today. Yet the local loyalties of Rhode Islanders and their yearning to be left alone to run their own affairs are still very strong, even if frequently frustrated. Of one thing we can be quite sure: despite the theoretical appeal of taking the final step and turning the state into a single city-state, it will not happen. Gradually more and more governmental activity has been centralized. But, as they have with school system consolidation, Rhode Islanders are certain at some point to say "this far and no farther." That point will come long before the cities and towns lose their individual identities entirely.

Epilogue

"Poor Little Rhode Island, the smallest of the forty-eight . . ."

This popular song of a few decades ago, captures in a few words some important facts about the Ocean State. It is indeed the smallest—in area but not in population—of the now fifty states. At various times in its history it has been poor and, with the exception of Narragansett Bay, it lacks extensive or remarkable natural resources. These factors have done much to shape the history and culture of the state.

From the very beginning the colony's small size and relative economic insignificance (as seen from London) proved to be a curious boon. English authorities were apparently quite willing to confer a unique degree of local authority on Roger Williams's renegade settlements. The King Charles Charter of 1663 conferred remarkable democratic self-government and religious freedom on them that were enjoyed nowhere else in the colonies and certainly in few, if any, places in Europe. The phrasing of this unusual privilege of self-determination may well suggest a willingness to gratify the handful of subjects in light of "the remote distance of those places," as the charter put it. In other words, an experiment in this small remote place would be little threat to other British domains or to the uniformity imposed by the Church of England. The charter thus gave Rhode Island a measure of autonomy and freedom to regulate its own affairs enjoyed by none of the other colonies. Structurally the charter made the General Assembly, the representative body close to the people, the repository of most governmental power. The constitutions that followed essentially retained this structure, and the state still supports a representative body close to the people. Moreover, the size of the state continues to sustain a tradition of vocal and at times ornery citizen groups with access to and substantial influence on the political process.

Size has also affected the state's position in New England. During much of its early history its position as a small slice of territory sandwiched between Massachusetts and Connecticut tempted those two colonies to cast greedy glances and to mount strategies to split the colony between them. Not until the nineteenth century were Rhode Island's boundaries finally established; this experience only added to the outcast or rogue status of the state and further encouraged a kind of tough bravado and defensive pride among its citizens that remains evident today.

Clearly the availability of natural resources shape the history, development, and culture of any state. Narragansett Bay certainly did that for Rhode Island. That important body of water is often cited as the state's only significant natural resource. The state has no oil, few mineral resources of consequence, and no striking natural features other than the bay. It does not even have, within its thousand-plus square miles, a moderate amount of good agricultural soil.

As a result, Rhode Islanders throughout their history have had to live by their wits. This has engendered and the state has put to good use a considerable amount of ingenuity, grit, and entrepreneurial skill. The latter, in particular, has been displayed in an astonishing series of successful efforts to create and recreate a viable state economy. There have been numerous cycles of development, from the hardscrabble existence of colonial times to the state's prosperous economic zenith at the turn of the twentieth century, when Rhode Island enjoyed the second highest per capita income in the country. It has become fashionable in recent decades to argue that the state has serious and perhaps insolvable economic problems. Yet, at the turn of the twenty-first century the state is again on the rebound. A recent newspaper headline in the summer of 1999, just months before the beginning of the new millennium, noted that Rhode Island "survives the transition to [a] service economy," basically acknowledging the shift from defense contracting and manufacturing to a service-based economy. These economic transitions have caused profound demographic and political changes in the character of the state.

Early on, subsistence agriculture was partially supplanted by a movement to the carrying trade on ships constructed and home ported on the shores of Narragansett Bay. Sadly, the colonists' ingenuity and grit included the importation of slaves, a major element in the triangular trade that flourished during the eighteenth century. By the early nineteenth century the bay was the base for clipper ships and the China trade that produced enormous wealth. The manufacture of textiles, using waterpower produced by the rivers of the state, began at Slater's Mill in 1790 and eventually brought another major economic transition, making manufacturing the chief employer and wealth creator.

The textile industry continued to be the mainstay of the economy for the next 150 years. Beginning in the 1920s, however, the mills began to close or move to the cheaper labor markets in the South. Before they left they wrought massive demographic and political changes in Rhode Island. The early mills were staffed with workers drawn from the rural farms. Then came the Irish, driven out by the potato famine in their homeland. Still more workers were needed, so the mill owners actively recruited in French Canada and in Italy. Portuguese from the Azores further swelled the flood.

By the 1930s the population of the state was both vastly expanded and vastly changed in composition, from the original Anglo-Saxon stock to a polyglot array of immigrant groups and from overwhelmingly Protestant to two-thirds Catholic. Other states saw similar demographic shifts, but none to the extent of Rhode Island's. The intrastate geographic impact was huge. Small outlying towns lost population as the cities and mill towns grew rapidly. The result was the transformation of a small agricultural and trading state into one of the most highly industrialized and urbanized in the country.

The loss of textiles was partially replaced with other manufacturing, especially jewelry and machine tools and, in the years leading up to World War II, an increasing military presence. Eventually the U.S. Navy became the state's largest employer, until the pullout during the 1970s. Manufacturing employment continued to decline throughout this period, and the state slipped into a prolonged economic downturn. As of the late 1990s, however, the state has survived the rocky transition to a service economy. A strong educational base has been able to support the growing areas of modern technology, financial services, medical industries, and tourism, providing new economic directions and a rebound in the economy.

The impact of these economic and demographic shifts on the state's politics was great. Occupationally, a conservative farm and trading population was replaced by a large and growing blue-collar one. Not until the 1930s was the full electoral potential released and mobilized by what James Michael Curly of Boston called the "newer races." When it was liberated, a staunchly Republican state became solidly Democratic.

Following the Second World War the development of the interstate highway system spawned during the Eisenhower administration resulted in yet another population shift. Urban dwellers left the cities and began to populate the outlying towns. Urbanization gave way to suburbanization but with a Rhode Island twist. Because of the small size of the state, distance is a relative concept for Rhode Islanders, who regard a half-hour commute as burdensome. Hence, while the population of the city of Providence shrank (from a peak of 265,000 in 1925 to 150,000 by the latter part of this century), the population of Providence County remained fairly constant at about 500,000, as people moved to the suburban towns just a few miles away.

It was some time before the frustrations and resentments of the immigrants and their children, directed against those who had kept them marginalized on the political and economic sidelines, finally began to subside. That process was clearly helped by suburbanization. As the children and grandchildren of immigrants climbed the economic ladder and moved out of the crowded cities, political independence became more fashionable. At about the same time the national revulsion against machine politics and partisan ties, spurred by the Vietnam War and the Watergate scandals, further eroded traditional loyalties and behavior.

In terms of political culture, however, the more things changed the more they stayed the same. From the colonial period on, the entire history of the state has fostered a view of government and politics as individualistic. That is, politics is seen as a resource to be used for individual or group advantage: those in power claim the jobs, create the tax benefits, and reap political and economic advantages in other ways. The Republicans had done this with remarkable skill and struggled to hold onto power. Then, in the 1930s when the Democrats took over the levers of power, they in turn manipulated the system for their own group advantage. "Now it's our turn," you can imagine them saying.

Given this history and culture it is hardly surprising that reform movements in Rhode Island made little headway until the 1980s and 1990s. Nonetheless, notions that government must be honest, fair, even-handed, and used for the greater good rather than for group advantage have made considerable inroads in recent years. These ideas, of course, were spurred on by a few shocking and widely publicized scandals, but also no doubt by the growth of the suburban middle class and their changing expectations about efficient and effective government.

Successful reforms have altered the character of state government. Although flaws remain, citizens now enjoy more professional, accountable, and open government. Yet even in this changed environment echoes of the past reverberate. Despite the changes in economic patterns, social structure, religious affiliation, and population composition, they have played out against a remarkable continuity in constitutional and governmental arrangements. Structurally the royal charter made the General Assembly the representative body close to the people, the repository of most governmental power. The constitutions that followed essentially retained this structure, and a supreme court decision issued in 1999 affirmed the arrangement. Thus the legislature has sustained its premier position, resisting reformers' demands for restructuring the system and implementing the initiative and the referendum, both movements that have recently been successful in many other states.

Yet because of the state's small size, vocal and active interest groups still have the ability to access and influence the system. Even in light of legislative supremacy, and perhaps to some extent due to it, the political system is remarkably porous. In fact, as we move into the new century three of the most important issues facing Rhode Island will ultimately be left to "the people."

The first is the contentious issue as to whether Rhode Island should grant the Narragansett Indians the right to operate gambling casinos within the state's borders. In this case the Rhode Island Constitution does provide direction in that it mandates that any extensions of gambling in the state must be put to a public referendum. With the governor on one side and the General Assembly divided on the issue, various interest groups, from reformers and local government groups to the churches and big gambling interests, mobilized their resources and clashed in a heated and contentious debate reminiscent of Rhode Island politics as they have existed since colonial times. While the legislature opted not to put the question on the 2000 ballot, ultimately it will be left to the people, via a ballot question, to decide to allow the Naragansetts the right to initiate casino gambling.

Another issue concerns the economic development of the vast stretches of waterfront property at Quonset Point and its environs in the aftermath of the navy pullout. The land has reverted back to the state and it is now littered with abandoned and dilapidated shipping stations, storage spaces, airport runways, and loading docks. Buoyed by the economic recovery, in 1998 Governor Lincoln Almond charged the Economic Development Corporation to work with developers and shape proposals to redevelop the property as an industrial site that would include a high-volume container port and a rail link to the major Northeast corridor. As various proposals emerged (many of which required substantial dredging and landfill schemes), environmentalists, representatives of the fishing industry, boaters, and various local groups of citizens who live on or near the bay raised such a ruckus that the governor was forced to backpedal fast. He then initiated a "stakeholders process" through which representatives from all these groups can engage in a series of group encounters. The goal was to reach some form of consensus on the parameters of an acceptable plan that the governor would use as a baseline for further development proposals. Allowing all these groups input into the process, while highly democratic also resulted in something of an impasse.

Although the governor's office, the Economic Development Corporation, and the leadership in the General Assembly generally support industrial development, the idea of a container port is probably dead, and the likelihood that any significant industrial development will take place ultimately hinges on these groups reaching some form of consensus.

The final issue—one with profound long-term ramifications—relates to a restructuring of the institutional power of the governor vis-à-vis the General Assembly. In two majority opinions of 1999 and 2000 the state supreme court affirmed the premiere position of the General Assembly in the constitution. In these decisions the justices recommended that if the people of Rhode Island are unhappy with the existing constitutional arrangement they should change the constitution. As it happens, the constitution requires that the question of a constitutional convention be put to the people on the ballot every ten years. The political establishment over the years has been able to finesse this provision. (In 1994, for example, the question of calling a convention was placed on the ballot at the last minute with little publicity and it was defeated.) Reformers and other groups are already gearing up for the 2004 question, which may be the prelude to yet another massive and contentious "interest group encounter" in the form of a constitutional convention whereby the people of Rhode Island will once again shape their political future.

General Resources

Rhode Island is a small state, but one with a long and varied history. The following essay will illustrate the many and rich resources available to study the state's history and development. At the same time it should be noted that, with a few exceptions, not a great deal of recent scholarship has been produced, particularly on contemporary events. This is in some measure due to the fact that, unlike many states, the required study of Rhode Island history and politics has not been written into the curricula of the state's public colleges nor as a mandatory part of the secondary-school curriculum.

The following are the most important and fruitful sources of historical and political material about the state that, in addition to the sources cited in the notes, can be consulted by those interested in further study and research.

LIBRARIES

Any study of the state should begin at the library. The availability of journals, books, special collections, and government documents varies, but cumulatively these provide a rich source of materials.

The University of Rhode Island Library has extensive research material in its collection. The system houses a special collection, "Rhode Island Historical Manuscripts," which includes an array of early town records, letters, correspondence, and subject files. This collection also contains the political papers of many twentieth-century political figures, including former U.S. Senator Claiborne Pell, former governor and U.S. Senator John O. Pastore, Philip Noel, and Bruce Sundlun. It also houses the Rhode Island Collection, which contains historical material such as state publications printed prior to 1900, atlases, tax books, periodicals, maps, and early Rhode Island almanacs.

The university library is also a selective depository for U. S. government documents, and its collection of federal documents is the largest in the state. The Government Publications resource includes a collection of state budgets, legislative bills, state laws, Rhode Island supreme court decisions, current state almanacs, election results, population material and reports, and papers from the state's many departments and agencies.

The library is also part of the Helin consortium that has over fourteen thousand resources on the subject of Rhode Island. The consortium includes Rhode Island College, the Community College of Rhode Island, Providence College, Salve Regina University, Roger Williams University, and Johnson and Wales University. The URI library houses more than ten thousand of these holdings.

The Brown University Library, particularly the special collections found in the John Hay Library, is the repository of extensive and valuable materials relating to Rhode Island history, culture, and politics. The Sidney S. Rider Collection of Rhode Island History includes books, pamphlets, newspapers, manuscripts, engravings, posters, photographs, cartoons, and broadsides relating to Rhode Island prior to 1904. The library holds the papers of Thomas Wilson Dorr, lawyer, politician, reformer, and central figure in Rhode Island's "Dorr War" of 1842. The collection contains letters and speeches on suffrage, elections, banks, and state politics, and includes sixty scrapbooks of Dorr's personal and political correspondence, as well as other items relating to the Suffrage Party and Providence history. In addition there are collections of the papers of Rhode Island governors William Sprague (1830–1915) and Charles Warren Lippitt (1846–1924), and an official manuscript copy of the Acts and Resolves of the Rhode Island General Assembly (1678–1747).

The Rhode Island Manuscripts collection contains some three thousand items dating chiefly from 1638 to 1840, covering aspects of local history and tracing economic, political, legal, and cultural personalities and events. Papers on religious history reflect Brown University's Baptist origins, and include the papers of Roger Williams.

The John D. Rockefeller Library at Brown University houses the Government Documents department. Brown is a selective depository for U.S. federal government documents and United Nations documents, and is a full depository for Rhode Island state government publications. In addition, the Rockefeller library has files of theses and dissertations produced by graduate students and honors candidates, many of which contain valuable studies on various aspects of Rhode Island history and politics.

Providence College has made a major effort to build its collection of the papers of many of the key political figures in the recent history of

Rhode Island. The Philips Memorial Library of Special Collections holds the papers of Nelson W. Aldrich and the papers of many prominent twentieth-century mayoral, gubernatorial, and congressional figures. These include Joseph Doorley Jr., Dennis Roberts, Robert Quinn, Aime J. Forand, Edward J. Higgins, J. Howard McGrath, John E. Fogarty, and John O. Pastore. Other collections of interest are those from the Quonset Point Naval Station, the Urban League of Rhode Island, and the papers from the 1964 through 1969 and 1986 Rhode Island constitutional conventions.

The Rhode Island State Library in the statehouse has an extensive collection of reports, documents, and other materials pertaining to state government, including the files of the General Assembly Journals. The state library provides information on laws, regulations, and Rhode Island history. It also houses all past annual issues of the *Rhode Island Manual*, the virtual bible of those interested in state government research, with a range of information on past and present aspects of state government. Unfortunately, the secretary of state in 1994 discontinued publication of the manual and substituted instead a shorter "user's manual," the *Rhode Island Government Owner's Manual,* to replace the biannual publication. An alternate source, which is available at all libraries in the state, is the annual issue of the *Providence Journal Almanac*, a valuable source of updated information on the state.

The secretary of state's office also manages the Public Information Center, which tracks current legislative bills and provides updated information on lobbyist registration and administrative rules and regulations filings.

The State Archives and Public Records Administration contains comprehensive archives and records management services for all public documents. The archives also have the papers from the constitutional convention of 1842, the Journal of the House of Representatives, the Journal of the Senate, papers relating to the adoption of the constitution of the United States, petitions to the General Assembly, and the reports of committees of the General Assembly.

The Rhode Island Historical Society has a library with extensive archival collections, files of newspapers, and other valuable materials. It also publishes the journal *Rhode Island History,* which features numerous articles on all phases of Rhode Island history.

The Providence public library should also be visited. Along with other historical materials, the library has maintained a detailed index of articles appearing in *The Providence Journal.*

The Rhode Island Labor History Society holds an extensive collection of material relating to labor in Rhode Island, and has published a resource, the *Guide to the Historical Study of Rhode Island Working People*. This guide contains extensive listings of virtually all published material on labor in Rhode Island.

A key source of information about Rhode Island politics is newspapers, especially the *Providence Journal*, which is essentially the paper of record. Founded in 1820, it has been in continuous daily publication since 1829. In addition to a detailed index of articles located at the Providence Public Library, the *Providence Journal* has an archival room and an electronic research service that can provide copies of all articles printed after January 1, 1983. One can also consult the paper's web site at www/projo.com to access articles online.

Other regional papers that provide coverage of state politics include the *Kent County Daily Times*, the *Newport Daily News*, the *Pawtucket Times*, the *Westerly Sun,* and the *Woonsocket Call.* A highly respected source of business information is the *Providence Business News.*

Rhode Island History is published by the Rhode Island Historical Society. The *Roger Williams University Law Review* often publishes articles dealing with legal issues related to the Rhode Island courts and state government. *Rhode Island Monthly* is a popular magazine that covers politics, culture, and society.

Demographic, social, economic, and political data for the state and cities can be found in a number of publications. Primary sources are the *Book of the States* and the *Municipal Year Book* for various years. Comparative state and city data are also available in numerous U.S. Bureau of the Census documents such as *The Statistical Abstract of the United States,* the *State and Municipal Data Book,* the *Census of Governments,* and *State Government Finances* for various years. Extensive data tapes are available through the U. S. Bureau of the Census. Many of these same statistics are also published in government documents and can be found in the reference or documents sections of public and university libraries. The U. S. Department of Commerce, Bureau of the Census, publishes an *Annual Census Catalog and Guide* that provides a complete list of holdings in the archive. Another comparative guide for various years is Congressional Quarterly's *State Fact Finder: Rankings across America.*

Census information can be found at the state Department of Administration, Department of Health, Library Services, and the Department of Information, all designated as state data centers. Rhode Island has also developed a website (*www.info.state.ri.us/aslisthl.html*) which gives its citizens access to all state agencies. Most of the public libraries and all of the state colleges and universities provide computer access for the public.

RESEARCH CENTERS

For years the Bureau of Government Research at the University of Rhode Island published numerous studies of state and local government issues. Although the bureau no longer exists, its publications, housed at the University of Rhode Island Library, should be consulted.

The Rhode Island Public Expenditure Council is a business-supported organization but produces objective and valuable compilations of data on a variety of subjects. Its in-depth studies of governmental functions and agencies, as well as of policy proposals, are of excellent quality.

The Alfred Taubman Center of Public Policy and Institutions at Brown University produces various public policy studies that are extremely valuable for study and research. In addition, beginning in 1984 the center has conducted periodic public opinion surveys in the state relating to public affairs, issues, and personalities. The Public Opinion Laboratory publishes the "Public Opinion Report," a quarterly newsletter that provides descriptions and analyses of poll results.

The Rhode Island Economic Development Corporation can provide information such as economic data, tax information, and analysis and other studies related to development initiatives.

ELECTION DATA

The State Board of Elections publishes a volume containing the official count after each general election for state candidates and issues. For local races the handiest (though unofficial) source is the *Providence Journal Almanac*. For official counts, the city and town boards of canvassers may also be consulted.

Notes

1. RHODE ISLAND IN TRANSITION

1. *The World Almanac and Book of Facts: 1999* (Manwah NJ: Primedia, 1999).
2. A competing explanation holds that the state was named Rhode Island by the Dutch explorer Adriaen Block who termed it Roodt Eyland (red island) because of the red soil visible from the shore. Most people, including those at the Rhode Island Historical Society, hold to the other, more appealing, interpretation.
3. During the early twentieth century the state had the nation's largest foreign-born percentage of population. The 1930 census figures indicated that 30 percent of the population in Rhode Island was foreign born.
4. During the 1960s and 1970s the Eagleton Institute of Politics at Rutgers University, New Jersey, began sponsoring a series of state legislative conferences on professionalizing state legislatures and published a series of reports on the various states. The one written on Rhode Island was generally ignored. See Charles Tantillo, *Strengthening the Rhode Island Legislature* (New Brunswick NJ: Rutgers University Press, 1968).
5. See Kendra A. Holvey and Harold A. Holvey, *State Fact Finder: Ranking across America: 1998* (Washington DC: Congressional Quarterly Press, 1998).
6. Rhode Island ranks 33d among fifty states in total crime reported, below Massachusetts and Connecticut. The state has for decades had one of the lowest homicide rates in the country; while it formerly ranked high on car thefts, that number declined significantly throughout the 1990s. *Providence Journal*, 16 May 1995.
7. Tom Rice and Alexander Sumberg, "Civic Culture and Government Performance in the American States," *Publius: The Journal of Federalism* 27 (winter 1997): 99–114.
8. Richard McIntyre "Field of Dreams and Labor Market Outcomes in the 1990s,"

Proceedings of the Forty-sixth Annual Meeting (Boston: Industrial Relations Research Foundation, 1994), pp. 480–88.

9. National figures indicate that the nation went into a short, shallow recession during 1990 and 1991. This recession was longer and ran deeper in New England, and Rhode Island was particularly hard hit.

10. State figures indicate that number of state employees decreased from 18,000 in 1989 to just over 15,500 in 1998. *Budget Analysis, Fiscal Year 1999*, House Fiscal Advisory Report, 1998.

11. The federal court of appeals in 1999 found against the union pensions.

12. Robert Atkinson "How to Revive Manufacturing," *Providence Journal*, 13 May 1997.

13. McIntyre, "Field of Dreams," pp. 480–88.

14. See Darrell West, Thomas Anton, and Jack Combs, *Public Opinion in Rhode Island, 1984–1993* (Providence: Brown University, 1994). Also see Thomas Anton and Darrell West, "Trust, Self-Interest, and Representation in Economic Policymaking: Rhode Island Reconsidered," *New England Journal of Public Policy* vol. 3 no. 1 (winter–spring, 1987): 73–87.

15. Parts of this section are drawn from "The Rhode Island Legislature: The Center Still Holds," by Maureen Moakley and Elmer Cornwell. Paper delivered at the Annual Meeting of the American Political Science Association, 1996.

16. *Rhode Island Federation of Teachers,* AFT, AFL-CIO *vs. Sundlun*, No. 91–196-Appeal, 1991.

17. Before being appointed to the post of chief administrator of the state court system, Matthew Fay was the Speaker of the House of Representatives during the heyday of pension extensions and revolving-door appointments.

18. Fay was accused of offenses such as helping a friend move the court date for traffic tickets and having a real estate partner on a rotating list of court-appointed arbitrators. He also allowed Matthew Smith to use a court fund, established by his predecessor, for miscellaneous expenses like condolence flowers for court workers, deli deliveries, office water coolers, and office baseball trips. He pleaded guilty to two felony counts: one for wrongful conversion of money over $100 and another for "obstructing the judicial system." He resigned from the court, received a suspended sentence, and was disbarred.

19. See Maureen Moakley, "The New Face of the Rhode Island Legislature," *Providence Journal*, 13 January 1997.

20. The legislature passed some innovative responses to New Federalism, including the first-in-the-country plan for electricity deregulation as well as RIte-Care, a state health-insurance plan for working poor families which has been extended to all eligible populations under eighteen years old. These, along with Rhode Island's welfare reform legislation, have been recognized as national models.

21. See Scott MacKay, "Poll: Voters Divided on Stadium," *Providence Journal,* 25 September 1997.

22. Timothy Harman, "RI Residents Feel Confident on Economy," *Providence Journal,* 14 October 1997.

23. For a fascinating account of the redevelopment projects see Milly McLean, "Moving Heaven and Earth," *Rhode Island Monthly,* February 1989.

24. Approval of the plan to build the mall became a key campaign issue in the 1994 election. Both gubernatorial candidates, in response to public cynicism, campaigned against the mall and vowed to cancel the project once elected. After the election the winner, Republican Lincoln Almond, struck a deal just a bit different than the one he denounced and the development commenced.

25. 3 November 1997.

2. POLITICAL CULTURE IN THE OCEAN STATE

1. See the discussion of political culture in Daniel J. Elazar, *American Federalism: A View from the States* (New York: Thomas Crowell, 1966).

2. Elazar notes that these categories are merely labels and not literal terms.

3. Carey McWilliams, *The Idea of Fraternity in America* (Berkeley: University of California Press, 1973), p. 144.

4. Elazar, *American Federalism,* p. 87.

5. See, for example, Thomas J. Anton, *American Federalism and Public Policy: How the System Works* (New York: Random House, 1989). See also John Kincaid, ed., *Political Culture, Public Policy, and the American States* (Philadelphia: ISHI Press, 1982), and Alan Rosenthal and Maureen Moakley, *The Political Life of the American States* (New York: Praeger, 1984).

6. John Winthrop and Lawrence W. Towner, eds., "A Model of Christian Charity," in *An American Primer,* Daniel J. Boorstin, ed. (New York: University of Chicago Press, 1966).

7. McWilliams, *Idea of Fraternity,* p. 144.

8. Gordon S. Wood, *The Radicalism of the American Revolution* (New York: Vintage Books, 1991), p. 140.

9. Edmund Morgan, *Roger Williams: The Church and the State* (New York: W. W. Norton, 1967), pp. 118–20.

10. William G. McLoughlin, *Rhode Island: A History* (New York: Norton, 1986), pp. 4–5.

11. Wood, *Radicalism of American Revolution,* p. 122.

12. McLoughlin, *Rhode Island.*

13. See Perry Miller, *Roger Williams: His Contribution to the American Tradition* (New York: Athenaeum, 1962).

14. Emily Easton, *Roger Williams: Prophet and Pioneer* (Boston: Houghton Mifflin, 1930).

15. McLoughlin, *Rhode Island*, p. 58.

16. William G. McLoughlin, *New England Dissent* vol. 1 (Cambridge: Harvard University Press, 1971), p. 10.

17. McLoughlin, *Rhode Island*, pp. 106–8.

18. David S. Lovejoy, *Rhode Island Politics and the American Revolution: 1760–1776* (Providence: Brown University Press, 1958).

19. Lovejoy, *Rhode Island Politics*, p. 194.

20. Wood, *Radicalism of American Revolution*, p. 294.

21. McLoughlin, *Rhode Island*, p. 149.

22. For a fascinating account of the Bloodless Revolution see Matthew J. Smith, "The Real McCoy in the Bloodless Revolution of 1935," *Rhode Island History* xxxii (1973): 67–85.

23. Patrick T. Conley, *The Irish in Rhode Island* (Providence: Rhode Island Heritage Commission, 1988).

24. Albert K. Aubin, *The French in Rhode Island* (Providence: Rhode Island Heritage Commission, 1988).

25. Carmela E. Santoro, *The Italians in Rhode Island: The Age of Exploration to the Present, 1524–1989* (Providence: Rhode Island Heritage Commission, 1990), pp. 3–4.

26. Geraldine Foster, *The Jews in Rhode Island* (Providence: Rhode Island Heritage Commission, 1985).

27. Rachel Cunha, Susan Pacheco, and Beth Pereira Wolfson, *The Portuguese in Rhode Island* (Providence: Rhode Island Heritage Commission, 1985).

3. RHODE ISLAND AND THE FEDERAL SYSTEM

1. McLoughlin, *Rhode Island*, p. 41.

2. McLoughlin, *Rhode Island*, p. 84.

3. Patrick T. Conley, "Anarchiad, 1786–1787," *Rhode Island Bar Journal* 35 (May 1987): 11–19.

4. McLoughlin, *Rhode Island*, p. 128.

5. McLoughlin, *Rhode Island*, pp. 142–47.

6. Maureen Moakley, "Political Parties in Rhode Island: Back to the Future," *Polity* (winter 1997).

7. See "The Federal Budget and the States: Fiscal Year 1995" (Cambridge: Harvard University Taubman Center for State and Local Government, September 1996).

8. Jonathan Saltzman, "State Gets Bigger Return from Uncle Sam," *Providence Journal*, 13 August 1999.

9. *Providence Journal*, 3 February 1997.

10. See John Kincaid, "The Devolution Tortoise and the Centralization Hare," *New England Economic Review* (May–June 1998): 1.

11. Felice Freyer, "Almond Plans to Build on RIte Care," *Providence Journal*, 9 September 1998.

12. See Thomas Anton and Richard Francis, "Welfare Reform: Lessons from New England," paper delivered at the New England Political Science Association Meeting, 1998.

13. "Are States Improving the Lives of Poor Families?" Report issued by the Center on Hunger and Poverty, Tufts University, 1998.

14. Christopher Rowland, "Rhode Island Trails Most of U.S. in Reducing Welfare Rolls," *Providence Journal*, 1 February 1999.

15. Scott MacKay, "New England Governors Face Hard Times," *Providence Journal*, 31 July 1995.

16. Timothy Barmann, "Watch Out, Boston! RI Has Its Eye on Your Business," *Providence Journal*, 12 February 1998.

17. *Providence Journal*, 24 July 1997.

18. "EB's new edge," *Providence Journal*, 24 August 1995.

19. For a thoughtful discussion of Indian and settler relations in New England see William Cronin, *Changes in the Land* (New York: Hill and Wang, 1983).

20. McLoughlin, *Rhode Island*, p. 5.

21. Ethel Boissevain, *The Narragansett People* (Phoenix: Indian Tribal Series, 1975).

22. Bruce Sundlun, "Let's Have a Go at Gambling," *Providence Journal*, 13 July 1997.

23. Betsy Taylor, "Locals Salute Pequots' Plans," *Providence Journal*, 26 October 1997.

24. Katherine Gregg, "Tribe's Backers Gamble $9 million on Casino," *Providence Journal*, 1 April 1998.

25. For an excellent overview of the quest of the Indians for a casino, see John H. Mulligan, "Casino Is Elusive Dream for Tribe," *Providence Journal*, 9 August 1998.

4. THE CONSTITUTION

1. According to a tabulation by Albert L. Sturm in *Thirty Years of State Constitution-Making: 1938–1968* (New York: National Municipal League, 1970), as of 1969 the states collectively had adopted 137 constitutions, or an average of nearly three per state.

2. An earlier 1644 patent, obtained by Roger Williams from the parliamentary commissioners, failed to gain enough support to unify the colony.

3. The text of the Royal Charter may be found in most issues of the *Rhode Island Manual*. The charter has no article or section subdivisions which makes specific citations difficult.

4. See Patrick T. Conley, *Democracy in Decline* (Providence: Rhode Island Historical Society, 1977), p. 48.

5. Peter J. Coleman documents this shift in detail. Working with 1790 through 1840 census data, he divided the thirty-one towns into ten that were expanding rapidly, fifteen that were static, and six declining. The first group centered on Providence and in the Blackstone and Pawtuxet valleys. The six decliners were the towns most distant from these centers of economic development. Peter J. Coleman, *The Transformation of Rhode Island 1790–1860* (Providence: Brown University Press, 1969), p. 220.

6. Coleman, *Transformation of Rhode Island*, p. 256.

7. See chapter six in Coleman, *Transformation of Rhode Island* and McLoughlin, *Rhode Island*, pp. 126–37.

8. The text of the 1843 constitution may be found in issues of the *Rhode Island Manual* prior to 1986, when an edited version was accepted by the voters which inserted all accumulated amendment provisions in their proper place.

9. That it was the conscious intention of the framers to produce a weak governorship is interestingly illustrated in the wording of Article VII ("Of the Executive Power") section 1: "The chief executive power of this state shall be vested in a governor, who, together with the lieutenant-governor shall be annually elected by the people." The framers, here and elsewhere, must have been using the national constitution as a model. Note, however, the insertion of the word "chief" in phrasing that otherwise follows closely the comparable federal provision. This change probably reflects both the inclusion of other elected executive officers like the secretary of state and treasurer, but also the fact that the assembly would continue to play a major role.

10. For an example see Richard D. Bingham and David Hedge, *State and Local Government in a Changing Society* (New York: McGraw-Hill, 1991), p. 30.

11. Major efforts to revise the constitution using the amendment mechanism failed at the polls in 1898 and in 1899.

12. Opinion of the Court to the Governor in the Matter of the Constitutional Convention 55 R.I. 56, 1935.

13. Advisory to the Governor, 612 A2d (R.I. 1992).

14. Actually Rhode Island had begun this kind of regulation in 1974 when the General Assembly passed an act entitled "Require Reporting of Campaign Contributions and Expenditures, Limiting Election Campaign Expenditures, and Making an Appropriation Therefore" (1974 Public Laws, Ch. 298). This was amended three times between then and the adoption of the amendment. Five pieces of legislation

were passed after 1986 to further tighten the law and cover issues like public funding that had not been dealt with earlier.

15. The major change regarding impeachment was a specification of impeachable offenses, of which there was no mention in the original provision.

16. The original guarantee of "shore rights" was expanded to cover the overall protection of the natural resources of the state.

17. A 1996 study that took into account both statutory and constitutional provisions ranks Rhode Island with a large number of states at 3.5 on a scale of 5.0 (actual scores ranged from 4.0 down to 2.5). Virginia Gray and Herbert Jacob, *Politics in the American States* (Washington DC: Congressional Quarterly Press, 6th ed., 1996), p. 237. See also a discussion in chapter six of similar classification schemes.

18. See Advisory Opinion to the Governor, 732 A (R.I. 1999) and *Lincoln C. Almond v. the Rhode Island Lottery Commission*, 99–525-Appeal (R.I. 2000).

5. THE GENERAL ASSEMBLY

1. Lovejoy, *Rhode Island Politics*, p. 24.

2. Representation was constituted on the basis of population, always allowing one representative for any fraction exceeding half the population ratio. The population ratio as of the effective date of the constitution was 1,530 per representative. Nine towns had less than the ratio, four with under one thousand inhabitants. Providence's population at that time would have entitled it to fifteen representatives rather than the twelve (one-sixth) allowed by the constitution.

3. Amendment XIX.

4. 95 R.I. 68, 183 A2d 296 (1962).

5. Report of the Blue Ribbon Commission on the General Assembly, "The General Assembly in Rhode Island, A Blue Print for the Twenty-First Century," December 1993.

6. See Lincoln Steffens, "Rhode Island, A State for Sale," *McClure's Magazine*, vol. 24 no. 4 (February 1905); McLoughlin, *Rhode Island*, chapter 5; and Garrett D. Byrnes and Charles H. Spilman, *The Providence Journal* (Providence: Providence Journal Company, 1980), pp. 201–12, for the nineteenth century and early twentieth century period.

7. Lovejoy, *Rhode Island Politics*, p. 24.

8. The "long count" was the result of a disputed outcome of the gubernatorial election of 1956. After a solid run of Democratic gubernatorial victories, Democrat Dennis Roberts appeared to have won the 1956 race by the slimmest of margins. In fact, when the absentee ballots were counted it appeared that Republican Christopher Del Sesto was ahead. A request to have some ballots invalidated by the courts was successful and Roberts was able to retain his office. However, the press played

this up as an election steal and in the rematch in 1958 Del Sesto, a Republican, won.

9. Moakley and Cornwell, "Rhode Island Legislature: Center Still Holds."
10. Karen Hansen, "Are Coalitions Really on the Rise?" *State Legislatures* vol. 15 no. 4 (April 1989): 11.
11. Charles Tantillo, *Strengthening the Rhode Island Legislature* (New Brunswick NJ: Rutgers University Press for Eagleton Institute, 1968).

6. THE EXECUTIVE AND THE ADMINISTRATION

1. Gray and Jacob, *Politics in American State*, p. 237.
2. Article of Amendment XV, now section 14 Article IX of the 1986 edited version of the constitution.
3. James Q. Dealey, *Political Situations in Rhode Island* (privately published by author, 1928).
4. Erwin L. Levine, *Theodore Francis Green, The Rhode Island Years* (Providence: Brown University Press, 1963), p. 181.
5. Levine, *Theodore Francis Green*, p. 185.
6. Chapter 2188, Public Laws of 1935, section 1.
7. Chapter 2188 was essentially skeleton legislation that was fleshed out in chapter 2250, Public Laws of 1935, approved 1 June 1935, entitled "An act relating to the civil administration of the state government and amending or repealing certain general and public laws."
8. General Laws of Rhode Island, 1938, chapter 7, sec. 4, clauses A and C.
9. 1951 Public Laws, chapter 2727; currently chapter 11 of title 42 of the General Laws.
10. Former Governor Noel provided considerable insight into his staffing of the governor's office in a telephone interview.
11. These currently appear in the General Laws as chapters 63 and 64 of title 42. In 1995 Governor Lincoln Almond secured passage of legislation (1995 Public Laws, chapter 370) which folded both the department and the Port Authority into a new entity called the Rhode Island Economic Development Corporation.
12. Much of this information on both the Sundlun and Almond administrations comes from an extensive personal interview with an individual who had served on the policy staffs in both administrations, 22 January 1997.

7. THE COURTS

1. See the discussion of the courts in Lovejoy, *Rhode Island Politics*.

2. Lovejoy, *Rhode Island Politics*, pp. 7–30.

3. Steffens, "A State for Sale."

4. Constitution of Rhode Island, Article X, section 4, as cited in *Rhode Island Manual*, 1991–1994. But see Advisory Opinion, 507. A. 2nd 1316, 1323, RI, 1986, wherein a majority of the justices opined that the General Assembly's power to declare such offices to be vacant had ceased to exist as early as 1854 when the annual session to exercise such power was eliminated.

5. Matthew Smith, "The Real McCoy."

6. It was not uncommon for legislators to "trade" their electoral slots during periods of reapportionment that consolidated their districts for cushy and secure court positions with extensive pension benefits.

7. A summary account of this episode was taken from "The Chief Justice Resigns: A Look Back," *Providence Journal*, 29 May 1986.

8. Smith headed a commission that dealt with reforming the court structure and initiated many of the reform proposals the commission had recommended. But, as one member of the commission recalled, "Matty would get red in the face whenever we brought up the idea of changing the judicial selection system."

9. See editorial in the *Providence Journal*, 3 November 1997.

10. Scott MacKay, "Legislators Ready to Pare Incentives for Clerks," *Providence Journal*, 27 March 1994.

11. Karen A. Bordeleau, "A Study: The Rhode Island State Court System," unpublished paper.

12. Brief descriptions of the courts were taken from *The 1996 Report on the Judiciary* prepared by the Administrative Office of the State Courts, 1998.

13. Additional information on the superior court was taken from a booklet "Rhode Island Superior Court: 1996," which was issued under the direction of Justice Joseph F. Rogers, Presiding Justice.

14. See Maureen Moakley, "Reinventing Government in Rhode Island," paper presented at the annual meeting of the American Political Science Association, September 1998.

15. While Judge Arrigan is regarded as a leader who was responsible for the significant overhaul of the workers compensation court, he made some enemies in the process and was scantioned by the supreme court for violating ethics standards. Although many observers believe that charges against him—for inappropriately promoting the wares of missionaries in his court—which led to a hearing against him before the Judicial Performance Evaluation Committee, were prompted by individuals who were unhappy with the changes he had instigated in the court system. Some of the charges were upheld and Judge Arrigan was censured for pressuring attorneys to contribute to favorite charities of the judge.

16. William J. Donovan, "Workers Comp Law: A Dying Profession," *Providence Journal*, 22 February 1998.

17. An excellent series, "Disorder in the Court," by Christopher Rowland and Jonathan Saltzman, charted the abuses in the system. See *Providence Journal*, 8–9 February 1998. The report prompted a review of the system and subsequent significant changes.

18. Christopher Rowland and Jonathan Saltzman, "Traffic Court Shifts Gears," *Providence Journal*, 11 February 1998, was part of the follow-up effort.

19. Cited in the *Providence Journal*, 10 June 1998.

20. Rhode Island Supreme Court advisory opinion 93–120, 1993.

21. *Rhode Island Federation of Teachers*, AFT, AFL-CIO v. *Sundlun*, 91–196-Appeal, 1991.

22. RI 97–81-MP 28, 1997.

23. Susan Fino, *The Role of State Supreme Courts in the New Judicial Federalism* (New York: Greenwood Press, 1987).

24. John Kincaid, "The New Judicial Federalism" (Lexington KY: Council of State Governments, September–October 1988).

25. See *Sundlun v City of Pawtucket et. al.* 94–203 MP, 1995.

26. Edward Beiser, "The Rhode Island Supreme Court: A Well-Integrated Political System," *Law and Society Review* 90 (1974): 489–504.

27. See *Bandoni vs State of Rhode Island*, 95274, 1998.

28. Robert Flanders, "The Utility of Separate Judicial Opinions in Appellate Courts of Last Resort: Why Dissents Are Valuable," *Roger Williams University Law Review* vol. 4 no. 2 (spring 1999): 401–23.

29. See Kincaid, "New Judicial Federalism." Kincaid argues that there has been a shift from an ethic of communitarianism to one of individualism. A communitarian ethic would expect citizens who choose to live in a given community to abide by the rules of that community. The individualistic ethic, on the other hand, would be more concerned with the protection of the rights of individuals against powerful majorities.

30. Tracy Breton, "High Court Voids Conviction but Allows Most Key Evidence for Retrial," *Providence Journal*, 27 April 1984.

31. See Wayne Swanson, *The Christ Child Goes to Court* (Philadelphia: Temple University Press, 1990). See also John Kincaid and Robert F. Williams, "The New Judicial Federalism: The State's Lead in Right's Protection," *The Journal of State Government* 65 (April–June 1992): 50–52.

32. *Weisman v Lee*, 505 U.S. 577, 1992.

8. POLITICAL PARTIES

1. Significant portions of this chapter are drawn from Maureen Moakley, "Political Parties in Rhode Island: Back to the Future," *Polity* (spring 1997): 95–112.
2. See John Bibby, "Parties and Elections," *Politics in the American States*, Virginia Gray and Herbert Jacob, eds. (Washington DC: Congressional Quarterly Press, 1996).
3. After 1888 the suffrage question continued to be an issue. In fact, the unrestricted right to vote in city council elections for non-property holders was not secured until 1928.
4. See McLoughlin, *Rhode Island*, p. 161.
5. Kristi Anderson, *The Creation of a Democratic Majority* (Chicago: University of Chicago Press, 1979).
6. Duane Lockard, *New England State Politics* (Princeton NJ: Princeton University Press, 1959), p. 72.
7. Moakley, "Political Parties in Rhode Island," p. 103.
8. Kennedy had a tough first race for an open seat and drew on the considerable political resources of his family. An award-winning PBS documentary, "Taking on the Kennedys," underscored the considerable force with which the Kennedy machine took on Patrick Kennedy's opponent.
9. See "Taking on the Kennedys."
10. For a similar perspective on partisan activities in the 1980s see Darrell West, "Stalled Realignment: Party Change in Rhode Island," in Maureen Moakley, ed., *Party Realignment and State Politics* (Columbus: Ohio State University Press, 1992).
11. Moakley, "Political Parties in Rhode Island," p. 109.
12. Scott MacKay, "York's Finances Catching Up with Almond's," *Providence Journal*, 15 April 1998.
13. MacKay, "York's Finances Catching Up."
14. Scott MacKay, "More and More, Endorsements Mean Less and Less," *Providence Journal*, 27 June 1996.
15. Jonathan Saltzman, "Whitehouse Wins in a Landslide," *Providence Journal*, 16 September 1998.
16. Cianci was in a tight race against a capable and well-known Democratic incumbent, Joseph Doorley, who, although weakened in the Democratic primary was expected to carry Federal Hill, an Italian district in Providence that normally supported the Democratic party. A few days before the election signs mysteriously appeared all over Federal Hill that stated, "Keep the Garlic Out of City Hall." This naturally enraged and mobilized Italian voters to support Cianci, who is Italian.
17. See the *Providence Journal*, 28 July 1994.

18. Fromma Harrop, "Yankee GOPers Go Democratic," *Providence Journal,* 26 November 1996.

9. INTEREST AND GROUP REPRESENTATION

1. 1912 Public Laws, chapter 847.
2. 1988 Public Laws, chapter 436; chapter 10 to title 22 of the present General Laws.
3. *Providence Journal,* 27 June 1997, pp. l and 12.
4. *Providence Journal,* 29 June 1997, p. A8.
5. See Clive S. Thomas and Ronald J. Hrebnar, "Interest Groups in the States," in Virginia Gray and Herbert Jacob, *Politics in the American States* (Washington DC: Congressional Quarterly Press, 1996).
6. Jay S. Goodman, *The Democrats and Labor in Rhode Island, 1952–1962* (Providence: Brown University Press, 1967), p. 103.
7. 1988 Public Laws, chapter 486.
8. 1985 Public Laws, chapter 486.
9. Milly McLean, "Moving Heaven and Earth," in *Rhode Island Monthly* (February 1989): 30–68.
10. For a discussion of the changing dynamics of local corporate activity see Thomas J. Anton, "Globalization and the Decline of Community Investment," paper delivered at the Annual Meeting of the American Political Science Association, September 1998.
11. Garrett C. Byrnes and Charles H. Spilman, *Providence Journal: One Hundred and Fifty Years* (Providence RI: *Providence Journal* Press, 1980).
12. See Darrell M. West, Thomas Anton, and Jack Combs, *Public Opinion in Rhode Island, 1984–1993,* in John Hazen White Sr., ed. and Public Opinion Laboratory (Providence: Brown University, 1994), p. 14.
13. West, Anton, and Combs, *Public Opinion,* p. 20.
14. University of Rhode Island poll on voter attitudes, 1998.
15. McLoughlin, *Rhode Island,* p. 120.
16. See Rhode Island General Laws, chapter 16–21.1 and section 16–23.2.
17. That particular case, *Lynch v. Donnelly,* was reversed by the U.S. Supreme Court in March 1984. But the practical effect was to set restrictions for religious displays on public property.

10. BUDGET POLITICS AND POLICY

1. The authors would like to thank Michael O'Keefe for his help in revising this chapter.

2. Rhode Island Constitution, Article IX, section 15.
3. See chapter 780, Rhode Island Public Laws, 1926. For a review of Republican attempts to hold back Democratic access to power during this period see McLoughlin, *Rhode Island*, pp. 162–82.
4. John Chafee, a popular incumbent governor, campaigned in 1968 in support of a state income tax as the only way to balance the budget. He was defeated by Democrat Frank Licht, who vowed not to support such a tax. In 1971, however, a permanent income tax was passed. Licht retired the following year.
5. The boom or recovery of the early 1980s was a short-lived result of the Reagan administration's defense buildup.
6. See Robert Tannenwals and Jonathan Cowan, "Fiscal Capacity, Fiscal Need, and Fiscal Comfort among U.S. States: New Evidence," *Publius: The Journal of Federalism* 27 (summer 1997): 113–25. Note: these data are based on 1994 figures, before two major property tax reductions were put in place.
7. These data are drawn from U.S. Census Bureau figures, found in *Government Finances* (which the government stopped publishing in 1993). It was formally available in *Significant Features of Fiscal Federalism* published by the Advisory Commission on Intergovernmental Relations.
8. The study was conducted by KPMG, Peat Marwick Policy Economics Group, in November, 1993.
9. Christopher Rowland, *Providence Journal*, 30 March 1999.
10. The Sundlun administration enjoyed a highly knowledgeable and savvy fiscal staff who assisted the governor in dominating the budget process. When a Republican administration came into power in 1995, they replaced that budget director with their own appointment. The house promptly hired the former governor's budget officer, giving them considerable knowledge and leverage in the budget process.
11. The Brown Poll, June 1995.
12. Russell Garland, "Almond Fights to Retain Budget Say," *Providence Journal*, 8 July 1996.
13. Russell Garland, "DEPCO Money Off-limits, Panel Decides," *Providence Journal*, 24 March 1998.
14. Scott Mackay and Christopher Rowland, "What To Do with All That Extra Money?" *Providence Journal*, 26 May 1998.
15. Darrell West, as quoted in "Budget Skirmish Signals Shift in RI Politics," *Providence Journal*, 14 June 1998.
16. This section draws heavily on the Rhode Island Public Expenditure Council Report, *Analysis of the FY 1999 State Budget: Managing Prosperity, 1998*. Special thanks to Peter Marino, principal author.
17. RIPEC, *Analysis of 1999 Budget*.

18. Rhode Island Public Expenditure Council Newsletter, vol. 2 (August 1998).
19. "General Assembly Passes Landmark Bills; Senate Adjourns before Finishing Business," *Providence Journal,* 1 July 1998.

11. THE POLITICS OF EDUCATION

1. Much of the data for this chapter was drawn from a series of reports prepared by the Rhode Island Expenditure Council, especially *Results: Education in Rhode Island, 1999.* One other important source was an excellent series called "Teaching Matters," a five-part series that was published by the *Providence Journal* in May 1998.
2. Estimates of the number of teachers are often cited as over 12,500, but that figure includes administrators as well as classroom teachers.
3. Among younger groups the picture has improved; presently, high school completion rates are just under 90 percent, ranking the state twenty-first nationally.
4. See "How Rhode Island Schools Compare," Rhode Island Public Expenditure Council, 1996.
5. "How Rhode Island Schools Compare," p. 37.
6. For a brief and engaging history of public education in Rhode Island, see the supreme court decision *Sundlun v. Pawtucket,* 1995.
7. See Swanson, *Christ Child Goes to Court.*
8. School population estimates vary slightly. The 1996 nonpublic school population from the Rhode Island Department of Education gives a figure of 16.8 percent.
9. Carl Senna, "It's Time to Share the Burden," *Providence Journal,* 12 July 1995.
10. *Results: Education in Rhode Island, 1999,* Rhode Island Public Expenditure Council, p. 29.
11. This result was documented in the RIPEC report of 1996.
12. See RIPEC report, 1999.
13. *Sundlun v. Pawtucket,* 1995.
14. D. Morgan McVicar, "Proposed State Budget Ups Education Funding in Every Community," *Providence Journal,* 29 June 1996.
15. Elliot Krieger and Elizabeth Rau, "We Must Try Harder and Do Better," *Providence Journal,* 8 April 1998.
16. D. Morgan McVicar, "A Force in Education," *Providence Journal Bulletin,* 3 May 1998.
17. For an excellent summary of the role of teachers unions in Rhode Island see Elliot Krieger and Elizabeth Rau, "Teachers Turned to Unions," *Providence Journal,* 6 May 1998.
18. Although strikes are technically illegal, in each case the courts must hold a hearing

and find that the strike is doing "irreparable harm" before teachers can be ordered back to work.

19. Russell Garland, "Almond Calls for More Charter Schools," *Providence Journal,* 4 March 1998.

20. Celeste Tarricone, "Coventry Will Reward Teacher Performance," *Providence Journal,* 29 September 1999.

21. RIPEC report, 1999.

22. See Scott MacKay, "Arena Deal a Coming-of-age for URI," *Providence Journal Bulletin,* 17 June 1998.

23. The report was issued by *Education Week.*

12. LOCAL GOVERNMENT

1. For the general historical pattern of Providence's economic development see Margaret D. Uroff, *Becoming a City: From Fishing Village to Manufacturing Center* (New York: Harcourt, Brace, and World, 1968). For more details see James B. Hedges, *The Browns of Providence,* 2 vols. (Providence: Brown University Press, 1952 and 1968).

2. Sidney V. James, *Colonial Rhode Island* (New York: Scribners, 1975).

3. James, *Colonial Rhode Island,* p. 56.

4. James, *Colonial Rhode Island,* p. 72.

5. James, *Colonial Rhode Island,* p. 145.

6. James, *Colonial Rhode Island,* p. 147.

7. The creature theory is often referred to as "Dillon's Rule."

8. Dealey, *Political Situations in Rhode Island.*

9. Article of Amendment XX, Rhode Island Constitution.

10. See McLoughlin, *Rhode Island,* pp. 188–91.

11. See "Central Falls: Fiscal Emergency Act, title 45, chapter 52.1," General Laws of Rhode Island, enacted 1991.

12. Article of Amendment XVIII, since 1986 Article XIII of the constitution.

13. One of the first bills the Democrats passed in January 1935 when they gained control of the General Assembly abolished the Providence police commission.

14. This legislative charter went into effect in 1941.

15. See *Flynn v. McCaughey,* 81 R.I. 143 (1953).

16. Pawtucket, Central Falls, Woonsocket, and Newport, all in 1952.

17. Legislation granting to groups of city employees the right to organize and bargain was passed during the 1960s.

18. See title 23, chapter 2 of the General Laws.

19. See title 42, chapter 17.1 of the General Laws.

20. See title 23, chapter 27.3, section 100.1.1 and subsequent sections of the General Laws.
21. See title 45, chapter 22.2 of the General Laws.
22. See title 45, chapter 55 of the General Laws.
23. See title 42, chapter 99 of the General Laws.
24. See chapter 332 of the Public Laws of 1981, section 2.
25. See title 42, chapter 63.5 of the General Laws.

Index

244   Index